THE COMPLETE BUSINESS MANAGEMENT GUIDE
FOR KITCHEN AND BATHROOM PROFESSIONALS
Starting and Staying in Business

by Hank Darlington

The National Kitchen & Bath Association (NKBA®) is the leading international organization exclusively serving the kitchen and bathroom industry. NKBA® is dedicated to researching and providing information on all facets of kitchens and bathrooms, and will continue to pursue timely subjects that affect the industry and those working in it.

ISBN 1887127-07-0

Information about this book and other NKBA® publications, membership and educational seminars may be obtained from the National Kitchen & Bath Association, 687 Willow Grove Street, Hackettstown, NJ 07840; phone 800-THE-NKBA; fax 908-852-1695; and e-mail educate@nkba.org. Visit our Web site at www.nkba.org.

This book is intended for professional use by kitchen and bathroom business professionals. The procedures and advice herein have been shown to be appropriate for the applications described, however, no warranty (expressed or implied) is intended or given. Moreover, the user of this book is cautioned to be familiar with business management and accounting principles.

FROM THE PUBLISHER

Dear Industry Professional,

A common belief held by many business owners and managers is that their success is guaranteed solely because they possess the skills and craftsmanship of the trade, and that they can hire the business and financial management capabilities necessary for success. This may have been true at one time, but it will not be so in the years ahead. If you have studied the industry, understand the changes that are happening and observe the shift in distribution and consumer purchasing attitudes, you are seeing that just the opposite is true. Most of your competitors possess strong business and financial management resources, and will hire the skill and craftsmanship talent of the trade.

Where the small business' stock in trade may be design and technical application, your competitor's stock in trade will be in business systems, finance management, inventory turnover, buying and selling strategies, marketing, public relations and personnel. As part of a series of books published by NKBA® on the elements of business, this book, correlating management to the element of fire, will assist you in developing the business skills necessary to compete and excel within this industry.

The Complete Business Management Guide for Kitchen and Bathroom Professionals was created for the existing and future business owner/manager. The second in a series of business and finance publications created by the Association, it has been assembled to help entrepreneurs in our industry become familiar with the necessary base upon which all successful businesses operate.

Serving as a resource for small kitchen and bathroom businesses, it is designed to renew your commitment to success and profitability. For those yet to become business owners, this publication will help you set in motion the planning criteria necessary for success.

NKBA Professional Development Department

NKBA®'S ELEMENTS OF SUCCESS

Earth, fire, water and air are the elements necessary to sustain life. In similar fashion, a business needs a solid startup, successful management, profit and good business information to thrive. NKBA® recognizes these basic business needs and offers this new three-book series which focuses on the elements of success essential to your kitchen and bathroom firm.

The Complete Business Management Guide for Kitchen and Bathroom Professionals ...Starting and Staying Business   by Hank Darlington
The Element of Fire

Fire provides the warmth that keeps us alive, the energy that moves us and powers machines, and a source of light when things get dark, just as innovative management propels a business forward and ensures that it continues on its path. Good management can lead a company through good and bad times, while poor management or no management, like an untended fire, destroys. Learn to manage every area of your company to keep projects moving, employees energetic and your business HOT!

Managing Your Kitchen and Bathroom Firm's Finances for Profit   by Don Quigley
The Element of Water

Just as you can't survive without water, your business can't survive without profit. Profit should flow through your business, buoying up the equipment, the people and the services you provide. The key is to plan, and to work with your financial records to keep the profit reservoir full. If you don't, profit will slow to a trickle, and your business will eventually fail. Use this guide to help keep profits flowing in your business.

The Kitchen and Bathroom Dealer Operating and Performance Survey   by NKBA®
The Element of Air

Our intake of air is essential to life. For a company, the intake and use of business information is essential for survival. This publication will provide important financial and management comparisons for kitchen and bathroom businesses. You'll be able to assess your own business practices and make modifications accordingly to stabilize your business atmosphere. A must-have for every business. Available to NKBA® members only.

CONTENTS

INTRODUCTION

GOT A MATCH?

Success is not spontaneous combustion. You have to set yourself on fire.
                                                            - Robert W. Johnson

You know how to light a fire. Even if you're not an expert, you can strike a spark and probably have some success. However, a short-lived fire is probably what most of us manage. You may hope that it will grow to a roaring blaze, but you know that the fire is not going to happen just because you are looking at it or pushing the kindling around with your foot. Critical to the process is knowledge of how to lay a proper fire, understanding of fuel and air to feed it and experience to maintain it. Being successful in business is very much like starting a fire. It's not going to happen without your expertise, excitement and effort.

My wife and I started a business from scratch and grew it to 40 employees with over $7 million in revenues. When we were starting out, there were no books to help us with basic start-up and management guidelines for the kitchen and bathroom industry. Many dealers are using good management tools, but others could use some guidance and practical applications. Managers often know what to do, but lack the necessary focus and discipline. In order to be successful, we need more than business plans, good pricing techniques and loyal employees; we need to motivate ourselves, and put our vision into action. To be successful in your business, you must have a fire burning within you. No one else is going to light that fire.

In terms of your standard of living, as well as your personal satisfaction, there's no limit to what you can achieve through private enterprise. To increase the probability of your success, this book provides practical information in an easy-to-understand format, with checklists and visual examples. Here are just a few of the business questions you will explore in the following chapters:

- How can I raise enough money to get started?
- Which is better—a sole proprietorship, partnership or corporation?
- How much insurance should I have?
- What is the best way to find good workers?
- How much merchandise should I inventory?
- What should I charge?
- Can I afford to advertise right away?
- Do I need a complicated bookkeeping system?
- What if I need outside help?
- How do I motivate my staff?
- Do I really understand profitability?
- How can I increase my profitability?
- Can I control my expenses?
- Am I really cut out to own my own business?

Whether you're thinking about starting your own kitchen and bathroom business or already operating a successful business, you'll find the answers you've been looking for in these pages. I hope this book will help you in starting and/or growing your business.

Hank Darlington

Remember, you are in business to succeed and make money. It is unlikely that you will become successful without good planning, hard work and constant reassessment of your situation. If you and your staff want to warm yourselves by the fire, you'll have to find some sticks.

Chapter 1

RUB TWO STICKS TOGETHER
How To Start and Grow Your Business

The beginning is the most important part of the work. **- Plato**

In any successful business operation, the secret ingredient is planning. The adage that "failing to plan means planning to fail" is especially true of running a business. Without good plans, a business is at the mercy of fate, ruled by laws based on random probability, rather than sound judgment. Instead of you running your business, it runs you. A way to avoid this is by taking the time to review your reasons for being in business or formulate your objectives before starting your business.

"What's in it for me?" is the first question you should ask yourself. Forming and operating your own business requires an investment of money, time and energy. In exchange for the opportunity of owning your own business, you give up the benefits that employees take for granted: job tenure, a regular paycheck, paid holidays, vacations, sick leave, a company insurance plan and the ability to leave your job at the end of the day. It is only logical that you should want to know what to expect in the form of a return on your investment—not just in dollars, but in satisfaction.

THE ADVANTAGES OF OWNING A BUSINESS

The number of new businesses started in the United States each year is currently growing at a faster rate than the population. These figures indicate a perception that owning a business offers certain advantages. Those advantages include:

- **Control** - The authority to make decisions rests with you. As the owner, you have the power to direct all the activities of your business.

- **Creative Freedom** - Without the restrictions imposed by the policies of others, and the need to go through channels, ideas and talent can be freely expressed.

- **Profits** - The more successful your business is, the more money you can make. Where employees' salaries are generally dependent on budget approvals and cost of living increases, yours is directly linked to performance.

- **Job Security** - You cannot be fired, laid off or forced to retire.

- **Pride** - There is the satisfaction that comes from knowing you have built your business into a successful operation through your own efforts.

THE DISADVANTAGES OF OWNING A BUSINESS

However, being the boss also has its disadvantages, such as:

- **Risk Of Investment** - If a business fails, you could lose your entire investment. In addition to this, your personal assets may be jeopardized.

- **Long Hours** - Keeping your business going is rarely just a "9-to-5" proposition, especially in the beginning. Be prepared to put in 12-plus hours a day, six or even seven days a week to make it work.

- **Income Fluctuation** - Instead of receiving a regular paycheck, your income is subject to the ups and downs of the business.

- **Responsibility** - The freedom to make decisions carries the burden of standing by them. If anything goes wrong, ultimately, you're the one who is responsible.

- **Pressure** - There is always the pressure to please customers, meet your payroll and satisfy creditors' demands.

- **Regulations** - You must abide by federal, state and local laws, as well as the safety stipulations imposed by your insurance carrier.

Only you can determine if the advantages of owning a business outweigh the disadvantages. Just as some individuals are happy only when working for themselves, others prefer to work for an employer. In planning your own business, it is important that you keep sight of your own needs and wants. Will owning a business enable you to satisfy them, and, at a price you're willing to pay?

HOW SUITED AM I TO OWN AND RUN MY OWN BUSINESS?

Do you have what it takes to own and operate your own business? Are you an entrepreneur? It isn't a matter of how smart you are; it's more a matter of personality and behavior. Researchers have found that individuals who possess certain characteristics are more likely to succeed as business owners than those who lack these characteristics. Although there is no total agreement as to the characteristics that are the most important, those frequently cited include:

- *Motivation* - The drive (mental and physical) to succeed, to accomplish the tasks of your own choosing, on your own terms.

- *Confidence* - The firm belief in your own capabilities and your own chances of success.

- *Willingness To Take Risks* - The readiness to sacrifice your own security, if need be, in order to accomplish your goals.

- *Ability To Make Decisions* - The talent to analyze complex situations and draw the conclusions that will make your business succeed.

- *Human Relations Skills* - The ability to get along with others, to inspire cooperation, confidence and loyalty.

- *Communications Skills* - The ability to express yourself and to understand others, so that ideas can be shared.

- *Technical Ability* - The expertise to produce the goods and services of your business.

One of the most important things you can do as an entrepreneur is to be honest with yourself. The following questions will help you evaluate your qualifications for running your own business. Write down the reasons why you gave a "yes" or "no" answer.

APPRAISING YOUR ENTREPRENEURIAL QUALIFICATIONS		
	YES	**NO**
1. Do you like to take charge of a given situation and make your own decisions?		
2. Do you enjoy competing in challenging business environments?		
3. Are you a self-directed individual with strong self-discipline?		
4. Do you like to plan ahead and do you consistently meet your goals and objectives?		

APPRAISING YOUR ENTREPRENEURIAL QUALIFICATIONS	YES	NO
5. Are you good at time management and do you regularly get things done on time?		
6. Would you lower your standard of living until the business produces a solid income?		
7. Do you have the stamina to work long hours?		
8. Can you take advice from others?		
9. If your business fails, are you prepared for the loss?		
10. Can you withstand stress?		
11. Can you adapt to new situations and implement changes when necessary?		
12. Are you a self-starter who can work on your own?		
13. Can you make decisions quickly and not regret bad decisions?		
14. Do you trust people and do they trust you?		
15. Do you know how to solve problems quickly and with competence?		
16. Can you maintain a positive attitude even in the face of adversity?		
17. Are you able to explain your ideas to others in a way they can understand?		

Scoring the Questionnaire

If you answered "yes" to 15 or more of the questions, you are probably well suited to be an entrepreneur. If you answered "no" to four or more, you may want to review your answers and be sure owning a business is what you want to do.

RISK

One of the most important components for success for entrepreneurs and business owners is the willingness to take risks and understand the degree of risk which makes sense for their business. Every business venture represents a gamble, for it is difficult to predict the future. Even with a well-conceived business plan, adequate financing and managerial experience in the field, you will still find the chances for success hovering around the 50/50 mark at best.

Generally, the risks of a small business are greater than larger ones and the risk is higher for new businesses. The risk diminishes as the business puts on some age.

The market that a small business serves can change because of local demographics, general economic conditions, technological developments, unexpected governmental edicts and local competition. If the market declines or disappears, the firm may have to move or shut its doors. Our area in California was hit relatively hard by a recession in the early 1990s. Before the recession, we had five good competitors in the kitchen and bathroom field. Today, there are two of us. For varying reasons, four owners took a risk and lost.

As part of the research you do before starting a business or opening a second location, identify the risks entailed. Be honest and objective about them, weigh them carefully and have a contingency plan. Remember, not every crisis that can affect a small business will necessarily prove fatal. For example, when that recession hit us, we changed the emphasis of our marketing,

From: *75% / 25%*   *New Construction / Remodeling*

To: *85% / 15%*   *Remodeling / New Construction*

We also added lower-priced product lines to meet the more conservative spending habits of our customers.

The do-it-yourself trend has been thought of as a serious threat to the traditional family-owned "mom and pop" kitchen and bathroom dealer. However, in my opinion, this has not proven to be the case. The do-it-yourself project often leads to complications which drives the amateur to you for solutions (in design, product selection and installation). Therefore, if you are serving a market with do-it-yourselfers in it, you can limit your risks of losing business by freely offering advice to those trying to cope with plumbing, carpentry and design problems.

As you research the kitchen and bathroom business, look for trends in taste or usage which may affect it, such as changes in aesthetic attitudes. Using cabinets as an example, the period look is currently very popular. Those dealers who change their displays to show these products will reduce their risks. Being flexible, adaptable and quick to respond all enhance your chances for success.

In looking at the acquisition of an established business, chase down all the common facts. Before investing in someone else's kitchen and bathroom business, find out why the former lessee or owner wants out. Is the location poor? What products are being represented? What kind of employees would you inherit? What marketing and pricing strategies are being used? Who is the competition and how effective is it?

A major part of the risk in owning a small business is financial. How much capital will it require to get started? How much money will be required to operate it? You will have leases and build-out to consider, as well as inventory, equipment and supplies. The single biggest reason for failure in small businesses is under-capitalization. A business can be doing very well on the sales and service side, but if cash flow can't keep up, the business will fail. This is all part of the risk.

For innovative ways to increase your cash flow, see NKBA®'s publication, entitled The Great Cash Hunt, by Stephen Vlachos, CKD, CBD and Leslie Vlachos, MEd.

A long time ago, I learned that there are certain qualities that are typical of a winning entrepreneur's profile. One of them is being a risk taker. Entrepreneurs are not afraid to take on tasks that are accompanied by some risk. However, they will avoid high risk whenever possible. They recognize that higher levels of achievement are possible only if they are willing to accept risk to accomplish their goals.

I remember the very day in 1983 that my wife and I walked into a brand-new bank, sat down with a brand-new president and explained that we, too, wanted to start a brand-new business. We presented a very well-prepared business plan with three years of financial projections, our personal credentials and financial status. We were enthusiastic and confident. We knew there would be risks, but with a wealth of experience and a lifelong dream to be "our own boss" (i.e., entrepreneur), we asked for a startup loan. We received a quick "yes" and have never looked back.

Even in the "cutting back" years of the recession, we maintained a confidence, built on success, hard work and good planning. In quiet moments, my wife and I would reflect on the wonderful experience that we were enjoying, and, if for some reason, we lost the business, we would still have had the experience of a lifetime. We took the risk—but from day one, when we met with the banker, we never once worried about it.

CHANGE

In addition to being willing to take risks, a small business owner/manager has to be willing to change—to be adaptable and flexible to new market conditions, new product development and new technologies.

As I look back over the past 15 years of starting, running and growing our business, I am astounded by the tremendous amount of changes that have taken place. Many have been dictated to us (demographics, economy, product changes, competitors) and many we have initiated (product mix, pricing, marketing strategies, growth and cutbacks). It has been our ability, willingness and adaptability to make these many changes that have contributed to our success.

Mr. Webster defines change as "the act, process or result of changing as (a) alteration; (b) transformation; (c) substitution." If you are running your business in the same way today that you were 10 or even five years ago, you've got problems.

We are in charge of many of the circumstances that dictate change, but not all of them. For example, we didn't cause three major military bases to be closed in a five-year period, putting 20,000 people out of work, nor did we cause a prolonged four-year recession. But, it was our decision to expand from only decorative plumbing products into decorative hardware, and into kitchen cabinets, appliances and countertops, i.e., "one-stop shopping." We did make the decisions to grow our number of employees during the good times and to reduce them during the bad.

The first four years we were in business, we were the only kitchen and bathroom showroom in town. Within the next five years we saw five competitors start businesses very similar to ours, and two major mass merchandiser chains opened multiple stores in our area. Then the recession came and four of our competitors closed their doors. The mass merchandisers are still there, but they market to their niche and we market to ours. Through all of this change, we were forced to change also. We believe we changed faster and better than the others. The proof of this would be that we are still expanding, growing and experiencing the best years of our business life.

To be successful, we must be good at planning, managing, finances and customer relations. In addition, we must be smart risk takers and as adaptable and flexible to change in business as chameleons are in their habitat.

GOAL SETTING

One way to improve your chances for success is to set goals for accomplishing the various tasks associated with forming and operating your own business. For each goal, indicate your plan of action and specify the target date for its achievement. Then, as each target date arrives, your actual performance can be compared with your intended performance. Whenever a goal is reached, set a new goal . In this way, you can keep both your momentum and your motivation going at a steady pace. Your list of goals might look like this:

Month One
- Read books and articles on starting and running a business.
- Visit your local chamber of commerce, the Small Business Administration, the library, and gather information on starting and running a business.
- Decide what direction your business will take.

Month Two
- Do market research on products, services, customers, competitors and demographics.
- Start looking for a location and building.
- Prepare a plan of action to obtain funds.
- Develop a comprehensive business plan.

Months Three to Four
- Open the business.

Year One
- Have the business break even.

Year Two
- Make a five percent or more return on investment.

Years Three to Five
- Possibly open a second store and/or expand the first store.

For the goal-setting process to work, the goals that you set for yourself should be **measurable**, **scheduled**, **realistic** and **in writing.**

Measurable

It isn't enough just to say that you want to do well or to be a success. You have to have a way to measure your goals. In other words, if you want to be a recognized leader in your field within three years, think of the criteria for judging whether you have obtained the goals—membership in specific organizations, write-ups in newspapers and magazines, sales and profit volumes. Unless there is some standard of measurement that can be used to determine what constitutes a recognized leader, there's no way to know if you are one.

Scheduled

Each goal that you set for yourself should have a specific time frame for its completion. If you have to move a date up or push it back, you can. But having a completion date to shoot for will make it easier for you to schedule the work needed to accomplish the goal and to monitor your progress. Are you on schedule, behind schedule or ahead of schedule?

Realistic

Setting unrealistic goals for yourself is just setting yourself up for failure. Few people become overnight millionaires or earn enough to retire within six months of starting their businesses. Look at what other business owners in your field have accomplished and how long it took them to do it. Then compare this to your own circumstances and set your goals accordingly. Keep in mind, too, that the closer your business goals are to your personal goals, the greater the likelihood that you will achieve both.

In Writing

A goal that isn't in writing isn't a goal, as management experts will tell you. By writing down the things that you want to accomplish, you help them to become real. Putting your goals in writing not only clarifies them, but enables you to keep them in focus as you work toward obtaining them.

MOTIVATION

Nick Geragi, Director of Education and Product Development for NKBA®, says, "One of the most difficult challenges for business owners is to retain the enthusiasm and motivation they possessed when they started their business. It's easy to get depressed and stagnate. Businesses, like people, periodically need their spark reignited.

"No one is immune, whether you experience downturns in the economy, loss of jobs to a competitor, radical changes in the marketplace or a need to increase your cash flow. On occasion, the daily challenges of running a business can take the wind out of your sails. Without question, our total focus on the daily issues often distracts us from seeing the bigger picture. While it is necessary to solve problems as they arise, I find it advantageous to focus on the complete operation. Here are some ideas to help you keep focused:"

1. Recognize that you can't possibly win every situation or sell every job. Pick your battles wisely. You are going to lose a few from time to time. Keep in mind that the economy always has its periods of peaks and valleys and that change happens in the business environment because it has to. *Remember, if nothing changes, nothing changes.*

2. Anticipate the daily situations and develop procedures and systems to overcome them. This will eliminate the negative effects they produce which tend to permeate the organization and affect everyone's morale.

3. Keep your eye on the overall picture.

    a. Remember why you got into business.
    b. Review your mission statement, goals and objectives.
    c. Study your competitors.
    d. Identify what is working successfully for others in our industry and improve upon it.
    e. Focus on what keeps customers happy and sending business to you.
    f. Send your staff out to visit with previous customers.
    g. Educate yourself and staff, go to an industry show, school, conference or seminar.
    h. Bring employees in on management decisions, allow them to make the decision, give them mental ownership. Better yet, tie their decision-making to their income. Ask them what they would do in a given situation. Utilize open-book management.
    i. Bring technology into your business. Find new and better ways to become efficient at delivering your services.
    j. Constantly challenge yourself by trying to improve the process and your customers' experiences.

IS A KITCHEN AND BATHROOM BUSINESS RIGHT FOR YOU?

Will your proposed business be able to support you both materially and emotionally? This depends on such difficult-to-predict factors as the economy, competition, resources and the political environment—all forces beyond your control. But it also depends on another factor you can control—yourself. The first thing you should do during the business planning stage is think about what you really want to do.

If you have been working in the kitchen and bathroom industry, perhaps as a designer or salesperson, your experience will certainly be an asset to owning and managing a business in the field. New businesses are generally very small, and your previous background may have given you experience in such tasks as business planning, budgets, forecasting and management. Starting with these abilities enhances your percentage of success.

If you're determined to start a kitchen and bathroom business, even though you know very little about it, what can you do to minimize your risk? Find out as much as possible about the industry before attempting to open your own business. Obtain additional education, take a job in someone else's business, research the business in the library and talk to people in the field. Even though this preparation may postpone opening the doors of your own business, the delay will be worth it. You'll be in a better position to stay in business.

As for uncontrollable factors that affect your business, stay tuned to what is happening in your area. Some new business owners get so caught up in the day-to-day operations of their business that they fail to keep track of events that may have a direct bearing on their operations. Read newspapers, magazines and trade journals. Listen to what people have to say, and observe changes in your environment.

Now that you have thought about your reasons for going into business, examined your temperament and considered the opportunities open to you, this checklist will help you get started. The questions relate to both the formation and the actual operation of your own business. Be as honest with yourself as possible. This will help you identify weaknesses that need improvement and topics that you need to research further.

CHECKLIST FOR GOING INTO BUSINESS	Yes	No
1. About you (See Chapter 1.)		
a. Are you the kind of person who is motivated to start and run a business?		
b. Do you want to own your own business badly enough to keep working long hours without any guarantee that it will succeed?		
c. Have you ever worked in a business like the one you want to start?		
d. Have you ever worked as a supervisor or manager?		
e. Have you had any business training in school?		
f. Have you researched your proposed business and tried to learn as much about it as possible?		
2. About money (See Chapter 2.)		
a. Have you saved any money to invest in the business?		
b. Do you know how much money you will need to get your business started?		
c. Do you know how much credit you can get from your suppliers—the people you will buy from?		
d. Do you know where you can borrow the rest of the money you may need?		
e. Have you figured out what your annual net income (salary plus profits) will be?		
f. Can you live on less than this amount if necessary?		
g. Have you talked to a banker about your plans?		
3. About a partner (See Chapter 2.)		
a. If you need a partner with the money or the know-how that you don't have, is there someone available you could work with?		
b. Do you know the pros and cons of doing it alone, having a partner or incorporating your business?		
c. Have you talked to a lawyer about your options?		
d. Have you consulted with an accountant about your start-up *pro forma* and short-term budgets (one to three years)?		
4. About customers (See Chapters 2 and 6.)		
a. Have you identified a niche for yourself in the marketplace?		
b. Is there a need for your particular product or service?		
c. Do you know who your customers will be?		
d. Do you understand their needs and wants?		
e. Will your product offering be competitive in all aspects—price, quality, etc.?		
f. Have you chosen a location that is convenient for your customers?		

GETTING STARTED	Yes	No
1. *Your building* (See Chapter 2.)		
a. Have you found a suitable building for your business?		
b. Will you have enough room when your business grows?		
c. Can you fix the building the way you want it without spending too much money?		
d. Is there adequate parking, maintenance, security or other necessary support services?		
e. Have you had a lawyer check the lease and zoning?		
f. Is it customer friendly (easy to find, easy to access, good parking)?		
2. *Equipment and supplies* (See Chapter 2.)		
a. Do you know what equipment and supplies you will need and how much they will cost?		
b. Can you save money by buying second-hand equipment?		
c. Have you compared the difference between buying and leasing?		
3. *Your merchandise* (See Chapter 5.)		
a. Have you decided what merchandise to carry?		
b. Do you know how much inventory you will need on opening day?		
c. Have you found suppliers who will sell you what you need at a good price?		
d. Have you compared the prices in credit terms of different suppliers?		
e. If a showroom is involved—how much product and build-out do you need to plan for?		
4. *Your records* (See Chapter 3.)		
a. Have you chosen a record-keeping system that will keep track of your income and expenses, assets and liabilities?		
b. Have you worked out a way to keep track of your inventory so that you will have enough on hand for your customers, but not more than you can sell?		
c. Have you figured out how you can maintain your payroll records and take care of tax reports and payments?		
d. Do you know what financial statements you should prepare?		
e. Do you know how to use these financial statements?		
f. Have you sought advice from an accountant, banker or some other outside source?		
5. *Your business and the law* (See Chapters 2, 8 and 9.)		
a. Do you know what licenses and permits you need?		
b. Do you know what business laws you have to obey?		
c. Do you know a lawyer who can give you advice and help with legal papers?		
d. Are you aware of the various risks that you should guard against?		
e. Have you talked with an insurance agent about what kinds of insurance you need?		
f. Have you made plans for protecting your business against thefts of all kinds— shoplifting, robberies, burglaries, employee stealing?		
6. *When buying a business* (See Chapter 2 and 9.)		
a. Have you made a list of likes and dislikes about a business that someone else started?		
b. Are you sure you know the real reason the owner wants to sell the business?		
c. Have you compared the cost of buying the business with the cost of starting a new business?		
d. Is the inventory up to date and in good condition?		
e. Is the building in good condition?		
f. Will the owner of the building transfer the lease to you and is it to your advantage?		
g. Have you talked to others in the area to see what they think of the business?		
h. Have you talked with the company's suppliers?		
i. Have you talked with a lawyer about the purchase?		
j. Have you conferred with an accountant and studied the company's financial reports in depth?		

MAKING IT WORK	Yes	No
1. Advertising *(See Chapter 6.)*		
a. Have you decided how you will advertise (newspapers, magazines, direct mail, etc.)?		
b. Do you know where to get help with your ads?		
c. Have you observed the types of promotions used by your competitors?		
2. Pricing *(See Chapter 4.)*		
a. Do you know how to calculate what you should charge?		
b. Do you know what other businesses charge?		
c. Do you know the difference between markup and margin?		
3. Buying *(See Chapter 5.)*		
a. Do you know what suppliers you intend to buy from?		
b. Will your plan for keeping track of your inventory tell what and when to buy?		
4. Selling *(See Chapter 6.)*		
a. Do you know what selling techniques to use?		
b. Have you thought about the reasons people buy and how you can convince customers to buy from you?		
c. Are you fully aware of the benefits associated with products and services you sell?		
5. Your employees *(See Chapter 7.)*		
a. If you need to hire someone to help you, do you know where to look?		
b. Do you know what kind of person you need?		
c. Do you know how much to pay?		
d. Do you have a plan for training your employees?		
e. Have you investigated writing job descriptions and perfecting job performance appraisals?		
f. Are you up to date on the laws involved with human resource management?		

A FEW MORE QUESTIONS TO PONDER	Yes	No
1. Will owning a business enable you to achieve your personal goals?		
2. Have you talked it over with your family and gotten their support?		
3. Are you willing to make the commitment to being the boss?		
4. Are you ready to begin developing your business plan?		

For every "yes" answer, think of yourself as one step closer to turning your business dream into a reality. Each "no" answer represents an area to work on—a temporary road block. Review the chapters indicated for more information on the subject.

GOING OUT OF BUSINESS

One of the factors of starting a business is planning to go out of business. Good management includes a plan on how to transfer ownership of your business or how you will close up shop. At some point, you will exit your business. It may be your choice to sell the business and retire or pursue another avenue. Circumstances, such as health, bankruptcy or misunderstandings among partners could dictate that you exit the business for reasons other than those you have planned. Over 50 percent of all new businesses fail within the first three years of being started. Circumstances change!

Regardless of the reason or the timing of your exit from your business, you need to have a documented plan. As in your day-in, day-out business plan, your exit plan will need to be updated at regular intervals. Business may be booming today and non-existent tomorrow. You may have money in the bank today, and face a lien or a lawsuit tomorrow.

Do some research and learn how to determine an accurate valuation of your business.

Hard work alone will not prevent the demise of a business. Most of us pride ourselves on persistence in the face of adversity. But, it is possible that this determined attitude could drive you deeper into disaster. Often owners will try to hang on longer than they should when indications are that the business is failing.

Generally, exiting sooner rather than later is wise. Business problems may fester and the situation worsen. Move quickly. Don't wait for the situation to escalate to catastrophic proportions. As soon as you sense it is time to get out—begin the severance process. Even if you don't see the early subtle clues, heed the more obvious warning signs.

If you routinely cannot meet all of your monthly obligations and you are making no progress at paying off the principal of your major debts, you might need to consider bankruptcy. Bankruptcy laws are designed to help people who have become overburdened with debt. This requires a discussion with your attorney and a careful review of all of your financial circumstances.

First and foremost—seek advise on how and when to exit your business. Use your banker, accountant, business mentors, consultants and a good business attorney. This applies to selling the business, merging the business or closing the business. Maximize the savings of dollars and personal well-being and minimize the losses and aggravation.

Handling the dissolution in a professional, orderly manner will benefit your employees and your family and friends, as well as yourself. Research all of your options and select what is best for your business. Putting the plan on paper will help you to move on when it is time.

The kitchen and bathroom field is geared for success as an important and necessary industry. What is your dream for your business? Financial success requires a balance of planning, skill, desire and a broad vision. There are many kitchen and bathroom businesses. To achieve success, yours must offer quality to your clients and a promise of solid jobs to your employees. The uniqueness that you alone bring to your business is what success is all about. A business that is run in a professional manner, respecting clients and employees alike, is a winner. If you plan and lay the groundwork, you will be in an excellent position to succeed.

Chapter 2

LAYING THE BASE
Business Basics

It's never too late to learn to play the piano. - **Anonymous**

You wake up in your vacation cabin in the North woods. It's October. It's cold. Your family wants a roaring fire—right now! If you throw wood and some paper in the stove and touch a match to it, you'll get a flash, a lot of smoke, and then—nothing. You'll have to start over. No matter how cold you are, it is worth taking the time to lay the fire properly.

Many kitchen and bathroom dealers are very knowledgeable in basic management skills. They understand the legalities in forming a business and know the components of a business plan. They relate well to their employees and their customers. But, somewhere between what they know and the day-to-day running of a business, getting the fire started immediately becomes more important than finding dry wood and ensuring an air space under the fire for ventilation. It's easier to run your business than to make the time to plan and execute your vision. You are in business and working hard at it. But, every so often, you wonder what you could do to improve your success. Maybe you are thinking of expanding. These are good reasons to spend some time reviewing what you know about business and management, learning something new and then getting up and doing it.

In any successful business operation, the secret ingredient is planning. Without good plans, a business is totally at the mercy of fate, ruled by laws based on random probability rather than sound judgment.

THE STRUCTURE OF YOUR BUSINESS

Your ability to make decisions rapidly, compete in the marketplace, and raise additional capital when needed is directly related to the legal structure of your business. Before deciding on a business structure, ask yourself these questions:

- What do I know about the kitchen and bathroom business?
- In what areas of the business do I need help?
- How much money do I need?
- What sources of money will be available to me later?
- What kinds of risks will I be exposed to?
- How can I limit my liability?
- What kinds of taxes am I paying?

An established business might benefit from a change in structure. Maybe you are thinking of expanding.

There are three legal forms from which to choose: *sole proprietorship*, *partnership* and *corporation*. No one form is better than another. Each has its advantages and its disadvantages. The important thing is to ascertain the legal form of business that will work best for you. The following section offers a comparison of these forms of businesses to give you more information on which to base your decision.

SOLE PROPRIETORSHIP

More than 75 percent of all businesses in the United States today are sole proprietorships, meaning that they are owned by just one person. And, more often than not, that person is directly involved in the day-to-day operation of the business. As a sole proprietor, you are in the driver's seat. In addition to having total control over your business, you have total responsibility for it. Just as all profits from its operation are yours, so are all of its debts and liabilities.

Advantages of a Sole Proprietorship

You are the boss. As a sole proprietor, you have the freedom to run your business in any legal way you choose. You can expand or contract your business, add or drop products or services, and hire, promote, and fire personnel. This ability to make decisions quickly, without having to wait for committee approval, lets you take advantage of timely opportunities. If you are looking for maximum control and minimum government interference, the sole proprietorship could be just what you need.

It's easy to get started. The sole proprietorship is by far the simplest legal form you can choose. There's no legal expense or red tape in getting started. All you need to do is obtain the assets and commence operations. Sometimes, local or state licenses may be required, for instance, if a contractor's license for installation is required. But, more often, it is just a matter of hanging up your shingle.

You keep all the profits. All profits from a sole proprietorship go to the owner. You are not obligated to share them with anyone else. It is up to you whether to keep them for your personal use or reinvest them in the business.

Income from the business is taxed as personal income. The government considers income derived from the sole proprietorship to be part of the owner's income. As such, you will have no separate income tax to pay. Furthermore, losses incurred by the business can be deducted from your personal income tax.

You can discontinue your business at will. Should you decide that you want to go on to something new, dissolving your business is quite simple. Without having to obtain a second opinion, divide up shares or process paperwork, you will need only to cease operations.

Disadvantages of Sole Proprietorship

You assume unlimited liability. A sole proprietor is responsible for all business debt or legal judgments against the business. In the event that these exceed the assets of the business, your own personal assets—home, automobile, savings account, investments—can be claimed by creditors. In other words, your financial liability is not limited to the amount of your investment in your business, but extends to your total ability to make payment. This unlimited liability is a sole proprietorship's worst feature.

The investment capital you can raise is limited. The amount of investment capital available to your business is limited to the money you have or are able to borrow. Unlike partnerships or corporations, which can draw on the resources of others, sole proprietors have to provide the total investment for their business.

You need to be a generalist. Anyone who starts a sole proprietorship must be prepared to perform a variety of functions, ranging from accounting to advertising. Most new sole proprietorships cannot afford the luxury of hiring specialists for these tasks. Even if you can, you have to understand what you are doing, since you are the one who will be held responsible for their actions.

Retaining high-caliber employees may be difficult. You may have difficulty in holding on to your best employees if they want more than you are offering them—namely, part ownership in your business. For these employees, a good salary and bonuses usually won't be enough. Your only recourse is to let them go or to convert your sole proprietorship to a partnership.

The life of the business is limited. The death of the owner automatically terminates a sole proprietorship, as does any other unforeseen occurrence (long-term illness, for example) which keeps the owner from operating the business. Since there is no one else to carry on, the business just ceases to function.

PARTNERSHIP

A partnership exists when two or more people share in the ownership of a business. By agreement, they determine the amount of time and money each partner will invest in the business and the percentage of the profits that each will receive. The extent of each partner's authority and liability must also be made clear.

To avoid misunderstandings later, everything that has been agreed to should be put in writing, preferably with the assistance of an attorney. The importance of a written partnership agreement cannot be overemphasized. In the absence of such a document, the courts can resolve any disputes that arise, but the outcome might not be to your liking.

Here is some of the information that should be included in your partnership agreement:

- Each partner's responsibility and authority.
- Extent of each partner's liability.
- The amount of capital each partner is investing in the business.
- How profits and losses are to be shared.
- How disputes between partners are to be resolved.
- Arrangements for the withdrawal or admission of partners.
- How assets are to be distributed should the business be dissolved.

Advantages of Partnership

Two heads are better than one. In a partnership you have the advantage of being able to draw on the skills and abilities of each partner. Ideally, the contributions that each partner is able to make to the business complement those of the other partners. For instance, one partner oversees accounting functions, another is in charge of production and another handles design and sales.

It's easy to get started. Starting a partnership is relatively easy. Although it entails additional cost and more planning than a sole proprietorship (e.g., selecting partners, preparing the partnership agreement), red tape is minimal.

More investment capital is available. Your company's ability to increase capital can be enhanced simply by bringing in more partners. Unlike a sole proprietorship, which can draw on the financial resources of only one individual, in a partnership, you have the combined resources of the partners.

Partners pay only personal income tax. Partnerships are taxed in the same way as sole proprietorships. The total income of the business is considered to be the personal income of the partners. This means there is no separate business income tax to pay and business losses are deducted from each partner's income tax.

High-caliber employees can be made partners. Partnerships are able to attract and retain high-caliber employees by offering them the opportunity to become partners. This method of employee motivation can be particularly successful.

Disadvantages Of Partnership

Partners have unlimited liability. Like sole proprietors, partners are responsible for all debts or legal judgments against the business. This liability is even worse for partners than it is for sole proprietors because, as a partner, you are responsible not only for your own debts, but for those of your partners. And remember that, even though your investment in the business may be minimal, your losses could be substantial. Your liability extends beyond the amount of your investment to include your personal assets as well.

Profits must be shared. All profits resulting from the partnership must be distributed among partners in accordance with the partnership agreement. The percentage of the profit to be reinvested in the company must be decided on by the partners. Your wishes in this matter represent only one point of view.

The partners may disagree. Disputes among partners can literally destroy a partnership. One partner's desire to expand the business can go against another's goal of cutting costs. Should your money be spent on improving your product or on promoting it? When key decisions must be made, the feelings, trust and admiration that drew you together as partners can disintegrate. If this is to be avoided, you must give your full attention to selecting partners and drawing up the partnership agreement. Foresight in the planning stage can pay off later.

The life of the business is limited. As with a sole proprietorship, the life of the partnership is limited. Should one of your partners withdraw from the business or die, or become too ill to carry on, the partnership is automatically dissolved. Though it is possible for the remaining partners to reorganize the business, the financial interest of the departing partner must be handled first. Furthermore, any time a new partner is admitted to the business, dissolution of the partnership is mandatory. A new partnership reflecting the addition of the new partner must be formed.

Limited Partnership

Because of the unlimited liability that partners are subject to, you may be reluctant to assume the risk. One way around this is to form a limited partnership. In a limited partnership, there are two kinds of partners—**general** and **limited**.

General partners assume unlimited liability for the business. The liability of limited partners is confined to the amounts of their investments. However, in exchange for this limited liability, limited partners are restricted from taking an active role in the company's management. The withdrawal of a limited partner from the business does not necessarily dissolve the partnership, should others wish to continue.

In a limited partnership, the risk can be shifted from one partner to another. It cannot be avoided entirely, though, since every limited partnership must have at least one general partner. If you decide to set up a limited partnership, public notice stating that one or more partners have limited status must be made. Otherwise, it is assumed that a general partnership exists in which all partners have liability.

Other Partners

Within the scope of the partnership format, there are four other types of partners you may wish to consider. Depending on your company's needs, one or more of these kinds of partners may be right for you.

- **Silent partners** invest money in a business, but take no active role in its management nor do they share liability. They are primarily interested in getting a return on their investment.

- **Secret partners** are active in the management end of the business, but are not known to be partners. Although they want to participate in running the business, they don't want the public to know about their involvement.

- **Dormant partners** are neither active in the business nor known to the public. Like silent partners, they are concerned with getting a return on their investment. Like secret partners, they want to maintain their privacy.

- **Nominal partners** aren't partners at all, but, by their behavior, they lead the public to believe that they are. An example of this is the person who permits his or her name to be associated with the business in exchange for a fee.

Depending on your company's needs, one or more of these kinds of partners may be right for you and your business.

Joint Venture

The kinds of partnerships described above all share the intention of being ongoing businesses. A joint venture differs from these in that it is a partnership set up for a specific purpose of limited duration. For example, suppose you and a friend decide to buy, renovate and resell a house together. Your joint venture would start when you purchased the house and end when you sold it. As for your taxes, joint ventures are taxed the same as partnerships.

During the life of such a joint venture, each partner is subject to unlimited liability. So the same caution should be exercised in selecting a joint venture partner as in selecting any other partner. Also, problems can be avoided by consulting an attorney and putting the terms of your joint venture agreement in writing.

CORPORATION

A corporation differs from other legal forms of businesses in that the law considers it to be an artificial being, possessing the same rights and responsibilities as a person. Unlike a sole proprietorship or a partnership, a corporation has an existence separate from its owners. As such, it can sue and be sued, own property, agree to contracts and engage in business transactions. Additionally, since a corporation is a separate entity, it is not dissolved with every change in ownership. The result is that corporations have the potential for unlimited life.

The Corporate Charter

To form a corporation, you must be granted a charter by the state in which your business resides. Each state sets its own requirements and fees for the issuance of charters. The cost for incorporating a small business usually ranges from $1,000 to $3,000. Generally, your charter must include such information as:

- Corporation's name.
- Names of principal stockholders.
- Number and types of shares to be issued.
- Place of business.
- Type of business.

Stockholders

Each person who owns stock in your corporation is a co-owner of the business. This does not mean that every stockholder will actively participate in your company's management, or even be associated with it in any way, other than by purchasing shares of the corporation's stock. Stockholders are guaranteed the right to vote on the members of the corporation's board of directors and on certain major corporate policies.

Enabling people to become co-owners in a business in this way benefits both the corporation and the stockholders. A corporation is able to obtain investment capital and the stockholders can share in whatever profits the corporation earns. These profits are distributed to stockholders in the form of dividends. Furthermore, since stock is transferable, stockholders are free to sell their stock at any time and receive the current market value for it.

The Board of Directors

The board of directors represents the stockholders and is responsible for protecting their interests. Board members are elected annually, usually for one-year terms, which can be renewed indefinitely by means of the election process. Since the number of votes that stockholders can cast is related to the number of shares they have, major stockholders can virtually elect themselves to the board.

The board of directors generally concerns itself with determining corporate policies, rather than taking care of day-to-day operations. To handle these, the board appoints a chief executive officer and other top corporate officers, e.g., vice presidents, secretary, treasurer. They, in turn, see that the policies stipulated by the board of directors are implemented.

Advantages of a Corporation

Stockholders have limited liability. One of the most attractive advantages of the corporate form of business is that the owners have limited liability. Investors are financially liable only up to the amount of their investment in the corporation. This limited liability ensures that the creditors of the corporation cannot touch personal assets.

Corporations can raise the most investment capital. You can increase the investment capital in your corporation simply by selling more shares of stock. Whereas sole proprietorships and partnerships are limited in the number of owners they can have, corporations can have any number of owners.

Corporations have unlimited life. Because of its status as a legal entity, a corporation has its own identity. Unlike sole proprietorships and partnerships, whose life spans are linked to those of their owners, it is possible for your corporation to exist indefinitely. The withdrawal of stockholders, corporate officers or employees will not terminate its existence.

Ownership is easily transferable. Ownership in a corporation is easily transferable from one person to another. Investors can buy and sell shares of stock as they please without seeking any prior approval. In addition to providing investors with maximum control over their investments, this enables your corporation to go on operating without disruption.

Corporations utilize specialists. Because of the separation of ownership and management, the corporation form of business can most effectively utilize the services of specialists. Unlike sole proprietorships and partnerships, which tend to rely on the skills and abilities of the owners to provide each function, corporations employ specialists. Availability of specially trained personnel leads to higher productivity and increased efficiency.

Disadvantages of a Corporation

Corporations are taxed twice. Unlike sole proprietorships and partnerships, corporations and their owners are taxed separately. In what amounts to double taxation, both the income your corporation earns and the income you as an individual earn are taxed. This is the primary drawback to the corporate form.

Corporations must pay a capital stock tax. In addition to paying a corporate federal income tax, corporations must pay a capital stock tax. This is an annual tax on outstanding shares of stock which is levied by the state in which the business is incorporated.

Starting a corporation is expensive. More expense is involved in starting a corporation than is involved in starting any other form of legal business. There are the costs for legal assistance in drawing up your charter, state incorporation fees, and the purchase of record books and stock certificates. All these require expenditures not only of money, but of time.

Corporations are more closely regulated. The government regulates corporations much more closely than it does any other form of business. Numerous state and federal reports must be filed regularly. Each year, corporations are required to prepare, print and distribute an annual report summarizing the company's activities during the preceding year. Often specialists are retained on staff solely for the purpose of providing the data for these reports.

S Corporations

If you are interested in forming a corporation, but hesitant to do so because of the double taxation, there is a way to avoid it. You can do this by making your business an S corporation. The Internal Revenue Service (IRS) permits this type of corporation to be taxed as a partnership rather than as a corporation. However, to qualify for "S" status, your business must meet the specific requirements set forth by the IRS. These include limits on the number and type of shareholders in the business, the stock that is issued and the corporation's sources of revenues. For more information on forming an S corporation, consult with your attorney, your accountant or the IRS.

SUMMARY

Advantages and Disadvantages of Each Legal Form of Ownership

SOLE PROPRIETORSHIP	
Advantages	**Disadvantages**
1. You're the boss.	1. You assume unlimited liability.
2. It's easy to get started.	2. The investment capital you can raise is limited.
3. You keep all the profits.	3. You need to be a generalist.
4. Income from business is taxed as personal income.	4. It may be difficult to retain high-caliber employees.
5. You can discontinue your business at will.	5. The life of the business is limited.

PARTNERSHIP	
Advantages	**Disadvantages**
1. Two heads are better than one.	1. Partners have unlimited liability.
2. It's easy to get started.	2. Profits must be shared.
3. More investment capital is available.	3. The partners may disagree.
4. Partners pay only personal income tax.	4. The life of the business is limited.
5. High-caliber employees can be made partners.	

CORPORATION	
Advantages	**Disadvantages**
1. Stockholders have limited liability.	1. Corporations are taxed twice.
2. Corporations can raise the most capital.	2. Corporations must pay capital stock tax.
3. Corporations have unlimited life.	3. Starting a corporation is more expensive.
4. Ownership is easily transferable.	4. Corporations are more closely regulated.
5. Corporations utilize specialists.	

You may own a family business or be considering adding a family member to your business. Some rules you may want to follow to minimize problems:

- Clearly define responsibilities.
- Establish working hours to avoid misunderstandings.
- Establish reporting requirements.
- Deal objectively with family member's qualifications.
- Discuss salary in advance.
- Work together on estate planning.

GOVERNMENT REGULATIONS

Depending on what you sell and where your business is located, there will also be various permits and paperwork to take care of and trademarks, patents and copyrights to consider. To protect the legal standing of your business in the community, it is important to find out which local, state and federal regulations apply.

LOCAL REGULATIONS

At the local level, regulations pertaining to businesses are primarily concerned with taxation, public health and safety, and zoning. Although each community is different, the most typical forms of regulations are:

Business taxes and permits. Commonly referred to as a business license, a permit is issued by the city and/or county in which a business is located and is usually valid for one or two years. The fee for it, which is based on the gross sales of your business, can range from less than $50 to more than $250. To find out if a business license is necessary in your particular circumstances and/or which agency issues it, check the white pages of your telephone directory under your city for the business tax or license division or city clerk.

Fictitious business name statements. If you are planning to operate your business under a name other than your own, such as ABC Kitchens, then you will probably need to file a Fictitious Name Statement with the county clerk's office. The purpose of this statement is to inform the public of your identity and the identities of any others who are co-owners in the business. Providing this public notice is a two-part process that involves filing the statement with the county clerk and having the statement published in a newspaper in general circulation. You can usually do the first part, though, by going directly to the newspaper who is going to run your statement. As a convenience to their customers, most newspapers keep fictitious name forms on hand and will file the completed statement for you. The total cost for filing and publishing the statement should be somewhere between $30 and $100.

Zoning restrictions. Just as some people are more inclined to be entrepreneurs than others, so are some communities. Whereas one city may encourage businesses to locate there, another may not. Typically regulated things include the type of businesses that are acceptable, the size and placement of signs, exterior merchandise displays, inventory storage, parking and hours of operation. Since the main purpose of zoning restrictions is to protect the rights of people and property, a business that is noisy, smelly or unsightly can expect to run into trouble. To find out the zoning restrictions for your community, contact your local planning department.

Other regulations. Depending on the nature of your business, other local regulations may also apply. For instance, if you are engaged in food preparation, processing or serving (mail-order cheesecakes, pizza restaurants, catering), you must stay within the county health department codes. Kitchen and bathroom dealers who make their own cabinets or install cabinets may fall into zoning codes for that type of business. Other departments that have jurisdiction over businesses include the fire and sanitation departments.

STATE REGULATIONS

At the state level, regulations pertaining to businesses center around taxation and monitoring of specific professions. Each state sets its own standards in these areas, but the most common regulations involve the issuing of seller's permits and occupational licenses.

Seller's Permit. Many states require anyone who buys and sells merchandise to obtain a seller's permit. This permit exempts you from paying sales tax on the merchandise you purchase for resale through your business, and authorizes you to collect sales tax from your customers. Usually there is no fee to obtain a seller's permit, but, depending on your estimated growth sales for the year, you may be required to post a bond. This is to ensure that you collect and remit to the state all sales tax due. To find out more about the seller's permit and whether or not you should have one, check your telephone directory white pages under your state listing for taxes.

Occupational License. To maintain set standards of performance and protect the safety of consumers, most states regulate entry into specific occupations or professions, such as those in the health services, cosmetology, accounting, real estate and construction. If your business is in a regulated field, you must first meet the standards set forth by the state licensing board. Once you have demonstrated your competence, you will be issued a license, which is usually valid for a period of one to two years and is renewable. To determine if any occupational license is required for your business activity, check your state's consumer affair's office.

FEDERAL REGULATIONS

Federal regulations pertaining to business focus on taxation, employer responsibilities, consumer protection and the registration of trademarks, patents and copyrights.

Employer Identification Number. If you employ one or more persons in your business, the federal government requires you to have an employer identification number. This enables the government to verify that you are paying all appropriate employer taxes and withholding the proper amounts from employee paychecks. Even though you may not have any employees in the beginning, it is still advisable to obtain a number, especially if you sell to businesses, because customers often need it for their records. If you should decide to hire someone later, take in a partner, or incorporate, you will need the number for tax purposes. Obtaining your identification number is an easy matter. What's more, there is no fee for it. Just fill out the IRS Form #FS-4 and submit it to the IRS.

Consumer protection regulations. To protect the rights of consumers, the federal government regulates business practices in a variety of areas. Businesses that engage in mail order sales or sell their products in more than one state are subject to regulation by the Federal Trade Commission, Interstate Commerce Commission and/or the U. S. Postal Service. The Federal Trade Commission also oversees product packaging and labeling, product warranties and advertising claims. With nutritional supplements, health care products or cosmetics, the Food and Drug Administration steps into the picture. Financial services and businesses may come under the jurisdiction of the securities and exchange commission. To familiarize yourself with the regulations that apply to your type of business, write to the Federal Trade Commission, Washington, DC 20580.

Trademarks, patents and copyrights. In addition to protecting the rights of consumers, the federal government also protects the rights of entrepreneurs. In this case, it protects your right to use and profit from your own name (or business or product name), inventions and artistic creations. The following information outlines the protection provided by trademarks, patents and copyrights, as well as how you can use them to your advantage.

- ***Trademarks:*** By definition, a trademark is any word, name, symbol, device or combination of these used to identify the products or services of a business and to distinguish them from those of other enterprises. Often, one of the businesses most valuable assets, a trademark, can help to define its image, increase customer awareness and stimulate repeat purchases. Although a business isn't required by law to register its trademark, this is advisable since it offers the greatest protection. Once a trademark is registered, the holder's right to use it extends for a period of ten years, at which time registration is renewable. For more information on trademarks write to the U.S. Department of Commerce, Patent and Trademark Office, Washington, DC 20231, and ask them to send you their pamphlet, "General Information Concerning Trademarks."

  When we started our business, we immediately registered our company name and our logo with the state—for the *whole* state. It is good that we did, because, over the years, we had two cases where another business had the same name (not in our immediate trading area, but in our state) and one case where our logo was challenged. In all three instances we were registered and they were not. So, even though we were newer in business, we "owned" the name and the logo.

- **Patents:** In granting a patent to a business, the federal government gives it the right to exclude all others from making, using or selling the invention in the United States. Patents for new and useful products or purposes are valid for 17 years. A design patent, covering only the style or appearance of a product, may be valid for a period ranging from 3½ to 14 years. If you develop a product, process or design that you believe has commercial possibilities, obtaining a patent may be advisable, given the protection it affords. The government recommends that inventors not attempt to prepare their own patent applications without the help of a registered attorney or agent skilled in patent procedures. Taking this into consideration, when legal phases are added in, the total cost of obtaining a patent runs between $2,000 and $5,000. Once again, information pertaining to obtaining a patent is available from the U.S. Department of Commerce, Patent and Trademark Office, Washington, DC 20231.

- **Copyrights:** A copyright protects the right of an individual to keep others from copying his or her creations. Although most commonly associated with literary works, copyright protection extends to your kitchen and bathroom designs, graphic designs, paintings, sculpture, musical compositions, sound recordings and audio/visual works. A business doesn't have to be in the arts to benefit from this protection. A sampling of the works that come within the broad scope of copyright coverage includes brochures, catalogs, advertising copy, newsletters, books, audio cassettes, video tapes, reports, charts, technical drawings and computer programs. Obtaining a copyright is relatively simple. All you need to do is to provide public notice of the copyright of the work itself and file an application form. The fee is currently $20, and, once granted, the copyright is for up to 50 years after the holder's death.

Protecting Your Kitchen and Bathroom Plans

It is a good business practice to ensure that your company's design plans for your clients will not be copied or used by a competitor. This may be done by copyrighting the design plans that you or members of your firm prepare.

Copyright is an international form of protection/exclusivity provided by law to authors of original works, despite whether the work is published or not. Original works of authorship include any literary, pictorial, graphic or sculptured works, such as your design plans, provided they are original works done by you.

Copyright protection exists from the moment the work is created in its final form and will endure 50 years after the author's death.

If two or more persons are authors of an original work, they will be deemed co-owners of its copyright. For example, if you as the kitchen specialist collaborate with an interior designer, you will both be co-owners of the design copyright.

An original work generated by two or more authors is referred to as a "joint work." Generally, a joint work results if the authors collaborated on the work or, if each prepared a segment of it with the knowledge and intent that it would be incorporated with the contributions submitted by other authors. Accordingly, a joint work will only be found when each co-author intended his or her respective contribution to be combined into a larger, integrated piece. There is no requirement that each of the co-authors work together or even be acquainted with one another.

A work created by an employee within the scope of his or her employment is regarded as "work made for hire," and is normally owned by the employer, unless the parties explicitly stipulate in a written agreement, signed by both, that the copyright will be owned by the employee. If you are an independent contractor, the "works made for hire" statutes do not include architectural drawings or other design plans, therefore, the copyright in any kitchen or bathroom design created by you will remain vested with you until you contractually agree to relinquish ownership.

To secure copyright protection for your plans, you are required to give notice of copyright on all publicly distributed copies. The use of the copyright notice is your responsibility as the copyright owner and does not require advance permission from, or registration with, the Copyright Office in Washington, DC.

A proper copyright notice must include the following three items:

- The symbol ©, or the word "copyright," or the abbreviation "copy," (© is considered as the international symbol for copyright);
- The year of the first publication of the work; and
- The name of the owner of the copyright in the work, or an abbreviation by which the name can be recognized, or a generally known alternative designation of the owner.

An example of a proper copyright notice would be: **Copyright© 1997 Joe Smith**. The notice should be affixed to copies of your design plan in such a manner and location as to give reasonable notice of the claim of copyright.

As mentioned previously, you or your firm continue to retain copyright protection of your design plan even if the plan is given to the client after he or she has paid for it. Although the copyright ownership may be transferred, such transfer must be in writing and signed by you as the owner of the copyright conveyed. Normally, the transfer of a copyright is made by contract. In order to protect your exclusive rights, however, you should include a clause in your contract which reads: "Design plans are provided for the fair use by the client or his or her agent in completing the project as listed within this contract. Design plans remain the property of (your name)."

This clause should also be in any agreement between you and a client who requests that you prepare a design plan for his or her review. Such a design plan usually serves as the basis for a subsequent contract between you and the client for the actual installation of the kitchen or bathroom. This type of agreement will prevent the client from obtaining a design plan from you and then taking that plan to a competitor who may simply copy your plan. As long as you retain the copyright of the design plan, you will be able to sue any party who has copied it for infringement.

To make sure that you have selected a legal form that is appropriate for your business and are familiar with the government regulations that apply to it, complete this checklist. A review of this chapter will help you with the answers.

STRUCTURING-THE-BUSINESS CHECKLIST		
	YES	NO
1. Do you know the advantages of Sole Proprietorship?		
Of a Partnership?		
Of a Corporation?		
2. Do you know why you should have a written partnership agreement?		
3. Do you know what information to include in a partnership agreement?		
4. Are you aware of the differences between a general partnership and a limited partnership?		
5. Can you describe the characteristics of each type of partnership?		
Of a Silent Partnership?		
Of a Secret Partnership?		
Of a Dormant Partnership?		
6. Do you know what a Joint Venture is?		
7. Do you know the steps to incorporate?		
8. Do you know the benefits of an S Corporation?		
9. Are you aware of local, state and federal regulations?		
10. Are you aware of licenses and permits?		
11. Are you aware of trademarks, patents and copyrights?		
12. Have you estimated costs?		
13. Have you consulted an attorney and an accountant?		

CREATING A BUSINESS PLAN

A sound business plan can mean the difference between success and failure. Rather than pursuing conflicting goals or allowing the business to develop haphazardly, you can use the plan to help you solidify ideas, and keep your business on track. Some of the questions your plan should answer are:

- What is my business?
- What are my products or services?
- Who are my competitors?
- Who is my target market?
- What is the best marketing strategy?
- How should my resources be utilized?
- What is the business' profit potential?

Even though you may not be able to work out all the answers in advance, or may find that they change later, the important thing is to have a set of assumptions about the business and its environment that you can share with others. This will make it easier for you to enlist their support in launching the business and in carrying out their respective tasks and yours as a cohesive unit.

Given the rapid changes occurring in the marketplace and the increasing levels of competition that all businesses face, you can't afford to proceed blindly, hoping that hard work alone will be enough to make your kitchen and bathroom business a success. To succeed, a business must have clearly defined objectives and a fully developed strategy for achieving them. In short, what is needed is a business plan.

Far from viewing a business plan as a luxury reserved for big businesses or something created solely to impress the financial community, entrepreneurs should see it for what it is—one of the most important tools a business can have. Just as an organization chart shows the working relationships of the people within a business, a business plan presents the purpose of the business and what it intends to accomplish. A good business plan helps to give form and substance to an entrepreneurial vision, providing a mechanism that enables owners, managers and workers to function effectively. The better the business plan, the better equipped your business will be to recognize and assess the opportunities and risks that lie ahead.

WHEN TO USE A BUSINESS PLAN

If you are setting up a business, you need a business plan to verify that you have covered all elements needed for startup and obtaining financing. However, much like a Swiss Army knife with its multitude of tools, your plan can serve many purposes. Once you are in business, you will use your business plan when you are:

Expanding Your Business

Your business plan can help reduce the added risks involved in expanding your business. A plan is especially critical during an expansion phase since this is one of the most dangerous times for a business. If you try to expand a business too quickly, before mastering its current level of activity, the quality of your products and services may suffer. On the other hand, if you wait too long, the market could be saturated with similar products and services offered and the opportunity may be lost.

By addressing such issues as timing, the rate of expansion (should the business grow at an annual rate of 5 percent or 20 percent?), and the type of expansion (a bigger building, additional locations, new products), your plan can help you to make the right choices. In this way, instead of being overwhelmed by growth, you should be able to maintain a manageable level.

Developing New Products

For most businesses, the need to develop new products is brought about by the continuing challenge of satisfying customers' changing needs and making effective use of new technologies by developing new products and services or by improving existing ones. The company that developed the new "lifetime" light bulb knew this; they invented a product that lasts years longer than traditional incandescent and fluorescent bulbs, and is more energy efficient.

Unless the business has a plan to guide it, though, the chances of coming up with profitable ideas for new products, product modifications or improvements are minimal. To make the most of your resources as your business grows, you must have a systematic plan for developing new products and services and managing your current ones.

Obtaining Financing

Commercial lenders, such as banks and finance companies, expect to see a business plan as a matter of course before they will lend money to a business. The same holds true for government lenders. Even when there is sufficient collateral to pledge a security for the loan, a business plan is still likely to be required because it shows where the business is going and how the money will be utilized.

A business plan is even more important if you are seeking investment capital. Investors, especially venture capitalists, tend to be more demanding than lenders because their risks are greater. Unless the plan can convince them that financing a business will enable them to earn a substantial return on their investment, the standard response is "No go, no dough." This puts the burden on you to demonstrate through your business plan that the investment will be worth their while.

Making Management Decisions

Perhaps the most valuable use of a business plan is in making management decisions. By stating what the business wants to accomplish in assessing both its internal and external environments, a business plan shows the big picture. This gives you a real advantage. Instead of operating in the dark or looking at just one aspect of a problem, you can consider it from all points of view and make decisions that are in the best overall interest of your business.

Along with this, your business plan can also help you to maintain your objectivity, enabling you to see the business as an outsider would. Putting sentiment aside, you can then focus on what needs to be done to achieve your goals, making hard decisions when necessary.

Maintaining Control

Another key use of a business plan is as a control device. Are goals being met? Did sales reach their target? Are sales and production increasing according to schedule? Are costs staying in line? Is the business doing what it set out to do? You should be able to get the answers to these questions and more by examining your business plan. Then, by carefully rating your performance against your goals, you can determine if you are moving ahead or merely stepping in place. If a method or strategy is not working, or if you find that the business is going in a different direction, you can act quickly to bring these back in line or chart a new course.

GUIDELINES FOR SUCCESSFUL PLANNING

The following guidelines should help you to master the planning process and become more proficient at preparing, updating and using a business plan.

1. *Set aside time for planning.* Recognizing the need to plan is one thing, allocating the time to do it can be another. Call it planning phobia or simply procrastination, for your business to succeed, you must spend sufficient time on planning.

2. *Determine in advance what you want to accomplish.* What is the purpose of the planning effort? To prepare a business plan for a new venture? To update an existing plan? To obtain financing? By identifying your specific planning goals, you can focus your attention on the key issues or activities that need to be addressed.

3. *Be sure you have access to the necessary facts.* Information is what fuels the planning process. To plan effectively, your information must be relevant, accurate and up to date. This means having access to internal information, such as accounting records and sales reports, and external information, such as industry trends and consumer buying habits.

4. *Coordinate your planning efforts with the efforts of others.* Ensure that each person involved in the planning process knows what everyone else is doing. To avoid working at cross purposes—pursuing one planning objective while a partner or employee is pursuing another—your efforts must be coordinated. This is the only way to maintain harmony and guarantee that the goals set for the business are compatible.

5. *Keep an open mind.* To achieve the best results as a planner, it is important not to get locked into one approach to a problem or situation. Different strategies must be given a chance to develop and possible courses of action explored. Above all, let yourself be creative. Rather than starting out with a preconceived idea of what your business should do or not do, take the time to consider the alternatives.

6. *Solicit input from others.* Don't be afraid to ask for advice and get others' viewpoints. As your business grows, this will become increasingly important. The planning process works best when it is a collaborative effort bringing together those responsible for creating the business plan with those who will be called upon to implement it.

7. *Review your business plan.* Once your business plan is completed, go over it to see that it clearly depicts your business and adequately states your intentions. Before implementing the plan, be sure that it will enable you to achieve your objectives.

8. *Update the plan.* Business experts often recommend updating a business plan every six months. That way, you can determine whether the plan is continuing to meet the needs of your business. As circumstances change or as new information becomes available, the plan should be updated accordingly.

9.   *Make the plan accessible.* All too often business plans are kept from the very people who need to see them. Keeping proprietary information from your competitors makes sense; keeping it from your own people does not. For key employees to fully contribute their talents and abilities to the business, they must know what it stands for and where it is going.

10. *Use the plan.* Most important of all, you must use your business plan. A plan that is gathering dust on the shelf or buried in a filing cabinet can't do you any good. If your plan is going to be the blueprint for a successful business, you must put it to work.

I consider myself to be very fortunate to have been exposed to an excellent education, but, more importantly, my formative years in business were with larger businesses—businesses that were sophisticated in how they were run. I learned at an early stage the importance of a mission statement, a business plan, a budget and good human resource management. I know that there are owners and managers in our great kitchen and bathroom industry who have not had the advantage of these experiences. But, there are many books, classes and mentors that are available to anyone who is willing to invest his or her time and energy in learning how to become a more professional manager.

Before I started *The Plumbery*, I did a complete three-year business plan, which included marketing, financial and human resource information. I took this package to a bank and they immediately agreed to be a partner. Every quarter, we review our budgets and business plan, and revise, redo and extend the numbers as dictated for that particular period in time. This is our road map to keep us on course. It eliminates surprises. It has been a major contributor to our success. Gathering the following information will aide you as you develop your plan.

I.   An Overview of the Business
      A.   Name of the company
      B.   Nature of the business
      C.   Major business objectives
      D.   Legal form of the business
      E.   Desired image

II.   The Physical Plant
      A.   Description of desired location (state, town, area, neighborhood, site)
      B.   Transportation facility requirements
      C.   Parking facilities
      D.   Building (size, condition, description, façade, remodeling/renovation required)
      E.   Terms of lease/purchase and all occupancy details
      F.   Utilities (availability, costs, arrangements)
      G.   Permits and licenses required
      H.   Zoning regulations
      I.   Machinery, equipment and fixtures required
      J.   Leasehold build-out (costs, products, displays, etc.)

      K.   Interior layout and design
      L.   Supplies required

III.   The Financial Plan
      A.   Initial investment requirement
      B.   Additional financial needs and possible sources
      C.   Projected sales
      D.   *Pro forma* balance sheet (two to three years)
      E.   *Pro forma* income and expense statements (P&Ls) (two to three years)
      F.   Cash flow projections
      G.   Insurance requirements
      H.   Bookkeeping method
      I.   Expected taxation liabilities and responsibilities
      J.   Internal risk-reduction measures to be utilized

IV.   The Marketing Plan
      A.   Targeted customer groups: demographics, characteristics, market segment size
      B.   Analysis of competition
      C.   Product mix
      D.   Services mix
      E.   Pricing policy: discounting, price ranges, promotional pricing
      F.   Determining prices (markup or markdown)
      G.   Budget for advertising, promotion and public relations
      H.   Promotion calendar for each year
      I.   Advertising plans (media selection, schedules, cooperative advertising)
      J.   Salespeople requirements, i.e., inside selling or outside selling or both
      K.   Training program requirements
      L.   Sales promotion requirements
      M.   Window and interior displays (if retail business)
      N.   Distribution methods and channels
      O.   Market research requirements
      P.   Credit extension and management of accounts receivable

V.   Human Resource Plan
      A.   Organizational chart for the business
      B.   Key personnel (names, job titles, education, experience requirements)
      C.   Written job description for each position
      D.   Open positions
      E.   Sources for personnel
      F.   Details of employee compensation, including fringe benefits
      G.   Plans for employee training (initial and ongoing)

VI.   Inventory Plan
        A.   Initial inventory requirement (all details by item, quantity, cost, quality, depth and width)
        B.   Details for inventory management, planning and control
        C.   Projected rates of inventory turnover
        D.   Buying: names and addresses of suppliers
        E.   Buying: terms, delivery, warranties and representation

HOW TO PREPARE YOUR BUSINESS PLAN

Once you have decided that your business needs a plan, or your business plan needs to be updated, you are ready to begin. Much as you may be tempted to skip this step or hire someone else to do the work for you, *don't!* The effort you put into it and the knowledge you gain from creating the finished, written plan will be invaluable.

Although every business plan is different, reflecting the ideas and intentions of the person who wrote it, certain elements or sections are common to all plans. As shown in the business plan outline that follows, your plan should be organized so that it provides essential information in a concise and logical format.

BUSINESS PLAN OUTLINE

Title Page

The title page should include the name of your business, address and phone number, and the names of all owners. The important thing is to provide prospective lenders, investors and others who see the plan with a means of contacting you.

Table of Contents

A table of contents is absolutely essential. It not only provides an overview of what is in your plan, but enables readers to quickly find what they are looking for without having to thumb through all the pages. This makes a more reader-friendly plan which will, in turn, help to generate a favorable response.

Executive Summary

The executive summary is the single most important element of a business plan. Having the power to make or break your plan, it should provide a concise, but clear, picture of your business—within a maximum of two pages. Designed to stimulate a busy reader's interest, the executive summary must convince the reader to take the time to go over the rest of the plan in detail. Among the points that you should cover in the executive summary are:

1. The current status of your business, indicating when it was started (or when it is expected to commence operations).

2. A description of your products or services.

3. Information about your target market and your means for researching it.

4. The strengths inherent in your business that will enable it to achieve its objectives (e.g., experience, a unique idea, good location, product quality).

5. Your short-term and long-term plans.

6. Financial projections.

7. The amount of money, if any, you are currently seeking.

Condensing all this data to a two-page summary is not easy, but, by staying focused on the key facts, you can do it. And, remember, even though the summary comes first in your business plan, write it last. That way, you will have the business in perspective and the information you need in hand.

Business/Industry Description

This section should begin with a statement of the goals and objectives of the business, defining what the business does (or will do) and its purpose. This is the place to put background information about the founding of the business, its ownership and legal structure, the nature of its industry, and the role the business will play in it. Include any data you have about changes in the marketplace that will lead to an increased demand for what your business offers. As you can imagine, investors are particularly attracted to growth industries.

Products or Services Description

Explain what your business sells or proposes to sell, describing your products or services in detail, e.g., their features, quality, performance levels and functions. It is important to point out what separates them from competitors' product offerings, and the benefits customers will derive from them. In other words, what makes your products or services unique or gives them the edge? If you are utilizing a trade secret, such as a design, trademark or formula, or have (or expect to receive) patent protection, that should also be stated.

Organizational Data

In this section, outline the duties and responsibilities of the people involved in your business. Make it clear who does what (in production, sales, accounting, etc.), and who reports to whom. If you are currently an organization of one, describe the tasks you will be carrying out and estimate your future personnel needs. To further illustrate how your business is set up, it is a good idea to include an organization chart in this section, along with résumés showing each person's qualifications.

Marketing Strategy

The main reason for starting a business is to sell something. That's where marketing strategy comes in. The primary objectives in this section of your business plan are to:

1. Define your target market, describing your potential customers and why they buy.

2. Estimate the total market size and determine what share of it you can realistically hope to obtain.

3. Develop a pricing structure that will ensure you maximum profitability.

4. Determine what combination of advertising and publicity to use to promote the business.

5. Outline a distribution strategy that will enable you to reach customers most effectively.

In spelling out these objectives, try to be as specific as you can, basing your marketing strategy on facts, rather than on wishful thinking. Much of the information you will need to formulate your strategy can be obtained through books, magazines, government reports, trade associations, and your own observations and research.

Competitive Analysis

Your competitive analysis should identify the key players in your industry and explain how your business can compete with them. Focusing on your strengths and advantages (as noted in your product or service description), you want to show how you can capitalize on them to gain your desired market share. Your purpose is not to belittle the competition. Rather, it is to point out the customers whose needs your competition is failing to serve properly, if at all, and of limitations, such as being too large or having dated technology, that keep them from doing what you can do.

Operations Plan

This is the "nuts and bolts" section of your business plan—the place to describe how your product or service will actually be produced or delivered to the customer. Information about facilities, equipment and supplies is entered in this section. You should also explain what technologies, skills and processes are required to do the job.

Financial Information

Last is the financial section of your plan, and the one that lenders and investors often consider to be the heart of it. Consisting of the financial data relevant to your business venture, this section includes your current financial statements, as well as projected income and expense statement, balance sheet and cash flow statement. Covering a period of one to three years, these projections are meant to provide a financial picture of your business showing its expected revenues and expenses, assets and liabilities.

Doing the work to come up with the financial data you need takes time, but, with practice, you will be surprised how adept you become at number crunching. To find out more about financial statements and how to prepare and use them, see the following chapter.

See a sample kitchen and bathroom dealer's business plan at the end of this chapter.

To evaluate how your planning efforts are going and to identify those areas that need work, answer these questions.

PLANNING CHECKLIST	YES	NO
1. Have you developed a clear concept of what you want your business to be?		
2. Have you learned as much as possible about your business and its industry?		
3. Do you have the necessary information (financial data, marketing research and production requirements) to put together a business plan?		
4. Have you looked at other business plans (available at your local library or Small Business Development Center) to see how they were written?		
5. Are you willing to put in the necessary time to prepare a business plan?		
6. Have you talked about your plan with the people whose support you will need, and solicited their help with it?		
7. Have you taken steps to make the planning process inclusive, rather than exclusive, so that everyone involved in your business can contribute to it?		
8. Is planning an ongoing part of your business activities?		
9. Do you place as much importance on planning as you do on taking action?		
10. Is your mind open to new ways of doing things and new opportunities?		
11. Have you allowed yourself to be creative in forming a business vision that is uniquely your own?		
12. Is your business plan updated at least once a year?		
13. Do you currently have a business plan that you are satisfied with?		
14. Are you really using your plan as a tool in making management decisions and in shaping your business?		

DETERMINING THE BEST LOCATION

Where your business is located may seem a moot point—you're in business, right? But, always be aware of and consider your options. An opportunity may arise. The location of your business is too important to be decided casually, or solely on the basis of personal preference. To do so is to invite disaster. Major corporations are well aware of this. When seeking to relocate or expand their facilities, big business leaders sometimes spend years researching and analyzing the pros and cons of various locations. In our industry, and possibly in your case, spending that much time is probably not feasible or even advisable. However, the same scientific approach that works for big business can and should work for you.

CHOOSING THE COMMUNITY

When evaluating a particular community, ask yourself the following questions:

1. *Is there a need for my product or service?* A generally approved business strategy is to find a need and fill it. Will your new or preexisting business be able to fill a need in this community? If not, a change must be made—either in the type of business you're considering or in the community you are considering locating in.

2. *What is the customer potential, i.e., how many customers are there?* Is the number of potential customers large enough to justify locating your business in this community? The closer you are to your main market, the easier it will be to serve it. Local libraries are a good place to begin looking for this demographic information. The chamber of commerce is another.

3. *How strong is the competition?* Having determined that there is a market for your product or service, it is important not to overlook the competition. Do any businesses already have a foothold in this community? How many? How strong are they? What can you offer that will set your business apart from the rest? If yours is to be the first such business in the community, why haven't others already located there? Perhaps there is some drawback that you may have overlooked.

4. *Is the community prosperous enough to support my business?* To determine the community's level of prosperity, take a close look at its economic structure. Is it based on manufacturing, retail, services or a combination of all of these? Who are the major employers in town? What kind of work do the employees perform? How much unemployment is there? Could layoffs in one sector result in an economic collapse, if, for instance, a plant closed down? And will you be able to compete in terms of compensation with the local labor force?

5. *What is the community's growth potential?* Are people moving into the community or leaving it? Some positive indicators of growth are land development projects, the presence of department stores and other major businesses, well-kept homes and storefronts, active citizens' groups such as a chamber of commerce, PTA and adequate public services (health, education, safety and transportation).

6. *What kinds of people live there, what are the demographics (e.g., age, income, interests, occupations)?* In addition to the size of the community's population, you should be concerned about its makeup. What is the average age? How much does a typical worker earn? What percentage of the community is married, single, divorced? What is the average number of children per household? What is the per capita income? This type of statistical information, called demographics, can be obtained from local census tracts or your chamber of commerce. For a more complete profile of the local residents, you might examine their lifestyles as well. What do they like to do in their spare time? Read? Ski? Golf? Garden? Are they politically conservative or liberal? Data of this nature, known as psychographics, tells about the inner workings

of people, focusing on their activities, interests and opinions. This can be obtained through questionnaires, interviews and your own observations.

7. *What are the restrictions on my type of business (licenses, zoning, local ordinances)?* Each community has its own unique restrictions, instituted to either promote or discourage different types of businesses. In selecting your location, make sure you are aware of these restrictions. If not, you could find yourself prohibited from obtaining business licenses, expanding your facilities, receiving deliveries or maintaining certain hours of operation. By finding out ahead of time what to expect, you can avoid unpleasant surprises later.

8. *Will my suppliers have ready access to me?* If you are considering settling in a remote, out-of-the way locale, your privacy may come at a price. Unless your suppliers have ready access to you, you might be unable to obtain necessary shipments, or find yourself paying premium shipping costs. This will, of course, have a bearing on the merchandise you carry and the price you charge for it.

9. *Do my vendors need a supplier in this geographic area?* Are the best products and services that you are considering already committed to other competitors? Is there enough potential in this marketplace to entice the vendor to want to sell to you? Do the demographics of the area justify the vendors' interest in having their products or services sold in this area?

10. *Is the local labor force both adequate and affordable?* Whether labor is available and affordable depends on your type of business. In the kitchen and bathroom industry, finding a specialized or technical workforce could be difficult. This difficulty increases as the number of potential employees increases. As for wages, these vary with the community's standard of living. Will budgetary factors necessitate you locating in a community where labor costs might be lower?

11. *Do I like the community enough to live and work in it?* Regardless of your answers to the first 10 questions, if you can't say yes to this one, keep looking. Relying on personal preferences alone can be disastrous, but ignoring them all together can be equally so. The location that is best for your business must also be right for you and your family.

Once you've answered these questions, you will be in a much better position to rate a particular community's attractiveness. And, you will quickly see that an ideal location for one business can be totally wrong for another. A seaside resort, for instance, might just be the place to sell bathing suits, but a bad choice for a kitchen cabinet manufacturing business. Selecting the community where you wish to locate is only half the location process. The second, and equally important step, is to select the site within the community.

CHOOSING THE SITE

Regardless of the type of business you are in or growing into, be it a retail, wholesale, manufacturing or service, site selection plays an important role in its development. Evidence of this was found in a major study conducted by General Foods. The company wanted to know why certain grocery stores achieved greater profitability than others, so it compared seemingly identical stores carrying the same merchandise and utilizing the same operating and promotional procedures. Management effectiveness was also taken into consideration. Surprisingly, the stores that stood head and shoulders above the rest were not always the most well managed. Another factor was needed to explain this—the sites of the stores. Because of errors in site selection, some of the stores, though well managed, could never hope to achieve the success of the stores with better locations. Such liabilities as competition, declining neighborhoods and inadequate parking space were just too much to overcome.

The success of Sears and Roebuck after World War II can largely be attributed to its recognition of the importance of site selection. Instead of adding stores in the already overcrowded, downtown areas of American cities, where other major retailers were focusing their efforts, Sears decided to open its new stores on the outskirts of the cities. This was where it anticipated that post-war families would want to live. To further meet these families' needs, Sears made it a point to provide adequate parking space as well—something that downtown competitors were unable to do.

You've heard that "location, location, location" is so very important. Here's a personal experience: We have two showrooms. One is located on one of our city's busiest highways (an estimated 90,000 cars per day pass by our front window). We have large display windows and a big lighted sign facing the freeway. We ask all of our customers to "sign in" when they enter the showroom. One of the questions on the sign-in register is "How did you hear about us?" Referral is the number one answer. Another common answer is, "Saw you from the freeway." Our second store is well located, but it doesn't have the same exposure. If I could choose that location over, I'd try very hard to replicate the exposure of the first store.

Both stores are in retail "strip centers" with other building-product stores close by. Try and locate close to lighting, flooring, tile, design-oriented businesses. It makes it easier for clients to shop, and you'll draw potential clients from those businesses.

Our business is marketed toward the "higher-end" product. Thus, our clients are the more affluent. With this in mind, our store locations are in "nice" neighborhoods, surrounded by "nice" stores. There is excellent parking, lighting and accessibility. The whole atmosphere as you approach our stores is "upscale" in keeping with the niche toward which we have elected to market.

In contrast to this, if you elect to market in volume and sell the more competitive products, you might select a warehouse or industrial park location, giving the "bare bones" impression. The key is to be consistent from location, to type of building, to display, to products. If you choose to market both upper- and lower-end products and services, your job is a bit tougher.

Here you may need a location/building/display somewhere in the middle. My experience is that it is difficult to be all things to all people.

If your business is established, and you find nearby neighbors are neglecting their buildings and property, your business will be affected. Since the kitchen and bathroom business depends on image, the issue needs to be resolved. What is clearly an eyesore to you, may not be as apparent to your neighbors. Rather than confronting them, perhaps you can launch a cleanup campaign on your block. Your efforts to improve your property and the surrounding area may encourage your neighbors to do the same. Getting to know the owners may make an ally of them in revitalizing the area. If the situation is not improving, you may have to approach your landowner or the local code enforcement officials to determine your position. Moving to a new location is a serious consideration if your efforts are not successful.

THE ENVIRONMENT

Each of the following sites has its own unique characteristics, which you will want to consider. Then, given your particular kitchen and bathroom business needs, you can best select the environment.

The Downtown Business District. This is the part of town where finance, business and industrial concerns generally have their headquarters. Depending on the community in which you have decided to locate, this area can range in size from a few square blocks to many square miles. In this environment, a high percentage of your customers will be employees of the neighboring businesses. And, although they may commute great distances by car to reach their jobs, once there, they will generally confine any shopping to what is within walking distance. Peak shopping times, not surprisingly, are during lunch and before and after work. In the evenings and on weekends, sales are likely to drop off. The businesses most likely to flourish in the city's downtown areas are restaurants, shoe stores, bars, department stores, gift stores, bookstores, clothing shops and any other enterprise that caters to the working person.

A Shopping Center. The development of planned shopping centers and malls, which reached a peak in the 1980s, changed forever the way people shop and businesses operate. Shoppers could now do most of their shopping in a controlled environment, without having to leave a store, drive long distances and repeatedly search for parking places. Retail and service establishments could attract customers into their places of business simply by being in a popular shopping center or mall. Potential customers, who once might have driven by without shopping, now would stop to look and to buy.

Shopping centers seemed to be the way to go, but not for all businesses. Before you locate in a mall or center, take the time to find out what all the terms of occupancy are. What does your rent cover? Are there additional or hidden charges for shared facilities or services, such as parking, landscaping, decorations and signs, walkways, public rest areas, special programs, and joint advertising? What restrictions will you need to abide by? Would your business have to be open during specific hours on specific days? How much value would you really be getting for your money? Is the square footage adequate for your needs? Would your assigned space be in a good location in relation to the surrounding businesses as well as to the flow of customers' foot traffic through the shopping center or mall? Would your business be off by itself at the end of a side corridor, where customers would be likely to pass by without even noticing it?

Some other things to be aware of in evaluating a shopping center is the caliber of management operating it, and the mix of businesses represented. Are they compatible or competitive? What quality of goods and services do they offer? How many magnet stores (department stores) which draw customers to the center are there? You should also consider the vacancy rate of that shopping center.

Locating your business in a shopping center or a mall is expensive, and the various costs associated with such a location might be prohibitive. Furthermore, not all businesses derive any real advantage from a shopping center location. Some businesses, such as shoe-repair shops and cleaners, which provide essential services, probably would do as well, maybe even better, on a major street. The businesses that most benefit from a shopping center or mall location are the ones that cater not only to working people, but to non-working adults and to teenagers.

A Major Street or Highway. (Or a side street, near a highway access) Major streets have the heaviest flow of automobile traffic. Though perfect for fast food restaurants, and other "stop and shop" businesses, heavily trafficked streets can have drawbacks. Getting people to stop is one of them. If your business will be dependent on foot traffic or window shoppers, scouting a location will be more than just counting the cars passing by. What is your assessment of the array of businesses located there (antique shops or auto repair shops?), the desirability of the neighborhood, and the availability of parking? Does the street have a character that will make your potential customers feel at ease there?

If you have decided that relocating on a major street is the way to go for your business, and you have found the right street, the selection process still isn't over. Which side of the street is best? According to market experts, the "going-home" side of the street is better because people do their shopping on the way home from work rather than on the way to work. Businesses on the going-home side of the street tend to have bigger sales. Furthermore, when given a choice of shopping in sun or shade shoppers generally choose shade. This means that businesses on the shady side have bigger sales. If the going-home side and the shady side do not coincide, you might compensate for a lack of shade by erecting an awning.

An Industrial/Commercial Park. In recent years, the number of industrial/commercial parks being built has continued to increase. These sites are designed and built exclusively for businesses that engage in "business-to-business" selling or in industrial sales. Located on the outskirts of cities or in the suburbs where large parcels of land are available, these parks are often chosen by businesses for their headquarters or manufacturing operations. Among the advantages of this type of location are space, parking, desirable zoning laws and attractive leasing rates. Since most industrial/commercial parks are off the beaten track, retail and service businesses that cater to the general public may want to opt for more visible locations.

A Business Incubator. Business incubators are specially designed facilities for new or fledgling businesses. Created to provide entrepreneurs with affordable space and a support system, e.g., reception, secretarial services, computers, fax and copiers). Incubators provide a nurturing environment in which to grow a business. Protecting new businesses at the time when they are most vulnerable, incubators often sponsor workshops and seminars for their entrepreneur tenants on such subjects as financing, marketing and management.

PERFORMING A TRAFFIC COUNT

One way to gauge the potential sales volume of a site is to do a traffic count. This involves more than simply counting each car or person passing by. It requires that you analyze the flow of passersby to determine which are your customers. For instance, if you were planning to operate a women's health club, you would not be interested in counting the number of men who walk or drive by.

The accuracy of your traffic count depends on your ability to assess who your potential customers are. Prior to doing the count, you will want to spend some time drawing up a profile of your customers to help you recognize them when they pass by.

Having determined whom to count, the next thing to do is decide the scope of the count. Will it encompass just the area directly in front of your store or will it include nearby or cross traffic? Are you going to count people as they enter the area or as they leave it? If you count them at both times, there's a good chance you will be counting people twice. To guard against double counting, it is essential that you set up strategic checkpoints where your count is to be conducted. The timing of your count must also be carefully planned to coincide with a normal or typical period. If you conduct your count during a peak holiday, like during Christmas/Chanukah or the Passover/Easter vacation, it will be too high. Counting on Fridays or on the first day of the month could throw your tally out of balance also, since these are the times when many people receive paychecks and social security checks.

After you have chosen the time for your count, the final step is to divide the day into half-hour intervals. In this way, you can get both a total count of the day's traffic flow and subtotals for the flows at various intervals during the day. These subtotals will tell you when to expect the heaviest sales each day, which should help you plan your hours of operation. For additional information, many business owners find it helpful to do more than one traffic count and compare the data for various days. There are outside services available to help you achieve your traffic count. Refer to your local yellow pages for this information.

RATING THE SITE

You should find it easier to determine a site's desirability if you set up a rating system of some kind, against which each site can be judged. The following score sheet shown is just one example. Depending on the specific needs of your kitchen and bathroom business, you may very well wish to modify it.

CHARACTERISTICS	EXCELLENT	GOOD	FAIR	POOR
1. Centrally located to reach my market.				
2. Merchandise/raw material availability.				
3. Nearby competition.				
4. Transportation availability and rates.				
5. Parking facilities.				
6. Adequacy of utilities (sewer, water, gas, electricity, telephones, etc.).				
7. Traffic flow.				
8. Taxation burden.				
9. Quality of police and fire protection.				
10. Environmental factors (schools, cultural and community activities).				
11. Quantity of available employees.				
12. Prevailing rates of employee pay.				
13. Housing availability for workers and management.				
14. Local business climate and state of economy.				
15. Conditions of neighboring buildings.				
16. Your own personal feelings about the area.				
17. Accessibility for customers.				

YOUR BUILDING

Whether you plan to lease an existing building or construct a new one, care should be taken to ensure that the building is appropriate for your specific kitchen and bathroom business.

If you lease your building, verify the following:

- Rent - How much money for how much space? How often will it be raised?
- Sublease - Can you sublease if you need to move? Can you sublet a part of your space while you are there?
- Services - What services, utilities and insurance coverage are included?
- Improvements - Who pays for improvements? What changes can you make?
- Lease - Can your lease be renewed? How long does it run?

If you buy your building, protect yourself by the following:

- Have your lawyer prepare a purchase agreement that contains a legal description of the building, the property and all building fixtures.
- Include all details in the initial agreement that you sign.
- Determine if there are zoning or building code restrictions.

The building you finally decide on should be expected to do more than just keep the rain out. It should also promote your business and help it to function properly. Call the elements "looks" and "livability" if you will. Does the building have the looks to get a second glance from your potential customers and, better yet, to make them want to come inside. As for livability, how suitable is the building for your various business activities, e.g., selling, manufacturing, administration, shipping, receiving and storage? Unless your building gets a passing rating in both looks and livability, you are in for problems—the most common ones being lost sales, operations headaches and remodeling costs.

Forget what you've heard about not judging a book by its cover. Right or wrong, this is precisely what people will do every time they pass the building. Even those who never come inside, and know next to nothing about your business, will form opinions about it on the basis of its outside appearance—its looks alone. As such, the exterior of your building should be thought of as a communications medium, capable of transmitting messages about your business. If you are not careful, it's easy to transmit the wrong message. For instance, it would be a mistake for a store selling discount housewares and appliances to be in a building with a polished marble front and brass handles on the doors. Potential customers would take one look at the marble and brass and automatically assume that the store had high prices. A brick or stucco exterior, on the other hand, would get a positive reaction, encouraging people to associate the store with economy and practicability.

Retailing

Nowhere do looks exert a greater influence on the success and failure of a business than in retailing. Not only must your store's exterior accurately identify the nature of your business, but it must also be inviting enough to attract people inside. Achieving both ends, identification and invitation, requires planning and attention to detail. For best results, your store's architectural style, building materials, exterior colors, display windows and signs, should all be part of a coordinated effort. Ideally, each element complements the others and serves to reinforce your store's overall image. More than money, what's needed here is imagination and a clear idea of the kind of store you want it to be. Once you know that, it is easier to communicate the right message to others.

Manufacturing

Manufacturing establishments have a little more room for error in the "looks" department than do retailers. This is because they are less dependent on their ability to draw customers inside their places of business. Customers generally do not see the plants of the companies they do business with. Orders are usually placed through wholesalers and sales representatives or by mail. Potential customers who do visit a plant are generally more interested in examining the production facilities than in admiring the building. Although the looks of your building take a back seat to its livability, this is not to say that looks should be ignored. The exterior of your building makes a statement about the quality of the products you sell, your company's policies, and the level of success it has achieved. A rundown, unattractive building can only reflect badly on the business.

Services

Some services are so specialized that their clients actually seek them out and go to some trouble to find them (consultants, automobile repair shops, landscape architects, etc.). Others such as shoe repair shops and cleaners, are frequented so regularly that customers hurry in and out, barely even noticing how the facilities look. These places do not have to use looks to pull customers in because they are coming in already. But, not all services find it this easy to attract customers. Restaurants and hotels, for instance, rely on a great deal on drop-in customer traffic. The more inviting their buildings are, the better it is for business.

LIVABILITY

Because a building is deemed to conform to building codes doesn't make it suitable for any and all businesses. The difference between a livable building and one that's impossible depends on what you intend to do with it. The same building that is a dream come true for an automobile repair shop would probably be a nightmare for a jewelry shop. The best way to avoid going into the wrong building is to consider the building in terms of its construction, space, design and accessibility.

Is the building's construction such that it will be both safe and serviceable for your business? A manufacturer utilizing heavy equipment needs a building structure made of building materials that can reduce noise, resist fire and hold up to heavy wear. Cement and steel win out over wood and glass in this respect.

Does the building provide too much space or too little? Is there room for expansion later should the need arise? For optimum operating efficiency, it is important to strike a balance between your present and future needs for space.

Can effective use be made of the building's design? This requires that the relationship between the building's selling, work, and storage areas be compatible with your business activities.

Is the building readily accessible to both your customers and delivery personnel? Steps, entrances (their number and location) and loading facilities all play an important role in your day-to-day operating efficiency.

LAYOUT

Layout refers to the physical setup of furniture and fixtures, equipment, merchandise and supplies within your building. The better your layout, the easier it is for workers to do their jobs and for customers to shop. Conversely, a bad layout can be the cause of inefficiency and lost sales.

Arriving at the right layout involves more than just moving things around and hoping for the best. It involves arranging in a way calculated to display merchandise and services to their best advantage, conserve time and motion and fully utilize equipment. For retail businesses, this translates into increased customer traffic and sales, and for manufacturing service businesses, this means increased productivity and sales.

Retailing

In retailing, the main function of your layout is to direct the flow of customer traffic throughout the store. This is a two-stage process, first drawing customers into your store and then guiding them from one location to the next within it. Rather than having your customers wander haphazardly, or even turn around and walk back outside, an effective layout leads customers where you want them to go. En route, exposure to your merchandise increases the number of purchases made. It sounds easy, and it is, if you apply a few tested principles.

Study your customers' shopping habits. Find out which items customers purchase regularly and which ones only occasionally. Your observations should also help you differentiate between impulse items and demand items. Impulse items are purchased on the spur of the moment, without any planning. Demand items are purchased deliberately, according to plan.

Once you know how your customers shop, you can arrange your merchandise accordingly. An attractive kitchen display, seen by customers as they walk in the door, makes an impact and piques the curiosity. Walking through the kitchen display should lead customers to perhaps a second, different type of kitchen display. If you want your customers to look at a top-of-the-line kitchen, you can arrange your display area so that customers will naturally continue in that direction.

Create visually appealing merchandise displays. Unless your displays have eye appeal, customers will ignore them. How important is this? According to a group of independent retailers surveyed by the National Retail Merchants Association, one out of every four sales can be attributed to merchandise display. Other stores have credited displays for as much as 50 percent of their sales.

To improve your displays, look at displays in other stores, read trade magazines and ask your merchandise suppliers for tips. Many manufacturers will provide retailers with ready-made displays of their products at little or no charge. Keep displays inviting, making regular changes. You won't change a major display every week, but you could set out bowls of fresh apples one day, and a cluster of green plants another. If you have sales promotions or manufacturers' color displays, move them around. Customers come in several weeks in a row.

Our business is both decorative plumbing and hardware, and kitchen cabinets, appliances and countertops. It is our experience that keeping the plumbing and hardware displays current and appealing is much easier and less costly than the kitchen area.

We have about 10 different kitchen displays in both of our stores (approximately 3,500 square feet each). With ever-changing designs, styles, colors, wood and finish preferences, we try to change each vignette every three to four years. We've learned to rotate these so that the cost is spread over this period of time. But any way you approach this, it's expensive. It's all leasehold improvement and can be depreciated, but it is still expensive.

I've come to believe that a kitchen dealer could do an excellent marketing job with 2,500 square feet of showroom. Have two or three main vignettes and several smaller ones. Show a wide variety of product and design. Since a small room means less overall cost, you've saved on space and product. But, don't compromise on the quality of the build-out. Put in all the "bells and whistles."

- Have a wall of doors with different styles and finishes. Develop a complete job scrapbook with professional before-and-after pictures and testimonials.

- Incorporate large (24" x 18") back-lit color photographs of kitchens that you have done. They tell a great story and are easy to change-out at a reasonable cost.

- Accessorize, accessorize, accessorize, and make each display unique and complete, so that clients feel as though they are in a real working kitchen.

- Develop an "appliance room." We sell appliances (high end only). At first, we tried to incorporate as many as possible into the vignettes. Even with our larger showrooms, we were limited in how many appliances we could show, so we developed an "appliance room," where we can show 15 to 20 built-in appliances in a small, 10' x 10' room. They are easy to change-out and are all together for selling purposes. It's less expensive than building them into the individual vignettes.

- Solicit free materials and installation from subcontractors (flooring, tile, lighting, countertops) in return for displaying promotional material on their business in your showroom. Work out similar reciprocal arrangements for their showrooms.

Keep merchandise displays fresh. Even the most dramatic displays start to look commonplace when they have been left up too long. Do not let yours become permanent fixtures. Do not allow the displays to be robbed of particular items that customers may need on the spur of the moment. They should be 100 percent in completeness and cleanliness at all times.

Coordinate merchandise displays. Merchandise that goes together should be displayed together. In this way, customers are stimulated to purchase more than a single item. A customer purchasing a sink is likely to consider replacing an entire counter unit, if the sink he or she looks at is displayed attractively in a unit. In a bathroom business, it is easier and makes good sense to display all the various types, sizes, shapes and colors of toilets in one area so that the customer can go directly there to make his or her choice.

Create a pleasant shopping environment. Make sure your store is an enjoyable place in which to shop. In addition to being clean and attractive, it should have appropriate lighting and adequate temperature controls for ventilation. Conveniently located drinking fountains and restrooms are a plus. An inviting environment is one where a customer feels welcomed. If your sales associates are trained to focus their interest on the customers and always greet customers with a smile as they arrive, it makes an important, positive first impression. Most people don't want a salesperson to hover, but asking an open-ended question, such as "How may I be of service to you today?" might start a customer talking.

Utilize the space according to its value. Space directly in the path of customer traffic has the greatest sales potential and therefore the greatest value. The most valuable space of all is directly in the front of the store where customer traffic is the heaviest. The space having the least value is further from the traffic flow, generally in the back of the store.

Given these differences in value, it is advisable to differentiate between your selling and non-selling activities and allocate your least valuable space to non-selling activities (administration, shipping and receiving, storage and customer service). This allows more valuable space to be utilized in generating sales. In so doing, impulse items should be located as close to the traffic flow as possible (preferably at the front of the store) and demand goods can be located further away, in space having less value.

Manufacturing and Fabrication

In a manufacturing establishment, the main function of your layout is to increase productivity. Here, layout directs the flow through the production process. An effective layout provides for the most efficient utilization of personnel and equipment with minimal unnecessary movement of materials.

The two types of layouts most commonly used are product and process. A company that produces a steady flow of standardized products, such as the manufacture of sinks, would use a **product layout**. Here, equipment is arranged in an assembly line format that corresponds to the sequence of production steps for each product. Raw materials are then located at the points where they are needed and added to the line as the unfinished products pass by.

A company whose products are non-standardized or produced in varying quantities according to customer orders, such as a cabinet manufacturer or countertop fabricator, is unable to operate this way. Instead, he or she would use a **process layout**. Here, separate processing departments are maintained and each product passes through only those processing stages it requires. Unlike the product layout, this involves additional movement of unfinished goods and leaves some equipment idle, while other equipment struggles to function beyond capacity. These problems can be partially remedied through efficient scheduling and by keeping a close watch on production activities to streamline them whenever possible. In North America, manufacturers of "high-end" faucets basically utilize process layout, as they do not have large quantities of orders being processed at one time. Consequently, this manufacturer would use the process layout for manufacturing.

Services

Service establishments fit into two categories: those oriented toward **merchandising** (beauty salons, restaurants, hotels) and those oriented towards **processing** (automobile repair shops, cleaners, plumbers). Layouts for merchandise-oriented businesses normally are similar to those of retail operations, whereas processing services tend to follow manufacturing layouts. The reason for these differences stems from a respect of goals: to increase customer traffic or to increase productivity.

The following building-evaluation sheet can be useful in both selecting the building and designing your layout for optimum efficiency.

BUILDING-EVALUATION CHECKLIST				
Characteristics	Excellent	Good	Fair	Poor
1. Physical suitability of the building.				
2. Type and cost of the lease.				
3. Overall estimate of quality of the site in 10 years.				
4. Provision for future expansion.				
5. History of the building.				
6. Exterior of the building in promoting your business.				
7. Safe environment for customers and employees.				
8. Conformity to all zoning requirements.				
9. Ready accessibility for customers.				
10. Effectiveness of merchandise displays.				
11. Pleasant atmosphere as a place to shop.				
12. Quality of lighting.				
13. Utilization of space according to its value.				
14. Layout in facilitating movement of employees and materials.				
15. Layout potential for showroom, office, warehouse, production.				

You've laid the groundwork for your business, now consider the importance of good financial record keeping.

Chapter 2
Forms

- **Business Plan**

SAMPLE KITCHEN AND BATHROOM FIRM'S BUSINESS PLAN

This business plan template highlights a fictitious kitchen and bath firm known as Affluent Kitchen & Bathroom, Inc. Much of the wording in the plan is suggested rather than written out, because it is important that the plan be in your own words. After all, if you're going to show this plan to outsiders (i.e., banks), it is necessary for you to know and truly believe what you've projected in your plan. Lenders, while evaluating the merits of your business projections, will also be evaluating you—the person who is going to make the plan work. Make sure that your plan is realistic, honest and presented with integrity. If you do so, the plan will serve as a valuable benchmark for your business for years to come.

You may want to adjust the order of the material presented in this template, however, try to include all of the components. Every business is different so don't hesitate to be creative. No one has ever been turned down for financing for having too much information. Besides, as a business manager, you owe it to yourself to explore every possibility of success and failure that could impact your livelihood.

Good fortune is occasionally achieved with luck. Most good fortune, however, is created. Start by creating a plan that will get you there!

Provided by:
Stephen P. Vlachos CKD, CBD
Leslie L. Vlachos MEd
Atlantic Kitchen Center, Inc.
Portland, ME

BUSINESS PLAN

Current Date

Place your logo here in full color, if possible.

AFFLUENT KITCHEN & BATHROOM, INC.

2000 PROSPERITY AVENUE

CASCO, MAINE 04015

Your Name, Title
Address
City, State, Zip Code
Phone
Fax
E-Mail
Web Site

THIS DOCUMENT IS CONFIDENTIAL AND IS NOT FOR DISTRIBUTION.

TABLE OF CONTENTS

In this section list all of the areas that you are planning to cover in your plan and in the order you are covering them.

If you're planning to add services in an organized fashion you may want to break out the above headings in years, as in the following example.

> Business Services
> > Year One (kitchens and bathrooms)
> > Year Two (add full-scale remodeling service)
> > Year Three (open in-house countertop shop)

EXECUTIVE SUMMARY

This is your opportunity to sell yourself. More than just a résumé, this section is used to demonstrate why your experience makes you uniquely qualified to pull this venture off. You'll want to list all the obvious things such as education and work experience. Also, list all of your civic and volunteer activities. If you can demonstrate industry-recognition then, by all means, do it. As mentioned earlier, if someone outside your company is reviewing this plan for viability they will be taking just as close a look at you as they do your numbers.

When you're preparing this summary, look for areas where you are weak. While you may not want to broadcast to investors that you are not strong in financial management, for example, you owe it to yourself and your business to say something about your shortcomings.

This whole section should cover no more than one or two pages. Try to make your entries about yourself clear, concise and interesting. The goal is to capture the reader's attention and convince them that you have what it takes. You may want to enlist the aid of a professional résumé writer who can present you in the best possible light. The most important reader, of course, is you. If you are not absolutely convinced that you can be successful, then proceed no further.

MISSION STATEMENT

As clearly and concisely as possible describe what your company is all about.

Affluent Kitchen & Bathroom, Inc. will be the leading supplier of high-fashion European cabinetry in the State of Maine.

Explain, in brief, how you're going to accomplish that:

European cabinet manufacturers are the acknowledged world leaders in modern kitchen and bathroom styling. There are presently no other kitchen and bathroom retailers in our market area importing cabinetry. Affluent Kitchen & Bathroom, Inc. has targeted architects and interior designers for our marketing efforts, as they are the primary specifiers of high-fashion cabinetry. Affluent Kitchen & Bathroom, Inc. already enjoys a reputation for quality and this move is a natural progression for the firm.

Now it's time to briefly state what you need to accomplish your goal:

Affluent Kitchen & Bathroom, Inc. will need to add 1,000 square feet of showroom space and six new displays to accomplish our goal.

COMPANY PROFILE

Describe the history of the company, when it was founded and by whom. Explain how it has grown and changed. Be sure to include the legal name of the business in your description. If you are a start-up business, use this section to describe how you (and your partners) came to the point of needing or wanting to start your firm.

Include information as to the formation of your business. Are you an S-corporation, sole proprietor, etc.? Give specifics about the space where the business will operate. How many square feet. Is it expandable? Is it in a viable location? Put down a traffic count number if you can. You may want to refer to an exhibit number at the end of your plan where you will include a picture of the premises and a map cutaway showing where your business is (or will be).

Briefly mention the volume of business that can be expected from your location. If you are already in business, what are your monthly average sales now? What will it be when the showroom addition is built. If you are a start-up what is your target volume per month? In either case also mention what you feel is the maximum volume the location can produce without further improvements.

Does your location have compatible retailers nearby? Demonstrate how you can attract each other's customers. Is it near a major roadway? Can deliveries be easily made in and out? Will consumers find you easily?

Describe who your current and future suppliers will be. Demonstrate that they are industry leaders. Do they produce unique and highly sought after products? Can you demonstrate their loyalty to you? Do they offer you anything to make you unique among other kitchen and bathroom centers? Have you arranged any special terms or selling incentives with any suppliers?

Reference the proper exhibit number at the end of the plan, and include supplier brochures, letters from suppliers demonstrating favorable terms and industry articles about your suppliers and their products.

BUSINESS PROFILE

Tell how the business operates (or will operate)

Affluent Kitchen & Bathroom, Inc. is a retailer of high-end kitchens and bathrooms. The firm is located on 2000 Prosperity Avenue and services the entire state from that location.

The company is in a growth (start-up) mode and employs seven people. The firm recently sold its first six projects using imported cabinetry.

Is the firm a member of the local chamber of commerce? What national trade organizations do you belong to? NKBA? Do you have a Web site?

Has the business or the owner been featured in any newspaper, magazine or trade articles? Any television or radio recognition? Reference any of the above to the exhibit section at the end and include copies.

Does the business use cutting-edge systems to operate? CAD system?

Does the firm spend money on training? How much? How does the business do market research?

COMPANY SERVICES

Explain the services offered by your firm, e.g., measuring, designing, selling and installing kitchens and bathrooms. What is the average size (or anticipated size) size of the firm's projects?

What roles do subcontractors play in completing the projects? Have they been with you for awhile? Why will they stay with you?

Reference the exhibit section where you will include sample sales agreements, warranty cards, follow-up call reports and other documents which will demonstrate that your business is a well thought-out process.

Provide a history of products offered to your consumers. Demonstrate what has led your firm to offering European cabinetry. If you are a start-up, why have you chosen the products that you have?

Have you done any research showing why your firm and its products are needed in the marketplace? Demonstrate what makes (or will make) your firm unique. If you don't know what makes you unique or needed in the marketplace, then go no further!

MARKETING

This is a critical section for you—the owner. You need to clearly understand how big the market is and what your realistic chances are to capture a portion of it. Start by defining the market:

Affluent Kitchen & Bathroom, Inc. is competing in the custom kitchen and bathroom market. The National Kitchen & Bath Association (NKBA®) estimates that $21,000,000 worth of custom kitchen and bathroom products will be sold in the state this year. Affluent Kitchen & Bathroom, Inc. anticipates capturing $1,000,000 of that market with its unique offering of highly stylized cabinetry. NKBA® also estimates that the market will grow by 10 percent each year. Affluent Kitchen & Bathroom, Inc. will also grow by that 10 percent and plans to capture an additional 10 percent of the market with the introduction of fine European cabinetry.

Clearly define your segment of the market:

Affluent Kitchen & Bathroom, Inc. has identified its market segment as those consumers earning in excess of $70,000 per household. Private residences served by the firm range in value from $300,000-$1,000,000.

It is a good idea to include growth projections by a number of sources. For example, a Wall Street Journal article on the increase in luxury kitchens and bathrooms could be included and referenced in your exhibit section.

Detail your marketing plan. How are you going to reach architects and interior designers? Will there be direct-mail programs? How do you plan to reach the upscale customer that you mentioned above? Will your suppliers be assisting in this effort? Do you have an advertising strategy? Will you participate in trade shows? Home shows?

How much are you committed to spending on marketing? Can you afford it? How will you track results?

Try to detail all of the above without being too wordy or grandiose. You want the reader to believe that your marketing plan is well thought out. You also want the reader to believe it will work. Make sure that you believe it too!

COMPETITIVE ANALYSIS

Detail who and where your competitors are in the marketplace. Make sure your information is completely accurate. Provide a brief highlight on those you consider to be your primary competitors.

Mort's Kitchen Emporium is located at 112 Syllabus Street. It is a four-year-old family firm staffed by Mort and his cousin. They have a 1,000 square foot showroom which is attractive and located in an excellent part of town. Their focus, however, is on installation. When Mort and his cousin are out on job sites, the showroom is often closed to potential customers. Many clients have told us of trying to visit Mort's Kitchen Emporium only to find them closed. Their focus on installation has clearly cost them potential business.

As you detail your primary competitors you will want to accurately point out what they do that is different from the way you operate (or will operate). Does any competitor have an effective advertising campaign? Is there any one competitor that clearly stands out above the rest? Why?

It is important here not to kid yourself into thinking that you are better than your competitors just because you think you are. Make sure you prove it unequivocally to yourself!

BUSINESS OPPORTUNITIES/RISKS

In this section, deal with the opportunities ahead for your business. You also want to recognize the risks that exist and how you will deal with them.

Business Risks

Affluent Kitchen & Bathroom, Inc. will face a major risk in learning to become an effective importer. If cabinetry is damaged or mis-manufactured, there could be a long-lead time in getting replacements. This could damage our relationships with architect and interior design clients. Further, worldwide economic conditions could cause the product to rise dramatically in price. There is also the possibility of our government placing a significant import tax on products coming from our supplier's country.

Business Opportunities

Now you want to detail the opportunities and how you're going to deal with risks:

Affluent Kitchen & Bathroom, Inc. recognizes that risks exist. However, our firm has talked with other importers around the country to ensure ourselves that our supplier is reputable and quality oriented. Further, our supplier has agreed in writing not to adjust pricing upwards without first giving us six-month's notice. According to NKBA®, foreign-made cabinetry accounted for 17 percent of the cabinetry sold in the United States last year. Being the first to offer this unique and highly stylized cabinetry in our state gives us a tremendous boost over our competitors.

Go on to explain how you will build brand awareness. Detail what your suppliers will be doing to help you accomplish this goal. Again, any reprints of articles that will support your theory that European cabinetry is a leading style should be referenced and included in your exhibit section.

Above all, make sure that you truly believe that the risks that you are taking are outweighed by the opportunities!

CAPITAL REQUIREMENTS

This is the whole crux of why most people put together a business plan. Most small-business owners are nervous asking for capital. However, you can do greater harm to your business and yourself if you underestimate what you really need.

Affluent Kitchen & Bathroom, Inc. seeks a loan of $42,000 to fund the addition of showroom space. Further, when the showroom is complete, Affluent Kitchen & Bathroom, Inc. will also require a credit line of $25,000.

Go on to explain how the loan will be used, detailing construction costs, display costs, etc. Also detail how and why the credit line will be used.

Define how much time you will need to repay the loan and how you will generate enough cash to make the payments.

Affluent Kitchen & Bathroom, Inc. presently generates enough cash to support a five-year loan of $42,000. We anticipate, however, that the additional showroom opportunities will increase our sales by 10 percent which will make the impact of the loan on our cash flow more than manageable.

Finish with a strong concluding statement that emphasizes the benefit that this financing will have on the future prosperity of the firm.

FINANCIAL PLAN

Affluent Kitchen & Bathroom, Inc.

	ACTUAL 1996		PROJECTED 1997		PROJECTED 1998	
Sales	$1,000,000	100.0%	$1,200,000	100.0%	$1,452,000	100.0%
Cost of Sales	650,000	65.0%	780,000	65.0%	943,800	65.0%
Gross Profit	350,000	35.0%	420,000	35.0%	508,200	35.0%
Operating Expenses						
Salaries	150,000	15.0%	180,000	15.0%	217,800	15.0%
Payroll Taxes	45,000	4.5%	54,000	4.5%	65,340	4.5%
Rent	14,400	1.4%	14,832	1.2%	15,277	1.1%
Telephone & Utilities	24,000	2.4%	26,400	2.2%	29,040	2.0%
Insurance	12,000	1.2%	14,400	1.2%	15,840	1.1%
Advertising	20,000	2.0%	26,400	2.2%	27,720	1.9%
Maintenance & Repairs	2,200	.2%	2,420	.2%	2,541	.2%
Auto Expense	3,900	.4%	4,095	.3%	4,300	.3%
Depreciation	15,000	1.5%	18,000	1.5%	18,000	1.2%
Travel & Entertainment	1,750	.2%	2,160	.2%	2,614	.2%
Freight Out	4,940	.5%	5,434	.5%	5,977	.4%
Miscellaneous Expenses	30,000	3.0%	36,000	3.0%	43,560	3.0%
TOTAL EXPENSES	323,190	32.3%	384,141	32.0%	448,009	30.9%
Bank Financing ($42,00@10%-5years)	0		10,708		10,708	
NET INCOME	26,810	2.7%	25,151	2.1%	49,483	3.4%

Use the above format as an example only. Many lending institutions will require your projections to be carried forward through the length of their financing. It would also be of great benefit to you, the business owner, to do your future projections on a monthly basis rather than quarterly or yearly. That way you will be able to plot your progress each month and detect any problems or changes much more quickly.

The above numbers reflect a 10 percent increase in sales as predicted by NKBA® along with an additional 10 percent increase in sales due to the addition of the European cabinetry showroom. Some of your expenses will rise as a proportion of sales. Others will rise at a much slower rate as they are fixed expenses and not affected by sales volume.

Take plenty of time preparing this section. There are many bankers who will skip over all of the other information you have provided and go directly to the financial plan part of your presentation. They want to see if you will be viable before they waste much time talking with you! A big part of any lender's decision will rest on your ability to defend and support the numbers you provide in your financial plan. Understand, know and <u>believe</u> the numbers you are using before you submit them to anyone for review.

For further information, you may wish to obtain NKBA®'s publication, entitled <u>Managing Your Kitchen and Bathroom Firm's Finances for Profit</u> by Don Quigley.

EXHIBITS

Your goal up to now has been to keep your business plan as concise and interesting as possible. It was important not to clutter up any of the previous pages. This section is your opportunity to demonstrate and illustrate some of your earlier points.

Show the reader that you do know what you're talking about. This is where all of your background and research information should be made available. Remember to include the following:

- *Pictures and floor plans of your business.*
- *Maps detailing where your enterprise is (or will be).*
- *Product brochures and literature.*
- *Reprints of newspaper and magazine articles about you, your business or your suppliers.*
- *Reprints of articles supporting your forecasts.*
- *Copies of advertising and marketing material.*
- *Examples of business forms used such as sales agreements, purchase orders, client surveys and delivery forms.*
- *Patents and copyrights owned.*

Chapter 3

CHOPPING WOOD
Finances

The shortest answer is doing. - **English Proverb**

The failure rate of small businesses is huge (over 50 percent) and the main reason, by far, is poor management on the all-important financial side of the business. Most small business owners are good salespeople, excellent designers, talented marketers, but they tend to lack experience and a desire to learn in the area of financial management.

Of all of the information in this book, this is the most important. This is the area that will mean the difference between success and failure, or making a lot of money rather than a little.

I am the consummate salesperson. I am a good marketer, and, by hard work and study, I have become a strong financial manager. Finances are not my favorite part of the business, but they have earned the number one spot of importance. I doubt that our business would have survived the four-plus long years of recession in the early 1990s, if I had not had excellent financial record-keeping abilities and the skill to interpret what these figures meant.

Do not be intimidated by this chapter. Although, there is a lot of information, it is truly Finance 101. If you can maintain a checkbook at home, you can learn this. And, speaking of your personal checking account, you know how very important it is to keep it up to date and to know where you stand financially at all times. Why should it be any different at work? In fact, it's probably more important because you have more to lose.

Find **mentors** in your banker, accountant, a teacher, a financial person or a friend, and ask them to help you master this all-important part of your business. Take a class at your local college.

Your business may be large enough to allow you to employ a qualified accountant or a bookkeeper. However, don't use this as an excuse not to be involved. He or she can do the monthly numbers, but you have to analyze, tweak, massage, digest and fully understand what they mean. It's your business, you are in charge, and this has to be a major part of your total responsibility in running the business. You owe it to yourself, your family, your employees, your customers, your vendors, and, yes, your bank. I am certain that you will learn to enjoy this part of your business and that you will make more money! If this doesn't add fuel to your fire, I don't know what will.

Maintaining good financial records is a necessary part of doing business. The increasing number of government regulations alone makes it virtually impossible to avoid keeping detailed records. But just as important as the need to keep records for the government is the need to keep them for yourself. The success of your business depends on them.

RECORD-KEEPING PROCESS

An efficient system of record keeping can help you:

- Make management decisions.
- Compete in the marketplace.
- Monitor performance.
- Keep track of expenses.
- Eliminate unprofitable merchandise.
- Protect your assets.
- Prepare your financial statements.

By substituting facts for guesswork and continuity for confusion, day-to-day accounting records enable you to keep your finger on the pulse of your business. Any sign of financial ill health can be detected quickly and the appropriate corrective action taken before it's too late.

Business owners sometimes feel that record keeping is an unjustifiable waste of time when a good memory is all that is really needed. Unfortunately, memories can fail. Besides, the business owner cannot always be around when an employee needs to check an important piece of information. Taking time to set up and maintain your accounting system can actually save time by bringing order out of chaos.

By keeping good records, you will know at a glance:

- Last month's sales total.
- Sales commissions paid out in the past two weeks.
- Overtime charges for the previous quarter.
- Advertising expenses for the month.

- Percentage of sales made on credit.
- Customers behind on their bills.
- Amount of money tied up in inventory.
- Inventory shortages.
- Slow-moving merchandise.
- Effects of inflation on profits.
- Financial obligations coming due.
- Total value of your assets.

This information, and more, can be obtained readily from an adequate record system. The question isn't whether your business can afford to have one, rather, it's whether your business can afford *not* to have one.

Accountants

Once the importance of record keeping has been recognized, new business owners are often quick to delegate total responsibility for their records to accountants. Pleading ignorance ("What do I know about accounting?") or lack of time ("I can either run the business or keep the books"), they disassociate themselves entirely from the accounting function. And why not? After all, that's what accountants are paid for, isn't it? The problem with this tactic is that it gives your accountant free reign to make decisions affecting your business without receiving any input from you. There is even a greater reason for you to keep close tabs on your record system: You can't operate efficiently without access to its information.

Have your books audited. Many government loans, such as economic development loans, are easier to obtain if your books have been audited for the past three years.

For the best results, you and your accountant should work together as a team, supplying each other with accurate and timely information. Whether your accountant handles all your record keeping or just does your taxes, it's vital that you understand what is being done.

Setting Up The Books

The first step in setting up the books for your business is to determine which information to keep and which to discard. A good accounting system gives you only the information you need, not a lot of extraneous details.

Accounts are the foundation on which your record-keeping system is built. Each account represents a single category of business transactions (sales volume, rent expense, employees' wages, cash, notes payable). Any changes (increases or decreases) that occur within a specific category are shown in the appropriate account. In this way, when a sale is made, a bill is paid, or an expense incurred, you have a record of it. In its simplest form, an account looks like the following **T-Account**. All cash flowing into your business is entered on the left side of the cash account. All cash flowing out of your business is entered on the right side. Rather than changing the balance each time cash is added or subtracted, the account mechanism enables you to derive your new balance simply by totaling the two sides and subtracting right from left to get the difference. This not only saves time, but allows you to see the separate entries that affect the balance.

T-ACCOUNT
CASH

Increases		Decreases	
Beginning Balance	$15,000		$600
	3,000		250
	500		6,350
	1,200		
	700		
	$20,400		$7,200
New Balance	$13,200		

CASH ACCOUNT							
ACCOUNT: CASH						ACCOUNT NO. 101	
DATE	ITEM	DEBIT		DATE	ITEM	CREDIT	
19__				19__			
August 1	Balance	15000	00	August 1	Accounts Payable	600	00
2	Sale	3000	00	2	Supplies	250	00
3	Deposit	500	00	5	Payroll	6350	00
5	Sale	1200	00				
6	Sale	700	00				

In comparison to what a regular account looks like, the T account is just the bare outline or skeleton, lacking details. Your actual accounts will probably look something like the cash account above. The basic structure of the T account is still intact, but the refined format enables you to record more information.

Charts of Accounts are records of each individual account. As you go through the process of determining which accounting information to keep, the names of each account to be included in your records system should be added to your chart of accounts. This identifies your accounts by title and indicates their locations within the system. For example, the cash account in the previous illustration is numbered Account No. 101. This means that it falls under the assets category (arbitrarily assigned the series 10) and is the first account within that section. Depending on the number of accounts you wish to maintain, your numbering system can range from the simple to the sophisticated.

Double-Entry Accounting is an accounting method where for every transaction that is recorded, two entries are required. This is because any change in one account automatically results in a change in another account. For instance, if a customer purchases merchandise from you and pays cash for it, the balance in your cash account increases and at the same time your merchandise inventory decreases. Both changes must be recorded. The means for doing this is by way of debit and credit entries.

In double-entry accounting, for each transaction, the total debit must equal the total credit amount. If for any reason these amounts are not equal, the transaction has been recorded incorrectly.

How Debits and Credits Work is a topic which contains two common misconceptions. One is to think of them as being good things or bad things (as in "The firefighter was credited with rescuing the child from the burning building" or "That's more debit against you"). The other misconception is that debit means to subtract and a credit means to add. Although the outcome of the debit or credit entry can be good or bad, and call for addition or subtraction, the terms themselves have much simpler meanings.

To **debit** is to make an entry on the **left** side of the account.

To **credit** is to make an entry on the **right** side.

DEBIT AND CREDIT ENTRIES		
Type of Account	**To Increase the Account Enter the Amount as a:**	**To Decrease the Account Enter the Amount as a:**
Asset	Debit	Credit
Liability	Credit	Debit
Capital	Credit	Debit
Revenue	Credit	Debit
Expense	Debit	Credit

Depending on which account is receiving the entry, both debits and credits can be either positive (calling for an increase) or negative (calling for a decrease), as illustrated by the chart below.

SAMPLE CHART OF ACCOUNTS			
(10)	Assets (Debit)	(30)	Capital Accounts (Credit)
101	Cash	301	Owner's Capital
102	Accounts Receivable	302	Undistributed Capital
103	Inventory		
104	Materials and Supplies	(40)	Revenues (Credit)
105	Prepaid Expenses	401	Retail Sales
106	Land	402	Wholesale Sales
107	Buildings	403	Sales - Service
108	Reserve for Depreciation Buildings (Credit)	404	Miscellaneous Income
109	Furniture and Fixtures (Credit)		
110	Reserve for Depreciation Furniture and Fixtures (Credit)	(50)	Expenses (Debit)
111	Automotive Equipment	501	Accounting
112	Reserve for Depreciation	502	Advertising

SAMPLE CHART OF ACCOUNTS			
	Automotive Equipment (Credit)		
		503	Depreciation
(20)	Liabilities (Credit)	504	Insurance
201	Accounts Payable	505	Interest
202	Notes Payable	506	Miscellaneous
203	Sales Taxes - Payable	507	Payroll
204	FICA Taxes - Payable	508	Rent
210	Long Term Debt + (SBA Loan)	509	Repairs
		510	Supplies
		511	Travel
		512	Utilities

Single-entry accounting is a simpler accounting process. Although a double-entry accounting system offers the greatest degree of accuracy through its use of checks and balances, it can also be a difficult system to maintain for someone without bookkeeping experience. While your business is still small, you may prefer to use a single-entry accounting system instead. Based on your income statement, rather than your balance sheet, a single-entry system does not require you to balance the books or record more than one entry for each transaction. Quick and easy to use, it provides a simple way to keep track of your accounts receivable, accounts payable, depreciable assets and inventory. Depending on your needs, you can have an accountant or bookkeeper set up a single-entry accounting system especially tailored to your business, or you can purchase a ready-made system from an office supply or stationery store. Generally consisting of worksheets bound together in a spiral notebook, these ready-to-use systems usually cost less than $15.

Pegboard record keeping is a method which can simplify your record keeping even more. It is a single-entry system, but designed in the way you use it. An all-in-one system for keeping records, writing checks and issuing receipts, it derives its name from the fact that the checks and receipts it uses are overlaid, one after another, on top of your record sheets and held in place by pegs. Whenever you write a check or a receipt, the information is automatically transferred to the record sheet below. This eliminates the most common accounting error of all—forgetting to record an entry. For more information on pegboard systems, which range in price from $75 to $200, check the Yellow Pages under business forms and systems.

Whether you opt for a single-entry or a double-entry accounting system, to be successful, the important thing is to have some means for adequately tracking the financial information necessary for your business.

THE ACCOUNTING PROCESS

Entering information into your accounts is neither the first part of the accounting process nor the last. As shown in the chart, the process begins with the business transaction itself and continues until your financial statements have been prepared. Then the cycle begins again.

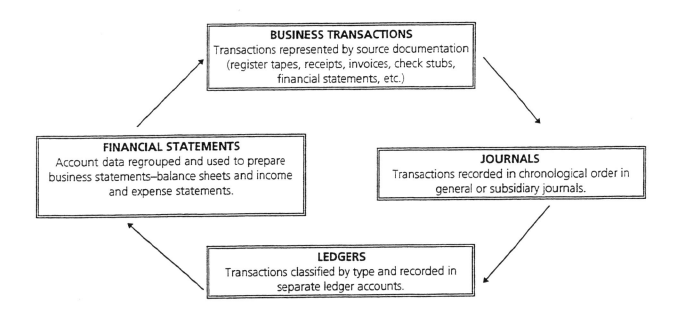

Journals

Once a transaction has occurred, information about it enters your accounting system through your journals. Often called the **books of original entry**, journals are merely chronological records of your business transactions. Each entry contains the date on which the transaction occurred, the specific accounts to be debited and credited and the amount of debit and credit.

Although one general journal covering all transactions is sometimes sufficient for a small business, the majority of businesses also maintain two additional journals: one for cash receipts and one for cash payments. Keeping separate journals saves time, space and reduces errors. These savings stem from the fact that, unlike the general journal, the separate journals offer these benefits:

1. *Headings are preprinted.* Less time is spent in recording the necessary information.

2. *Entries require fewer lines.* An entry that takes up three lines in the general journal will require only one line in the cash receipts journal.

3. *Column totals, rather than separate entries, are transferred later.* Reducing the number of entries to transfer also reduces the number of possible errors.

Source Documents for Journal Entries

Each entry that is recorded in your journals must be backed up by the appropriate source document—in other words, the written evidence, or business paper, that supports the entry. Examples of source documents are sales receipts, invoices, purchase orders, checks, check stubs, register tapes, credit memos, petty cash slips and business statements. These are necessary not only for tax-reporting purposes, but because they provide an additional safeguard against accounting errors and employee dishonesty.

Ledgers

To further consolidate the information contained within your journals and make it more meaningful, the next step in the accounting process is to transfer it to your ledgers. These are the books, files or computer records in which individual accounts are maintained.

All accounts can be grouped together in one general ledger, or, in addition to this, you may want to set up subsidiary ledgers such as an accounts receivable or an accounts payable ledger to track specific categories of high-activity accounts. The advantage is that these subsidiary ledgers make the general ledger less bulky and allow more than one person at a time to work on the ledger accounts. In place of each group of accounts removed from the general ledger, a control sheet, summarizing the group's activity, is inserted. This enables the general ledger to stay in balance by maintaining the equality of the debits and credits.

The process of transferring the information in the journals to the ledger accounts is called posting. During this stage, all data of the same kind is separated from the other journal data and entered into their respective accounts. Since the information recorded in each ledger stems from the journals, ledgers are called **books of secondary entry**.

To facilitate the process of entering information into your journals and posting it to the appropriate ledger accounts, there are a number of accounting software programs designed with small businesses in mind. These computer spreadsheet programs can assist you not only in keeping your day-to-day records, but also in preparing your financial statements.

CASH RECEIPTS JOURNAL								
			1	2	3	4	5
			GENERAL		SALES	ACCTS REC	CASH
			DEBIT	CREDIT	CREDIT	CREDIT	DEBIT
DATE		ACCOUNT TITLE						
19__								
November	1	Office Equipment	R1201		50.00			50.00
	1	Owner's Capital	R1202		700.00			700.00
	1	Sales	R1203			650.00		650.00
		Accounts Receivable	R1204				125.00	125.00

CASH PAYMENTS JOURNAL							
		CHECK	GENERAL		ACCTS PAY	CASH	
		NO.	DEBIT	CREDIT	DEBIT	CREDIT	
DATE	ACCOUNT TITLE						
19__							
November	1 Accounts Payable	1151				325.00	325.00
	2 Rent Expenses	1152	725.00				725.00
	2 Advertising Expense	1153	250.00				250.00

ACCOUNTS RECEIVABLE CONTROL SHEET					DEBIT
DATE		ITEM	DEBIT	CREDIT	BALANCE
19__					
October	29	Balance			9950.00
	29		150.00		10100.00
	30		300.00	225.00	10175.00
	31			140.00	10035.00
November	1			125.00	9910.00

ACCOUNTS RECEIVABLE LEDGER					
NAME:	George Jones			TERMS: Net 30 Days	
	2010 Harrison Street				DEBIT
ADDRESS:	Smith, AR 31022			CREDIT	BALANCE
DATE		ITEM	DEBIT		
19__					
October	1	Balance			85.00
	6	Sales Check #345	65.00		150.00
	15	Sales Check #384	50.00		200.00
	21	Sales Check #395	35.00		235.00
	31	Balance			235.00
November	1	Received on Account		125.00	110.00

GENERAL JOURNAL							
DATE		ACCOUNT TITLE	DEBIT			CREDIT	
19__							
November	1	Cash					
		Office Equipment	50	00			
		Receipt No. 1301				50	00
	1	Accounts Payable	325	00			
		Cash				325	00
		Check No. 1151					
	1	Cash	700	00			
		Owner's Capital				700	00
		Receipt No. 1302					
	1	Cash	650	00			
		Sales				650	00
		Receipt No. 1303					
	1	Cash	125	00			
		Accounts Receivable				125	00
		Receipt No. 1304					
	2	Rent Expense	725	00			
		Cash				725	00
		Check No. 1152					
	2	Advertising Expense	250	00			
		Cash				250	00
		Check No. 1153					

To help ensure that your business transactions are properly recorded and to measure the effectiveness of your record system, answer the questions in this record-keeping checklist. Any "no" answers indicate areas that need to be examined.

RECORD-KEEPING CHECKLIST	YES	NO
1. Do you know the reasons for keeping good records?		
2. Have you determined which records are important to your business?		
3. Are you using a chart of accounts to show the name and location of each account in your record system?		
4. Do you understand the reasoning behind the use of double-entry record keeping?		
5. Is the function of debits and credits clear to you?		
6. Can you identify the accounts likely to have debit balances?		
7. Can you identify the accounts likely to have credit balances?		
8. Have you set up your general journal and any subsidiary journals that will be used?		
9. Do you know what source documents are?		
10. Is each journal entry made solely on the basis of a source document?		
11. Does your filing system enable you to retain and locate all relevant source documents?		
12. Have you set up your general ledger and any subsidiary ledgers that will be used?		
13. Is information posted to your ledgers periodically?		
14. Are all ledger items based on journal entries?		
15. Are financial statements prepared at periodic intervals?		
16. Do you personally oversee all major business transactions?		
17. Are you thoroughly familiar with all aspects of your accounting system?		
18. Does your accounting system enable you to operate your business efficiently and get the full value out of your resources?		
19. Are you able to verify the following through your records? Cash on hand at the end of the day. All money owed to you by customers. Accounts that are past due. All money owed to suppliers and creditors. Bills that have been paid. Inventory that has been received. Salary and wages paid. All other expenses that have been incurred.		
20. Have you obtained the advice of an accountant in setting up your records system?		

FINANCIAL STATEMENTS

The information obtained through your system of financial record keeping is only as good as your ability to use it. In addition to compiling your financial data, you must also know how to summarize and interpret it.

SUMMARIZING FINANCIAL DATA

Summarizing involves taking the information contained within your ledger accounts and using it to prepare the financial statements for your business. The two most important of these are the **balance sheet** and the **income and expense statement** (often referred to as a profit and loss statement, or P&L).

The balance sheet is a summary of your business' assets, liabilities and capital on any given day.

The income and expense statement is a summary of your business' income and expenses during a specific period (month, quarter, year).

The difference between these statements can be compared to the difference between a photograph and a motion picture. The balance sheet is like a photograph, depicting your business as it appears in a single instant. The income and expense statement is like a motion picture, depicting your business as it changes over time. Since financial statements are prepared annually (or more often, as desired), it is common to see balance sheets dated, December 31, 19__, and income and expense statements dated "For the year ending, December 31, 19__."

The Importance of Financial Statements

Unlike day-to-day accounting records, financial statements provide an overview of your business. Instead of telling what you sold on a particular day, or how much a specific inventory item costs, financial statements give you the big picture—comparing what you own to what you owe, what you earned to what you spent. As such, they form the basis for any financial analysis of your business.

Financial statements are absolutely essential for the following:

- **Management planning** - To operate your business in the most profitable way possible, or lay the groundwork for future expansion, you need to know where your business stands and how it got there.

- **Raising capital** - Bankers and investors use financial statements as a way of evaluating your business. If you wish to obtain the support of either group, you must not only supply statements, but be ready to explain and defend them.

- **Preparing tax returns** - The **information** contained within your financial statements is needed to prepare your tax returns. Furthermore, in the event of an audit by the IRS, you will be expected to produce the relevant accounting records and statements.

THE BALANCE SHEET

A balance sheet, which indicates the financial condition of the business, has two main sections: one listing the assets of the business and one listing the liabilities and capital of the business. In accordance with the accounting equation, the two sides are always equal:

$$\text{Assets} = \text{Liabilities} + \text{Capital (Owner's Equity)}$$

This can be readily explained by the fact that all assets in a business are subject to the claims of creditors and owners.

ASSETS

An asset is anything of monetary value that is owned by the business. Assets are generally classified as being current, fixed or intangible. The order in which they appear on the balance sheet is determined by their liquidity—that is, their ability to be converted into cash:

$$\text{Assets} = \text{Liabilities} + \text{Capital (Owner's Equity)}$$

Current Assets consist of cash and assets that are expected to be converted into cash within the coming year. Included in this category are accounts receivable (money owed by customers) and inventory (merchandise, supplies, raw materials and parts).

Fixed Assets consist of tangible property to be used over a period of years in operating the business. Included in this category are land, buildings, machinery, equipment, motor vehicles, furniture and fixtures.

Intangible Assets consist of items that are usually non-physical assets. Included in this category are trademarks, patents, copyrights and goodwill.

LIABILITIES

A liability is a debt owed by the business. Liabilities are classified as being either current or long term:

$$\text{Liabilities} = \text{Assets} - \text{Capital (Owner's Equity)}$$

Current Liabilities consist of debts that are expected to be paid off within the coming year. Included in this category are accounts payable (money owed to suppliers and creditors), notes payable (money owed to the bank), and accrued liabilities (wages, interest, taxes, deposits and other amounts due but not paid as of the balance sheet date).

Long-Term Liabilities consist of those debts that are not due to be paid within the coming year. Included in this category are mortgages, term loans, bonds and similar future obligations.

CAPITAL

The difference between the assets of a business and its liabilities equals its capital or owner's equity:

Assets - Liabilities = Capital (Owner's Equity)

Capital represents the amount of owner investment in the business, as well as any profits (or losses) that have accumulated.

In a **Sole Proprietorship** or **Partnership**, capital is listed under each owner's name. Increases (or decreases) in capital are also shown there.

In a **Corporation**, capital is listed under the heading *capital stock.* This represents the paid-in value of the shares in stock issued to each owner. Corporate earnings that are not distributed to shareholders are shown here as *retained earnings*.

THE INCOME AND EXPENSE STATEMENT

An income and expense statement (or profit and loss statement) can generally be divided into the following sections, which demonstrate both the extent and the efficiency of the business' ability to generate income during the accounting period covered by the statement.

Net Sales represents the total sales during the accounting period, less sales tax and deductions for sales discounts, returns or allowances.

Cost of Goods Sold represents the total amount spent by the business to purchase the product sold during the accounting period. Businesses usually compute this by adding the value of the goods purchased during the period (less discounts offered by suppliers) to the value of the beginning inventory, and then subtracting the ending inventory.

Gross Margin represents the difference between the net sales and the cost of goods sold. It is also frequently referred to as the *gross profit.*

Expenses represents cost incurred as a result of operating the business. These can be divided into two categories: **selling expenses** (expenses such as sales, commissions and advertising, that are directly related to the business' sales activities), and **general and administrative expenses** (expenses incurred through activities other than selling, such as clerical salaries, rent and insurance).

Net Income represents what is left after all relevant expenses have been deducted from the gross margin. When total expenses exceed the gross margin, this is called a **net loss**.

Here is a sample profit and loss statement spreadsheet. It can be used to help in budgeting and/or tracking monthly activity.

PROJECTED PROFIT/LOSS														
	%	Jan	Feb	Mar	Apr	May	Jun	Jul	Aug	Sep	Oct	Nov	Dec	Tot
Total Net Sales														
Cost, goods sold														
Gross Profit														
Controllable Expense														
Salaries/Wages														
Payroll Taxes														
Legal/Accounting														
Advertising														
Automobile														
Office Supplies														
Dues/Subscriptions														
Telephone														
Utilities														
Miscellaneous														
Total Controllable Exp														
Fixed Expenses														
Rent														
Depreciation														
Insurance														
Licenses/Permits														
Taxes														
Loan Payments														
Total Fixed Expenses														
Total Expenses														
NET PROFIT/LOSS (before taxes)														

INTERPRETING FINANCIAL DATA

Interpreting financial data involves studying the various relationships that exist among the figures shown on your financial statements. These relationships are expressed in the form of **financial ratios**, which are comparative measurements that enable you to pinpoint the strengths and weaknesses in your business operations. What if you needed to know the answers to one of more of the following questions?

- Is there enough ready cash in my business?
- Are current liabilities at a safe level?
- How well could the business weather a financial setback?
- Are customers paying their bills on time?
- Is inventory moving as quickly as it should be?
- Are prices keeping pace with inflation?
- Are profits what they should be?
- Are assets being used wisely?
- How much of my business do I really own?

How could you get your hands on the necessary information? Call your accountant? Sure, if you had the time and money to spend waiting for an answer. But why bother when the information is already at hand, in your financial statements? Solving a few quick arithmetic problems is all it takes to find the answers.

Financial ratios can be used to find out a great deal of information about your business, ranging from the trivial to the significant. Among the ratios most closely examined by owners, investors and creditors are those pertaining to liquidity, profitability and ownership.

Liquidity Ratios

These measure your business' ability to pay its bills and to convert assets into cash.

Current Ratio compares current assets to current liabilities, and is used to assess your business' ability to meet its financial obligations within the coming year. The best known and most widely used of the ratios is computed by dividing current assets and current liabilities:

$$\text{Current Ratio} = \frac{\text{Current Assets}}{\text{Current Liabilities}}$$

$$\text{Current Ratio} = \frac{\$96,000}{\$42,000}$$

$$\text{Current Ratio} = 2.29:1$$

The generally accepted minimum current ratio is 2 to 1. This can vary, though, depending upon the specific circumstances of each business.

Quick Ratio compares cash and accounts receivable to current liabilities, and is used to assess the ability of your business to meet its current financial obligations in the event that sales decline and merchandise inventory cannot readily be converted to cash. Also called the **acid test** because it measures only ready assets, it is computed by dividing cash and accounts receivable by current liabilities:

$$\text{Quick Ratio} = \frac{\text{Cash} + \text{Accounts Receivable}}{\text{Current Liabilities}}$$

$$\text{Quick Ratio} = \frac{\$15,000 + \$34,500}{\$42,000}$$

$$\text{Acid Test Ratio} = 1.18:1$$

An acid-test ratio of 1 to 1 is considered acceptable, given the fact that an adequate means of collecting accounts receivable exists.

Working Capital Ratio compares current assets and current liabilities, and is used to assess the ability of your business to meet unforeseen expenses or weather a financial setback. It is computed by subtracting current liabilities from current assets:

Working Capital = Current Assets - Current Liabilities
Working Capital = $96,000 - $42,000
Working Capital = $54,000

Working capital needs vary from business to business. Frequently, though, lenders will insist that the level of working capital be maintained at or above a minimum level.

Average Collection compares your average day's sales to accounts receivable, and is used to assess the ability of your business to convert accounts receivable into cash. It is computed in a two-step process that first divides net sales by the number of days in the year; in the second step, this figure (average day's sales) is divided into accounts receivable:

Step 1:

$$\text{Average Day's Sales} = \frac{\text{Net Sales}}{365 \text{ Days}}$$

$$\text{Average Day's Sales} = \frac{\$300,000}{365 \text{ Days}}$$

$$\text{Average Day's Sales} = \$822 \text{ Per Day}$$

Step 2:

$$\text{Average Collection Period} = \frac{\text{Accounts Receivable}}{\text{Average Day's Sales}}$$

$$\text{Average Collection Period} = \frac{\$34,500}{\$822 \text{ Per Day}}$$

$$\text{Average Collection Period} = 42 \text{ Days}$$

What is deemed an acceptable average collection period depends on the credit terms. Generally, it should not exceed 1⅓ x the credit terms. Thus, since the ABC Kitchen and

Bathroom Company offers 30 days credit, its average collection period is slightly higher than it should be (1⅓ x 30 = 40 days).

Inventory Turnover compares your cost of goods sold to your average inventory level. Average inventory level is calculated as half the total of beginning inventory plus ending inventory. Inventory turnover is used to assess the ability of your business to convert merchandise inventory into sales. It is computed by dividing the cost of goods sold by the average inventory:

$$\text{Inventory Turnover} = \frac{\text{Cost of Goods Sold}}{\text{Average Inventory}}$$

$$\text{Inventory Turnover} = \frac{\$150,000}{1/2(\$46,600 + \$47,000)}$$

$$\text{Inventory Turnover} = \frac{\$150,000}{\$46,800}$$

$$\text{Inventory Turnover} = 3.2 \text{ Times}$$

Normally, the higher your turnover is, the better. This means you are moving the goods. However, as the turnover rate increases, so does the risk of stock shortages. By trial and error and by studying turnover rates of similar businesses, you can determine what rate is desirable for your business.

Profitability Ratios

These measure the ability of your business to use its assets to make a profit.

Profit Margin or Net Profit on Sales compares net profit to net sales. Used to assess the ability of your business to turn a profit on the sales it makes, it is computed by dividing net profit by net sales:

$$\text{Net Profit on Sales} = \frac{\text{Net Profit}}{\text{Net Sales}}$$

$$\text{Net Profit on Sales} = \frac{\$45,000}{\$300,000}$$

$$\text{Net Profit on Sales} = 0.15 \text{ or } 15\%$$

In this example, the ABC Kitchen and Bathroom Company makes 15¢ profit for every dollar in sales. Whether this is an acceptable level of profit depends on your objectives and the standard for your industry.

Return on Investment (ROI) compares net profit to total assets. Used to assess the ability of your business to turn a profit on the assets it holds, it is computed by dividing net profit by total assets:

$$\text{Return on Investment} = \frac{\text{Net Profit}}{\text{Total Assets}}$$

$$\text{Return on Investment} = \frac{\$45,000}{\$156,000}$$

$$\text{Return on Investment} = 0.29 \text{ or } 29\%$$

To determine if this is a good return on investment, you should compare your figures to those of comparable businesses.

Ownership Ratio

This measures the levels of ownership in the business, comparing the claims of owners to those of creditors.

Worth to Debt compares net worth to total debt. It is used to assess the ability of your business to protect creditors against losses. To compute it, divide net worth by total debts:

$$\text{Worth to Debt} = \frac{\text{Net Worth}}{\text{Total Debt}}$$

$$\text{Worth to Debt} = \frac{\$102,000}{\$54,000}$$

$$\text{Worth to Debt} = 1.89:1$$

For every dollar loaned to the ABC Kitchen and Bathroom Company, the owner has invested $1.89. Usually a ratio of 2 to 1 or better is preferred since this provides creditors with more protection. To improve this ratio, the owner can either invest more money in the business or reduce the debt.

Calculating the financial ratios for your business can be done fairly easily. To make it even easier to compare one set of ratios with another, there are several financial software programs on the market that you can use.

Once you have prepared the financial statements for your business, you can pinpoint the financial strengths and weaknesses by computing the ratios in the following checklist:

FINANCIAL RATIO CHECKLIST			
	Ratio	Satisfactory	Unsatisfactory
Liquidity			
Current Ratio			
Acid-test Ratio			
Working Capital			
Average Collection Period			
Inventory Turnover			
Profitability			
Net Profit on Sales			
Return on Investment			
Ownership			
Worth to Debt			

You've added to your business acumen by learning some of the specifics about financial statements, record keeping and accounting methods. The next chapter will help you stoke your fire by studying pricing and markup methods.

Chapter 4

STOKING THE FIRE
Pricing

Profit __and__ morality are a hard combination to beat. - Hubert H. Humphrey

Now that you've got a roaring fire, it needs to be maintained or it will go out. Continual attention to pricing structures and their effects on your kitchen and bathroom business is critical to the success of your business. In our industry, establishing prices on selling and making margins has been both a challenge and an opportunity.

When we first opened our doors, and for the first several years we were in business, we were the only kitchen and bathroom showroom in a town of 1.2 million people.

We had selected the "high-end" niche, so clients expected our prices to be higher. We looked and acted like a Cadillac, Lexus or Mercedes car dealer. But, in about our fourth year, a competitor came to town, then another and another. Soon, there were six of us. Needless to say, we felt pressure on our pricing.

Our first knee-jerk reaction was "we were here first, we are king of the hill, and we're not going to lose business to these new folks." Wrong. Our margins went down (from 39-40 percent to 34-35 percent) and we lost business, too. We regrouped and figured out what the pros and cons were of each of our competitors, matched this list against our own list of pros and cons, and developed a strategy to out-service and out-hustle, but not necessarily out-price our competitors. In other words, we got smart. Instead of reacting, we acted.

First, we studied our competitors' pricing very closely, including the new mass merchandisers that had come to town. We made sure that our pricing on popular like items was competitive. But, we got away from using the same discount across the board on a given product line or manufacturer. Kohler plumbing products, for example, are a big sell item for us. Before the competition came to town, we were able to discount Kohler's products 15-20 percent from list price. After the competition and the mass merchandisers arrived, we were forced to change to 25-30 percent off list, and sometimes that still wasn't good enough. This obviously caused a big impact on our margin (and bottom line). But, instead of offering a flat 25 percent on all Kohler items, we knew what the popular items were, those items that everyone "shopped." We made sure that we were competitive on these items, but used less of a discount on odd-ball, hard-to-get, unusual items. And, instead of always jumping in five percent increments from 20 to 25 to 30 percent, we started to use odd percentages, such as 27, 23.5 or 28.25 percent. Usually, if you've done a good job relating to and serving your clients, you won't lose a job for just a few percentage points. When it hits 5 percent or more, you probably will lose it. So stay close, but don't give it all away.

As owners/managers, we all have a perception of what our margins should be. We think we know what our competitors will allow us to make, but, in my opinion, we don't give ourselves enough credit for the quality products and great services we do offer, and we **don't** charge enough. Why do we work so darned hard but don't charge enough? The following is an example of how people's pricing perceptions vary.

A good friend of mine offers a great one-hour seminar on pricing. He's a kitchen and bathroom dealer in a major West Coast city. As part of the seminar, he gives everyone a blank sheet of paper and asks them to write in big numbers what the very best gross profit margin is that they can realize month in, month out, in their marketplaces. The attendees are from all over the USA and Canada. He asks everyone to hold up their answers and to look around the room at what everyone else has written. Answers range from a high of 50 percent to a low of 20 percent. These people are all in like businesses. How can this be? Sure, local demographics, economics and competition will dictate some variance, but certainly it shouldn't vary by 30 percent! My friend then proceeds to tell these participants they should expect—even demand—to make at least 35-40 percent gross profit margins, or they should reconsider whether they should even be in the business in the first place. I agree.

When we were faced with the new competition and let our margins slide by almost five percent, we developed an all-new pricing strategy to slowly move them back up to the 40 percent goal. We developed a new commission program for salespeople based on their individual gross profit margin, i.e., if they made more on a sale, they made more on their commissions.

It is important to point out that we pay all salespeople a base pay of $1,200 per month, paid bi-monthly. Their commissions, based on the attached chart, are paid once a month. The base pay is the variable, it can go up or down depending on local pay scales, competition, etc.

Monthly Gross Profit Average	Commission Earned on Gross Profit	Commission + Base = Percent of Sales*	Gross Profit for Owner After Commission + Base*
42 Plus	12	6.24	35.76
40-41.99	11	5.60	34.40
38-39.99	10	5.00	33.00
36-37.99	9	4.44	31.56
34-35.99	8	3.92	30.08
32-33.99	7	3.44	28.56
30-31.99	6	3.00	27.00
Less than 30	0	.0	.0

*These figures are based on the highest number, i.e., 42,40,38, etc.

We made everyone very aware of the importance of margin and educated them on how margin is figured, working from list down and from cost up. We showed them all the tricks of pricing (sell up, sell add-ons, mix the discounts, use odd discounts and sell preferred vendor products). It took two to three years to slowly move the margin back up. But we did it, and we did it during a recession.

Kitchen and bathroom dealers especially should be making 40 percent gross profit or more. They offer so much more in services (showrooms, design, professionalism, install and turnkey.). A kitchen designer really develops a longer-term relationship with his or her client than most salespeople are able to do. From the initial meeting to the finished project may take six months or more. This includes many meetings in the store and on site. Price really becomes secondary. As long as you've done a "ball park" price up front for budgetary reasons, you should be able to make excellent margins for all you put into it. Other professionals (e.g., doctors, accountants, lawyers) can charge $200 an hour plus or minus for their time. Shouldn't you?

As you read this chapter, remember that how you price your products and services can mean the difference between the success and failure of your business, and the size of your own paycheck. Those are pretty good incentives to do it well!

SETTING THE PRICE

In setting the prices for your products and services, some of the facts to be considered are the reactions of your customers, the stiffness of the competition and the state of the economy. Strange as it may seem, a price that is too low can be just as much of a turn off to customers as a price that is too high. Low prices are often interpreted as signifying low value or inferior merchandise. As for the competition, since your business does not exist in a vacuum, the role of other businesses in influencing your prices has to be recognized. Deciding to go head to head with competitors on prices, matching them dollar for dollar, or to undercut them, or to charge higher prices, is crucial to your pricing. Nor can the state of the economy be overlooked. Unemployment, inflation, interest rates, government policies and levels of investment all have an effect on consumer spending and therefore on your prices.

You must also take into consideration another factor: **profit** If your prices are so low that they fail to cover your expenses, or so high that an insufficient number of people want to buy from you, the result is a loss of profit. Your goal is to meet the demands of customers, keep an eye on competitors and the economy, and assure yourself a satisfactory profit.

Keep in mind that a stable pricing structure maintains credibility with the public, while allowing you to build a consistent marketing and advertising message, and makes it easy for employees to work with and remember. The disadvantages, however, may be that employees feel this makes you less competitive. You should not compete on price, but, if you have to, make sure everyone knows the point at which dropping your price costs you or them money.

PRICING AND CUSTOMERS

Part of knowing what prices to charge comes from knowing your customers. One customer's bargain may be another customer's extravagance. Affluent customers generally demand high-quality merchandise, personalized service, and an exclusive and attractive environment in which to shop. In exchange for these amenities, they are not only willing to pay more, but they expect to pay more. Low-income customers, on the other hand, are primarily concerned with stretching their dollars. They are willing to settle for less quality and service in a no-frills, discount-house type of environment in exchange for lower prices. In each case, the price is what counts.

In the beginning, formulating a pricing strategy to please your customers may seem like trying to solve the riddle of the chicken and the egg. Which comes first? Should you set your prices and then wait for your target customers to find you? Or should you wait to see what kind of customers you attract and then develop an appropriate pricing structure? The answer is both. To a great extent, your pricing strategy will be predetermined by your type of business, products sold, location, target customers, expenses, etc. But you also have to stay in touch with your customers to make sure that your prices, quality and service continue to reflect their needs and wants.

PRICING AND COMPETITION

Keeping tabs on competitors' prices helps you to assess your own pricing strategy. Are yours higher or lower than the competition? If your prices are higher, you are probably losing out on sales. If your prices are lower, you may be making more sales, but passing up additional profits. In comparing your prices with the competition, don't forget to compare service as well. Services add to the value of a product and therefore to its price. Such services as a prestige location, attractive facility, personal attention, credit, excellent parking, warranties and home deliveries benefit your customers. The more services you provide, the higher your prices are likely to be.

Here are some of the sources of information you can use to stay in touch with your competitors' strategies:

- **Customers** - Observing customers' shopping habits and listening to what they have to say can give you a pretty good idea of how your prices stack up against the competition.

- **Suppliers** - Since your suppliers are also their suppliers, this is another source of competitive information. But don't forget that information flows both ways. Your competitors can tap into the same source to find out about you.

- **Advertising** - Following competitors' promotional campaigns enables you to keep track of pricing changes and also to obtain current information about the quality and service being provided.

- **Industry Publications, Competitors' Catalogs and Price Lists** - These are excellent sources of information, particularly since the information is current.

- **Price Checkers** - These are shoppers employed by you to go out and gather information about competitors' prices. While pretending to shop, they actually record the prices of various key items. You can use employees to do some of this. Discuss and analyze the results.

- **Networking** - Within your community you may be able to meet with others in your industry on common ground—at trade meetings, chamber of commerce meetings, golf clubs or restaurants. This is a good way to stay in touch with what is going on in your area. You may even learn information from those outside of your field.

- **Information Gatherers** - Serious intelligence might be found by hiring professional market research firms, hiring a clipping service, talking to financial specialists. However, you may be paying for information that is overkill and not a help to your business. Protect your own secrets, and help employees to understand that keeping critical information is important to the business and to their jobs.

PRICING AND THE ECONOMY

Customer shopping habits reflect the state of the economy. During a recession or depression, customers are at their most price conscious. Worried about the high cost of living, threats of unemployment and cutbacks in credit, they want to make every dollar count. As the economy improves, customers become more optimistic about the future and are willing to pay higher prices. When the economy is at its peak and business is booming, customers offer little resistance to rising prices. The general feeling is that there is more money where that came from, so why not spend it?

As a business owner, your ability to recognize these fluctuations in the economy and to adjust your prices accordingly adds to your competitiveness. To keep your prices in line with customers' expectations, you may add or drop services, raise or lower quality standards, change your markups, or put together some combination of all of these.

PRICING AND PROFIT

Your prices should be set at a level sufficient to reimburse you for the cost of the goods or services sold, cover your overhead cost, and provide a profit. The amount of profit you receive will depend on your gross margin and/or markup. Gross margin, sometimes referred to as gross profit, and the term "markup" are not the same thing. Markup is the difference between the cost and the selling price of the goods sold. Example: A product costs you $100 and you sell it for $150. The difference between cost and sell is $50. The markup in this example is 50 percent. This is figured as a percentage of the seller's cost. The higher the markup, the greater your profit per sale. However, this does not necessarily mean that your overall profits will be higher. Why? Because higher markups usually result in reduced sales. This explains why discount stores are able to make healthy profits despite lower-than-average markups; their sales volume is higher.

Gross profit or margin in simple terms is the revenue remaining after deducting your costs for the product sold. Using the same $100 product cost example, the revenue remaining after deducting the $100 cost from a $150 sale is $50, but, as illustrated later in this chapter, it is a gross profit margin of 33 percent. This is figured as a percentage of the selling price.

PRICING METHODS

There are a number of pricing methods to choose from, ranging from the simple to the complex. Here are three of the most common methods:

Competitive Pricing - Prices are set at or below the competition's. Costs are made to conform to the prices that have been set.

Standard Markup Pricing - A standard markup is computed and then added to the cost of the goods or services sold. Some businesses apply a single markup across the board, while others have different markups for each sales category.

Cost-Oriented Pricing - Prices are set individually based on the cost of the goods or services sold, the overhead and the desired profit.

Of the three methods, cost-oriented pricing is the most accurate, but also the most complex and time consuming, since each product or service is evaluated separately. A standard markup saves time by eliminating the need to do individual computations. For a store that carries hundreds or thousands of merchandise items (SKUs - shop keeping units), this can make a big difference. Competitive pricing is the simplest method of all. Prices are virtually preset, being based on what is acceptable for your industry, or what the market will bear.

Common sense and a little experimentation will soon tell you which method or combination of methods works best for you. If you are in a highly competitive segment of the industry where the key determinant of sales is the price, you will have little choice but to use the competitive pricing method. For businesses with extensive inventories, time considerations alone will dictate that some sort of standardized markup be used. The cost-oriented pricing method is normally used by businesses offering one-of-a-kind products or specialized services.

MORE ABOUT PRICING

If you aren't careful in computing your selling price, you can easily shortchange yourself. A common mistake among new business owners is to forget to include all relevant expenses in the final price. As a result, potential profits are eaten up and sometimes even converted into losses. Your selling price needs to cover all administrative expenses, all selling expenses and all losses stemming from merchandise discounts, theft or damage. In addition, your selling price has to provide a measure of profit. This holds true regardless of which pricing method you use. In the standard markup method, these costs and profit considerations are all built into the mark-up figure itself. With cost-oriented pricing, they are added as you go. And in competitive pricing, you work backward from the price to figure the gross profit.

Gross Profit to Price

You can determine what the selling price would be, given a particular profit, by using this formula:

$$\text{Selling Price} = \frac{\text{Cost of Goods or Services} \times 100}{100\% - \text{Gross Profit }\%}$$

For instance, if a faucet cost $160 and your desired gross profit is 50 percent, you would calculate the selling price as follows:

Example #1: Faucet Cost $160 - Gross Profit 50%

$$\text{Selling Price} = \frac{\$160 \times 100}{100 - 50} = \frac{16,000}{50} = \$320$$

Selling Price = $320

Price to Gross Profit

If you are considering a particular price and want to know what the amount of your gross profit would be, you can figure that out, too:

$$\text{Gross Profit} = \frac{\text{Selling Price} - \text{Cost}}{\text{Selling Price}}$$

Using the cost and selling price from the previous example, the gross profit would be calculated like this:

$$\text{Gross Profit} = \frac{\$320 - \$160}{\$320} = \frac{\$160}{\$320} = 50\%$$

Example #2: Faucet Cost $160 - Gross Profit 35%

$$\text{Selling Price} = \frac{\$160 \times 100}{100 - 35} = \frac{16,000}{65} = \$246.15 \qquad \text{(Gross Profit to Price)}$$

Selling Price = $246.15

$$\text{Gross Profit} = \frac{246.15 - 160}{246.15} = \frac{86.15}{246.15} = 35\% \qquad \text{(Price to Gross Profit)}$$

A **Standard Markup** is the amount (often expressed as a percentage) of the original cost that you are **adding to the cost** to determine the **Sell Price**.

The equation you would use to determine a **Sell Price** from your cost would look like this:

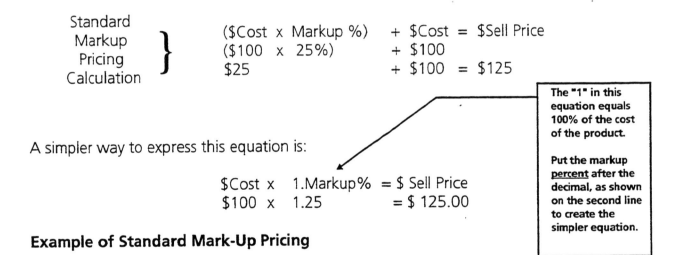

Standard Markup Pricing Calculation }

($Cost x Markup %) + $Cost = $Sell Price
($100 x 25%) + $100
$25 + $100 = $125

The "1" in this equation equals 100% of the cost of the product.

Put the markup **percent** after the decimal, as shown on the second line to create the simpler equation.

A simpler way to express this equation is:

$Cost x 1.Markup% = $ Sell Price
$100 x 1.25 = $ 125.00

Example of Standard Mark-Up Pricing

Assume your desired **Markup** is Y:

Cost x Markup = Sell

Y = 0% $100 x 1.00 = $100
Y = 20% $100 x 1.20 = $120
Y = 50% $100 x 1.50 = $150
Y = 100% $100 x 2.00 = $200
Y = 200% $100 x 3.00 = $300
Y = 300% $100 x 4.00 = $400

Note what happens in the following examples!

What is your **GROSS PROFIT** when you mark up the cost of the product to your sell price?

As a handy reference, the charts below have been created to help you understand that Gross Profit and Markup are not the same thing. Here, you will see that when you **Mark Up** your products, projects or services by a desired percent, you are not making that percentage as a **Gross Profit**.

Quick Reference GROSS MARGIN Matrix

Determining a Selling Price and Mark-Up from Known Gross Margin %

Target Gross Margin %	Multiplier Applied to Cost	Write Selling Price Here	Resulting Mark-Up %
1	1.01010		1.010
2	1.02041		2.041
3	1.03093		3.093
4	1.04167		4.167
5	1.05263		5.263
6	1.06383		6.383
7	1.07527		7.527
8	1.08696		8.696
9	1.09890		9.890
10	1.11111		11.111
11	1.12360		12.360
12	1.13636		13.636
13	1.14943		14.943
14	1.16279		16.279
15	1.17647		17.647
16	1.19048		19.048
17	1.20482		20.482
18	1.21951		21.951
19	1.23457		23.457
20	1.25000		25.000
21	1.26582		26.582
22	1.28205		28.205
23	1.29870		29.870
24	1.31579		31.579
25	1.33333		33.333

Target Gross Margin %	Multiplier Applied to Cost	Write Selling Price Here	Resulting Mark-Up %
26	1.35135		35.135
27	1.36986		36.986
28	1.38889		38.889
29	1.40845		40.845
30	1.42857		42.857
31	1.44928		44.928
32	1.47059		47.059
33	1.49254		49.254
34	1.51515		51.515
35	1.53846		53.846
36	1.56250		56.250
37	1.58730		58.730
38	1.61290		61.290
39	1.63934		63.934
40	1.66667		66.667
41	1.69492		69.492
42	1.72414		72.414
43	1.75439		75.439
44	1.78571		78.571
45	1.81818		81.818
46	1.85185		85.185
47	1.88679		88.679
48	1.92308		92.308
49	1.96078		96.078
50	2.00000		100.000

Target Gross Margin %	Multiplier Applied to Cost	Write Selling Price Here	Resulting Mark-Up %
51	2.04082		104.082
52	2.08333		108.333
53	2.12766		112.766
54	2.17391		117.391
55	2.22222		122.222
56	2.27273		127.273
57	2.32558		132.558
58	2.38095		138.095
59	2.43902		143.902
60	2.50000		150.000
61	2.56410		156.410
62	2.63158		163.158
63	2.70270		170.270
64	2.77778		177.778
65	2.85714		185.714
66	2.94118		194.118
67	3.03030		203.030
68	3.12500		212.500
69	3.22581		222.581
70	3.33333		233.333
71	3.44828		244.828
72	3.57143		257.143
73	3.70370		270.370
74	3.84615		284.615
75	4.00000		300.000

Target Gross Margin %	Multiplier Applied to Cost	Write Selling Price Here	Resulting Mark-Up %
76	4.16667		316.667
77	4.34783		334.783
78	4.54545		354.545
79	4.76190		376.190
80	5.00000		400.000
81	5.26316		426.316
82	5.55556		455.556
83	5.88235		488.235
84	6.25000		525.000
85	6.66667		566.667
86	7.14286		614.286
87	7.69231		669.231
88	8.33333		733.333
89	9.09091		809.091
90	10.00000		900.000
91	11.11111		1011.111
92	12.50000		1150.000
93	14.28571		1328.571
94	16.66667		1566.667
95	20.00000		1900.000
96	25.00000		2400.000
97	33.33333		3233.333
98	50.00000		4900.000
99	100.00000		9900.000

This matrix can be used to determine the **Selling Price** *and* **Mark-Up** *of any product or service at any Cost.*

NOTES:

Step 1: In the shaded columns, locate the "Target Gross Margin %" you want to make on a particular sale.

Step 2: Moving to the right, locate the corresponding "Multiplier Applied to Cost." Multiply COST times the number in this column to arrive at a Selling Price.

Step 3: Record the result in the space provided in the third column.

The third column tells you the actual Mark-Up % you are adding to your cost to earn the Target Gross Margin % you want (for reference only).

Quick Reference MARK-UP Matrix

Determining Selling Price and Gross Margin % from a Known Mark-Up %

Mark-Up %	Mark-Up Multiplier	Write Sell Price Here	Gross Margin
1	1.010		0.99%
2	1.020		1.96%
3	1.030		2.91%
4	1.040		3.85%
5	1.050		4.76%
6	1.060		5.66%
7	1.070		6.54%
8	1.080		7.41%
9	1.090		8.26%
10	1.100		9.09%
11	1.110		9.91%
12	1.120		10.71%
13	1.130		11.50%
14	1.140		12.28%
15	1.150		13.04%
16	1.160		13.79%
17	1.170		14.53%
18	1.180		15.25%
19	1.190		15.97%
20	1.200		16.67%
21	1.210		17.36%
22	1.220		18.03%
23	1.230		18.70%
24	1.240		19.35%
25	1.250		20.00%

Mark-Up %	Mark-Up Multiplier	Write Sell Price Here	Gross Margin
26	1.260		20.63%
27	1.270		21.26%
28	1.280		21.88%
29	1.290		22.48%
30	1.300		23.08%
31	1.310		23.66%
32	1.320		24.24%
33	1.330		24.81%
33.33	1.333		25.00%
34	1.340		25.37%
35	1.350		25.93%
36	1.360		26.47%
37	1.370		27.01%
38	1.380		27.54%
39	1.390		28.06%
40	1.400		28.57%
41	1.410		29.08%
42	1.420		29.58%
43	1.430		30.07%
44	1.440		30.56%
45	1.450		31.03%
46	1.460		31.51%
47	1.470		31.97%
48	1.480		32.43%
49	1.490		32.89%
50	1.500		33.33%

Mark-Up %	Mark-Up Multiplier	Write Sell Price Here	Gross Margin
51	1.510		33.71%
52	1.520		34.21%
53	1.530		34.64%
54	1.540		35.06%
55	1.550		35.48%
56	1.560		35.90%
57	1.570		36.31%
58	1.580		36.71%
59	1.590		37.11%
60	1.600		37.50%
61	1.610		37.89%
62	1.620		38.27%
63	1.630		38.65%
64	1.640		39.02%
65	1.650		39.39%
66	1.660		39.76%
66.66	1.667		40.00%
67	1.670		40.12%
68	1.680		40.48%
69	1.690		40.83%
70	1.700		41.18%
71	1.710		41.52%
72	1.720		41.86%
73	1.730		42.20%
74	1.740		42.53%
75	1.750		42.86%

Mark-Up %	Mark-Up Multiplier	Write Sell Price Here	Gross Margin
76	1.760		43.18%
77	1.770		43.50%
78	1.780		43.82%
79	1.790		44.13%
80	1.800		44.44%
81	1.810		44.75%
82	1.820		45.05%
83	1.830		45.36%
84	1.840		45.65%
85	1.850		45.95%
86	1.860		46.24%
87	1.870		46.52%
88	1.880		46.81%
89	1.890		47.09%
90	1.900		47.37%
91	1.910		47.64%
92	1.920		47.92%
93	1.930		48.19%
94	1.940		48.45%
95	1.950		48.72%
96	1.960		48.98%
97	1.970		49.24%
98	1.980		49.49%
99	1.990		49.75%
100	2.000		50.00%

NOTES:

This matrix can be used to determine the *Selling Price* and *Gross Margin* % of any product or service at any *Cost*.

Step 1: Simply locate the **Mark-Up %** (in the shaded columns) you want to apply to the cost.

Step 2: Move to the next column to the right to locate the "**Mark-Up Multiplier**." Multiply COST times the number in this column to arrive at a Selling Price.

Step 3: Record the result in the space provided in the third column.

The fourth column shows the resulting **Gross Margin** % you will earn when selling your product or service at the Mark-Up you desire (for reference only).

Keystone Markup

Avoiding percentages altogether, many retailers use a method called the keystone markup, which entails simply doubling the cost of an item to obtain its selling price. Although quick and easy, this method obviously can't be used in all situations.

PRICING STRATEGY

Now that you have the basics, it is time to consider strategy. If pricing were just a matter of plugging different numbers into a formula and coming up with the right figure, it wouldn't require any strategy at all, just a good head for numbers. This isn't the case. In addition to mathematical ability, you need marketing savvy.

Market Response: Elasticity

The first thing you need to find out is how responsive your market is to a change in price. This responsiveness is called "elasticity." Products such as eggs, baking soda, razor blades and medicine are highly inelastic. Regardless of whether their prices are raised or lowered, customers continue to purchase them in approximately the same quantities. Customer demand for some products, on the other hand, fluctuates with the price. A small change in price—up or down—results in a decrease or increase in the number of units sold. This type of response is said to be "elastic." For example, television sets, strawberries, clothing or jewelry are highly elastic.

As a rule, items that are considered to be necessities are less elastic than those that are considered to be luxuries. This is because the customer's need, rather than the product's price, triggers the purchase. For instance, a person with a broken cook top can't wait for a sale before buying a new one. The need to be able to cook takes priority over the price.

How does all this affect your pricing strategy? For one thing, the more inelastic your product is, the easier it is to raise your prices without hurting your sales, meaning more profit on the same volume. To increase your profits on highly elastic products, rather than raising your prices, you might try lowering them. Although this reduces your profit on each unit sold, the resulting increase in sales volume should improve your overall profits.

Other Determinants of Price

In addition to product elasticity, other pricing determinants include:

Volume - Are you selling to a mass market or just a niche? High-volume businesses generally employ low markups. Conversely, the lower your volume is, the higher the markup you will need to cover your overhead and provide a profit.

Image - Do you want your business known for its quality or for having the best buys? If you are after a quality image, you may decide to use a **prestige pricing** strategy. This strategy calls for deliberately setting prices high in order to attract affluent customers. The opposite of prestige pricing is **leader pricing**. Used to draw large numbers of customers into a store, leader pricing emphasizes low-price specials that have common appeal; it is also known as a "loss leader." Two-for-one sales and cents-off coupons are typical of this strategy.

Customer Psychology - According to market researchers, consumers react more favorably to certain prices than others. An item selling for $99.95 has a better chance of being purchased than an identical item at $100.00. Even though the difference in price is insignificant, there is a psychological difference.

Product Life Span - What's the life span of your product? If you're selling fashion or fad items that appeal to customers for only a brief time, you need to make your profits quickly. Otherwise, you could be left holding a bag full of expenses when the demand drops off. The longer your product's life span, the longer the period of time you have in which to earn your profits. This explains the numerous claims by advertisers that their products are new and improved. For the most part, such assertions are nothing more than attempts to stretch a product's life span and extend profits.

Profit Objectives - In formulating pricing strategy, the key thing to remember is not to lose sight of your overall objective: maintaining profitability. This may mean taking a loss on one product to stimulate the sales of another (leader pricing). It can also call for changes in your method of operation (high volume versus low volume).

Marketing Mix

Just as your business does not exist in a vacuum, neither do your pricing decisions. Price is only one of the four components that make up the marketing mix. The others—product, place and promotion—must all be in harmony with the prices you set. The product and services you decide to sell, your distribution system, and the messages you communicate about your business directly influence your pricing strategy and profitability.

Based on your marketing mix objectives, you may want to employ one or more of the following pricing strategies:

Skimming - Used for new, innovative products that are just being introduced into the marketplace, a skimming strategy calls for you to set your price high in the beginning, then to lower it over time as the product becomes more widely accepted. The advantage of this approach is that it enables businesses to quickly recoup their research, development and promotion costs.

Penetration - This strategy involves pricing your products low and keeping the prices low in an effort to penetrate the market and gain wide distribution and consumer acceptance. Since it entails shrinking your profit margins, this strategy only works with low-cost products that can be mass produced and are capable of achieving high sales volumes.

Price Bracketing - Businesses employing this strategy categorize their products within different price ranges or lines (high, medium, low), and price them accordingly. A plumbing retailer, for example, may carry faucets that sell for under $100, $100 to $200 and over $200. Depending upon what customers are willing to spend, they can then choose the preferred price range. This method makes it easier for businesses to price and display their products— and for customers to buy them.

Promotional Pricing - As the name implies, this strategy offers lower, limited-time-only prices on specific products to stimulate sales. It can be utilized for special purchase items that were bought at a discount or linked to customers' buying times, e.g., holidays, seasons, events.

Price Bundling - This strategy consists of bundling separate products or services together and selling them as a package. For example, a kitchen dealer might offer cabinets, plumbing and countertops all for one price.

Time-Period Pricing - This strategy raises or lowers prices based on a consumer-demand level at various times, charging higher prices at peak times and lower prices during slow times.

Value-Added Pricing - A business using this strategy offers an additional service or gift when a customer makes a regularly priced purchase.

Captive Pricing - With this pricing strategy, you set your price on one product, then make your profit by selling customers other products that go with it. Selling competitively priced appliances to help make a cabinet sale is an example.

These are just some of the most frequently used pricing strategies. By taking a creative approach, you should be able to adapt them to your own needs or come up with other pricing strategies that are uniquely suited to your specific kitchen and bathroom business.

For help in developing your pricing strategy and keeping it on target, answer the questions in the following checklist. Then, compare your answers to see if there are inconsistencies in your overall pricing strategy.

PRICING STRATEGY CHECKLIST	Yes	No
1. Do you try to evaluate the market forces affecting the demand for your products?		
2. Have you considered what price strategies would be compatible with your total marketing mix?		
3. Do you know which products are slow movers and which are fast?		
4. Do you know which products are elastic and which are inelastic?		
5. Do you know your competitors' pricing strategies?		
6. Are you influenced by competitors' price changes?		
7. Do you regularly review competitors' ads and quotes to update your information on their prices?		
8. Is your store large enough to employ a comparison shopper or use one of your own employees?		
9. Is there a specific time of year when your competitors have sales?		
10. Do your customers expect sales at certain times?		
11. Would periodic special sales, combining reduced prices and heavier advertising be consistent with the store image that you are seeking?		
12. Should any leader offerings (selected products with low, less-profitable prices) be used?		
13. Will discount coupons be used in newspaper ads or mailed to selected consumers on any occasion?		
14. Would odd prices, such as $9.95 or $99.99, be more appealing to your customers than even-ending pricing?		
15. Have you determined whether to price below, at, or above the market?		
16. Do you determine specific markups for each product?		
17. Do you use standardized markups for product categories?		
18. Are your prices set so as to cover the full cost on every sale?		
19. Are additional markups called for because of increases, or because an item's low price causes consumers to question its quality?		
20. Should employees be given purchase discounts?		
21. Should any group of customers, such as contractors or designers be given purchase discounts?		

For more information on pricing strategy, read NKBA®'s _Managing Your Kitchen and Bathroom Firm's Finances for Profit_ by Don Quigley.

Your inventory is probably your biggest investment. How do you use inventory to your best advantage?

Chapter 5

GUARDING THE FIRE
Inventory Management

An ounce of action is worth a ton of theory. - **Friedrich Engels**

In the kitchen and bathroom industry, inventory may or may not be an important factor. Many dealers may have a showroom, do design work, sell the job, follow through on installation, but do not have inventories. If this is the case, there is little inventory management or investment required. There are some dealers who make their own cabinets. Here, you have to manage the materials for each and every job, but still probably will not have any "regular stock" inventories. Then there are dealers who do stock cabinets or plumbing, hardware and appliances. These people need to digest, understand and practice what's in this chapter if they hope to be successful and to maximize their investment and return on investment. And, by maximizing their investments, they are, in effect, guarding the fire they have so carefully built.

Our business is a complete kitchen and bathroom business. We show and sell kitchen cabinets, high-end appliances, solid-surface countertops, decorative plumbing and hardware. But the only products we inventory are plumbing and some hardware. All the kitchen products are purchased by the job. No inventories. We even try to schedule deliveries of cabinets, appliances and countertops to go in "factory direct," so we don't even touch them. This doesn't always work, but at least this is our goal.

We have in excess of $1 million invested in plumbing and hardware inventories. We continually "close out" the slow movers and obsolete items.

If you do have inventories and you don't manage them properly, you can give away a major portion of your bottom line. Your goal must be to maximize your investment. This chapter will teach you how to do this.

CONTROLLING YOUR INVENTORY

Every kitchen and bathroom business, regardless of whether its primary function is retail, wholesale, service or manufacturing, has one thing in common: **inventory**. In fact, the major portion of your investment dollars is likely to go for inventory. Included in this are expenditures for merchandise, supplies, raw materials and parts, all of which are expected to earn profits for your business. To do so, however, they must be kept in proper balance. This is the aim of inventory control.

A good inventory control system:

1. Keeps inventory at the optimum level.
2. Uses just-in-time manufacturing for manufacturers.
3. Uses just-in-time delivery or cycle shipping for dealers.
4. Orders goods in the most economical quantities.
5. Speeds up merchandise turnover.
6. Reduces inventory shrinkage.

In other words, it enables you to get maximum value out of your inventory at minimum cost. But if it can do all that, it must be complicated. Right? Not really. Actually, it is pretty simple. Just as a thermostat is keyed to react to changes in temperature, an inventory control system reacts to changes (or the lack of changes) in your level of inventory. Once you have set up the system, it's almost totally automatic.

OPTIMUM LEVEL OF INVENTORY

Many businesses mistakenly abide by the philosophy that the more inventory you have on hand, the better, as a way of making sure that no sales are lost. What they don't realize is that the cost of carrying the extra inventory could more than equal the profits from the additional sales. Added to the cost of the inventory itself is the cost of shipping, storage, insurance and taxes. And there is always the danger that the inventory will become obsolete before it can become used or sold. That is a high price to pay for the security of having your shelves full.

Adopting a "let them eat cake" attitude isn't the solution either. Purposely letting your business run short on the inventory used for operations, activities or sales is guaranteed to alienate customers and employees alike. Among the costs incurred as a result of inventory shortages are: special handling charges and sacrificed purchase discounts, because of the need to trace rush orders; underutilization of personnel, equipment and facilities, and lost sales. When sales are involved, your loss can be far-reaching. This is because dissatisfied customers have a tendency to take their future business elsewhere.

This brings us to your objective—the **optimum level of inventory**. What is it? It is a level of inventory that is the most profitable. Rather than eliminating the cost of stock shortages altogether, by reducing inventory carrying costs to the lowest possible figure, it results in the lowest total of the two. For example:

Inventory Level	Costs of Stock Shortages	Costs of Extra Inventory	Total
A	$1,000	$8,750	$9,750
B	2,500	6,500	9,000
C	3,750	4,000	7,750
D	5,500	3,000	8,500

The optimum level at which to maintain inventory is level C, since this reduces the total costs by the greatest amount. Once you have established, through trial and error, the optimum level of inventory for your business, it is up to your control system to keep it at that level. This is accomplished by measuring the goods on hand, indicating the amounts needed and calculating delivery times.

Measuring the Goods on Hand

This is the way to find out what you have and what you don't have. Does that carton on the top shelf contain a dozen widgets, as marked, or is it empty? There are three ways to find out: make an educated guess, open the carton and count what is inside, or check your records.

1. *Educated Guess* - This method relies on your memory and the powers of observation to determine what is in stock. In the event that your business is small and you are able to keep close tabs on the day-to-day operations, it might be fairly accurate. But there is also a good chance it could be wrong. To be on the safe side, you should do a physical count at least once a year.

2. *Physical Count* - The most accurate, albeit time consuming, way to monitor your inventory levels is to do a physical count. This means tallying the goods on hand at periodic intervals to make sure that your estimated inventory matches up with your actual inventory.

   Two popular ways to verify inventory during the year with minimum effort are *zero counting* and *cycle counting*. In zero counting, when the physical location of an inventory area is empty, look at the records and determine it is zero. If no, adjust it to zero. In cycle counting, classify all materials into three categories, A, B and C. In the A Category, put all expensive items or items that have a long lead time. In the C Category put items that are inexpensive and can be purchased on short notice. All remaining items are classified as Category B. The intent is to spend 90 percent of your energy on the A Category and perhaps 1 percent on the C Category. Every month, count the A Category 100 percent (imported faucets, etc.), count 50 percent of the B Category (laminate sheets), and if you have time count the C Category items. If you find any discrepancies, adjust your records to actual. By cycle counting every month, it will help you reconstruct the month in your mind so that perhaps you can identify why there is a discrepancy between actual and book inventory.

3. *Perpetual Inventory* - A perpetual inventory system records changes in stock as they occur. Using the information obtained from stock tags, receipts and requisition forms, the appropriate stock number, size and color are entered into the inventory filing system at the time the goods are received, used or sold. This can be done manually or by computer. When using this system, supplement it with a physical count one or more times per year.

PERPETUAL INVENTORY FILE CARD					
Description		Location			
Product No.		Reorder Point			
Supplier		EOQ			
Received		Sold		Balance	
Date	Amount	Date	Amount	Date	Amount

Indicating the Amounts Needed

Having determined the extent of your inventory, you have reached the crucial point in the control process of deciding what to order and how much. This is where the automatic feature of your inventory control system comes into action. Based on your estimates of the minimum quantities of goods that are required to keep your inventory in balance, the system is programmed to react to specific reorder points. Each reorder point represents the level at which an inventory item needs to be replenished. The actual amount to be purchased is determined by such information updates as:

- Changes in operation's activities.
- Changes in customer preferences.
- Changes in seasons.
- Changes in products (improved, discontinued, new styles).
- Changes in profit margins.
- Changes in suppliers.

For instance, if the customer demand for a particular item is starting to taper off, you might decide to let that item drop below its reorder point without purchasing additional stock.

Calculating Delivery Time

The success of your inventory control system hinges on your ability to calculate delivery times. How long will it take the supplier to fill your order—not just to verify it over the phone, but actually process the paperwork, pack the goods and deliver them to your place of business? Unless the goods are on your shelves when you need them, not merely somewhere in transit, your hope of maintaining a balanced inventory is slim.

The way to minimize foul-ups in deliveries is to maintain good supplier relations. This means familiarizing yourself with each supplier's delivery capabilities, i.e., lead time needed, special order policy, dependability, minimum orders and freight requirements, so that you know what to expect. It also means keeping your requests within reason (not, "I needed it yesterday"). When suppliers find that you have an understanding of their business operations, they are more inclined to take an interest in yours. If this policy fails and you get poor service, don't be afraid to switch suppliers.

Economic Order Quantity

In addition to keeping your inventory at the optimum level, it is the function of your control system to determine the economic order quantity (EOQ) for each item. This is the number of units you must order so as to achieve the lowest total cost. Using your reorder points and estimated demand levels as a springboard, you already know what to order and how much. And you know the delivery capabilities of your suppliers. But, should you place one large order? Several small orders? A few medium-sized orders? What is the most economical order quantity?

The EOQ can be determined by offsetting the costs associated with each order. For instance, the larger your order, the greater your inventory carrying costs, but the smaller your ordering and delivery costs. Conversely, with small orders your carrying costs decrease and delivery costs go up.

At first, coming up with a winning combination might seem a little like trying to balance on a teeter-totter by yourself. Fortunately, you can use a specific formula to calculate the right answer. The formula is a bit complicated, but today's computer software on inventory control systems incorporates this and makes your job very easy. You simply need to add in such factors as sales, costs of ordering (clerical, shipping, delivery), inventory carrying charge (storage, insurance, taxes) and price per unit.

The hardest part of ascertaining the EOQ is figuring out the square root at the end. But don't let that discourage you from using the formula. An electronic calculator or square root table can solve the problem. Or, you can use the computer inventory control program to do the calculations. Whichever method you choose, once you have determined the EOQ for a specific item, it isn't necessary to recalculate it each time you order unless there are changes in demand, costs or delivery capabilities.

Purchase Discounts

In calculating the EOQ of the inventory items you need, it is important to pay close attention to purchase discounts. These are price reductions made available by suppliers on the basis of order size, total purchases per period, order season or credit terms.

1. *Order Size* - A discount is given when a larger order is placed. This encourages customers to order in larger quantities, thus reducing the supplier's shipping and handling costs while increasing revenues.

2. *Total Purchases* - A discount is given as a total amount of your purchases per period increases. This is done to stimulate repeat buying.

3. *Order Season* - A discount is given when your order is placed prior to the peak ordering season. In this way, suppliers can even out demand levels and reduce storage requirements.

4. *Credit Terms* - A discount is given when prompt payment is made for goods that have been received. The most commonly offered discount is two percent - 10 days, net 30. This authorizes you to deduct two percent from your bill if payment is made within 10 days; otherwise you are expected to pay the full amount in 30 days.

By taking advantages of these discounts, you can further reduce your ordering costs. However, this doesn't mean that you should purchase more than you can afford in an effort to save money. Each inventory item purchased should be justified on its own merits, exclusive of any accompanying costs.

MERCHANDISE TURNOVER

Your inventory control system can help you speed up merchandise turnover in a variety of ways. These include:

- Improving purchasing methods.
- Monitoring inventory levels.
- Identifying hard-to-move items.
- Adjusting for seasonal demand.
- Recognizing trends.

Rather than waiting until you are stuck with an oversupply of any one item, an effective system alerts you to the potential inventory problem before it happens. This enables you to stay on top of things by cutting back orders, modifying display and sales techniques, reducing markups or increasing promotional efforts.

UNIVERSAL PRODUCT CODES

If your inventory control system is equipped to make use of bar code data, the system can help compile inventory data. Bar codes, or universal product codes (UPCs) as they are officially called, are the vertical lines on packages and price tags that get scanned at electronic cash registers when a purchase is made.

In addition to giving you the price of an item sold, a bar code can help you to control your inventory by providing such information as the stock number, size, color, category, department and season.

When this data is scanned at the register and entered into your inventory control system, you can get a good idea of what is moving and what is not.

Although retailers are the greatest users of bar code data, manufacturers and others are making use of it, too, to process customer's orders, track inventory as it moves through the production process and monitor worker output. The only drawback to using UPC codes is the price of the electronic equipment. But, just as with computers, this has been steadily dropping. More and more small businesses are now utilizing UPC codes as an inventory control/accounting tool.

INVENTORY SHRINKAGE

Inventory shrinkage refers to unaccountable stock shortages. Inventory that should be in your stockroom or on your shelves may just disappear. This can be caused by employee or customer theft, misplaced stock or simply poor record keeping. Whatever the reason, missing inventory can be a source of frustration and mystification to the business owner, who often feels powerless to stop it.

One way to combat shrinkage is to tighten security. But the effectiveness of this method will be diluted unless it is backed up by inventory control. To reduce shrinkage, the following inventory controls are recommended:

- Log in inventory shipments when received.
- File purchase orders and invoices properly and promptly.
- Use requisition forms to keep track of supplies, materials and parts used in operating your business.
- Keep a written record of all sales transactions.
- Take a physical inventory at least once each year.
- Match perpetual inventory figures against physical inventory results.
- Limit access to inventory area.
- Assign one person to be in charge of the inventory area.

These controls will help you prevent most inventory shrinkage from occurring and to detect it quickly when it does occur.

To find out whether your inventory control system is doing all the things it is supposed to do, answer the questions in the following inventory checklist and use your "no" answers to help determine where you can improve your inventory management.

INVENTORY CHECKLIST	Yes	No
1. Do you have an adequate system for monitoring your level of inventory?		
2. Is a physical count taken at least once a year?		
3. Have you determined the optimum level of inventory for your business?		
4. Have you established reorder points for replenishing inventory items?		
5. Do you make adjustments for changes in customer demand when placing orders?		
6. Are you familiar with suppliers' delivery capabilities?		
7. Do you order in the most economic quantities?		
8. Do you take advantage of purchasing discounts?		
9. Do you keep track of slow-moving stock?		
10. Can you spot potentially fast movers?		
11. Is your merchandise inventory balanced by price line, color, size and type?		
12. Do you select merchandise items with your target customers in mind?		
13. Are you taking preventive action against inventory shrinkage?		
14. Is your inventory as profitable as it should be?		

For more information on inventory management, read NKBA's _Managing Your Kitchen and Bathroom Firm's Finances for Profit_ by Don Quigley.

With inventory management under control, let's move on to marketing your business and advertising successfully.

Chapter 6

DANCING AND CELEBRATING
Marketing

I want to see you shoot the way you shout. - **Theodore Roosevelt.**

As more and more people notice your fire, they will surely want to come closer. It's time to do some dancing and singing, and maybe even toast a few marshmallows.

I believe the marketing and advertising part of our business is the most fun and one of the most rewarding. You can try various combinations of media advertising, shows, events, mailings, and other innovative marketing ideas. The challenge is to find the best mix for your company.

The contradiction is that marketing and advertising can also be frustrating and difficult, because it is so very hard to measure results. We all advertise in the Yellow Pages, place ads in various media, work home shows and send out direct mailings, but very seldom can we say, "We received X amount of dollars in return for that activity." Sure, we end up with a "gut" feeling, but hard numbers are almost impossible to tie down. What we do know is if we don't keep our name, our products and our services out in front of the clients, we won't have clients.

Over the years of trying virtually every type of advertising and promotion feasible, we have learned what works best for us. The following outlines some of the advertising and marketing we do in our business.

Repeat customers and referrals by satisfied customers are certainly your best advertisement. It is vital to keep reminding those former customers that you are still in business and offering outstanding design, service and products.

Take time to plan your advertising program. Consider your budget and decide how to spend it most effectively. Have a graphics designer create a logo for your business and use it in all of your advertising. It takes time for your audience to actually "see" your advertisement, so run your ads often and keep the message simple. People will remember you when they decide to remodel, if your name, logo and message are familiar.

We do a fair amount of "prestige" **magazine advertising** in order to help create the image of "higher-end," or better products.

Direct mail of several kinds has been one of our best result winners. We subscribe to several services that provide "new job" information, e.g., job permits, size, type, owners, contractors and addresses. We select the jobs—new and remodels that we feel would apply to our products and services. We send a "congratulations on your new project" letter and a company brochure. We receive many (1,200 plus or minus a month) leads from the various manufacturers we represent. Every one of these gets a follow-up letter and brochure from our company.

Each month, we select 2,000 plus or minus names and addresses via zip code listings, based on demographics of income, size and age of the home. This direct-mail effort is geared primarily toward the remodel market. Our tangible results from direct mail seem to be the best of all the activities we try.

We offer three **sales** a year, promoted to both consumers and the trades. We have spring, summer and fall sales with the summer sale set up as a big parking lot activity. For all the sales, we promote through newspaper, radio and television advertising, we discount everything in the store and we stay open Saturdays and Sundays. Additionally, for the summer sale, we put up a big tent, fill the parking lot and the tent with products (new, old, good and not so good). We have cooking demonstrations, offer hot dogs and sodas, and try to make an event out of each one of them. They work! We see a big jump in sales and cash intake. The margins slip a bit, but it's our big opportunity to not only write new business and attract new clients to our store, but also to move obsolete and slow-moving merchandise.

We have a "love-hate" relationship with **home shows**. We love the exposure, but hate the work, staffing and expense. This may be our least-favorite form of marketing.

We have developed a series of four **seminars**, including finish plumbing products, kitchen cabinets, appliances and solid-surface countertops. To announce these seminars to consumers, we advertise and send out direct-mail invitations. The seminars last 90 minutes and are packed with useful information. We offer some food and sodas, and keep the sessions pretty non-commercial. We hold them in our showroom and include a short tour. These have been very successful.

Although we have cut back on our Yellow Pages advertising, it is still one of our biggest expense areas, and, I believe, one of the better information resources for potential clients.

"**Limo lunches**" or dinners are fun and successful. We've hosted builders, plumbers, architects and design firms, and companies with five to 10 product decision makers. We schedule a limousine to pick up the clients at their office and bring them to our showroom. We have a 45-minute tour/pitch and have the clients back to work in a timely manner. We offer either box lunches at noontime or heavy hors d'oeurvres, depending on the time of day and the number of people. The total cost for each venture is $250 to $300.

By far, our best advertising is "word of mouth" or **referral**. We ask all clients coming into our showroom to register at the front reception desk. One of the questions on our sign-in sheets is, "How did you hear about us?" Most often, the answer is, "referral." Thank goodness! It means we're doing a whole lot the right way. Yellow Pages, "saw you from the freeway" and various ads are next in order of highest response.

We facilitate many **events**, including once-a-month cooking demonstrations and hosting various trade-organization meetings, such as ASID, NKBA®, AIA and BIA. We've had several "celebrity" chefs come in and cook/lecture. Any reason to get people into your showroom should be considered very closely.

Part of our marketing program involves teaching classes to design students. There are several colleges in our marketing area that offer design classes. We try to schedule it so that the class can participate in a field trip to our showroom, because it is much more effective for students to feel, touch and see the products, as well as hear our comments. If this can't be done, we have a slide program we take to them. The design students of today will be our clients of tomorrow.

Many of your vendors have co-op advertising dollars available. Some will be formal, written programs, and some will not be in writing and you will not know about them unless you ask. Don't be shy, ask the question. Depending on your buying power with your respective vendors, you can judge how assertive you should be in asking for co-op advertising dollars. Develop a program, including a time line which incorporates the resources you are asking for, and go to your vendors with a request for help. I believe you'll be pleasantly surprised.

The challenge of good marketing and public relations is first being creative. Next is developing a plan that includes **what, when, how** and **how much**. It takes time and effort, but, if done correctly, will reap excellent rewards.

DEVELOPING YOUR PROMOTIONAL STRATEGY

If you build a better mousetrap, the world may indeed beat a path to your door, but not without a little help from you. In the first place, before people can buy your mousetrap, they have to know about it. In the second place, they have to know where to find your door. In the third place, it helps if the people you are trying to reach need your services.

The U.S. Patent Office has issued patents by the thousands for inventions that never made it. Putting aside the problems of unworkable designs or excessive production costs, many of the inventions fail simply because of poor or nonexistent promotional strategies. Having created their better mousetraps, the inventors didn't know what to do with them.

Successfully running a business is much the same as inventing a new product. To succeed, each needs to be promoted. At this point, you have a pretty good idea of who your potential customers are. Knowing this much is half the battle. What's left is to convert those potential customers into satisfied customers. That is where your promotional strategy comes in.

A promotional strategy is a game plan for reaching your target market—those people most likely to use your product or service. At the simplest, most direct level, your promotional strategy might consist of relying on a sign in front of your door and the word-of-mouth comments of your present customers. In some instances, if you are in a very small town, and if you offer unique products or services, or if you have a long-standing reputation, for example—this is sufficient. Normally, though, customers need more to go on before they are drawn to your business.

Hiring a full-time, customer-service employee is the newest trend for the small kitchen and bathroom dealer/designer who is interested in advertising and marketing as a way to compete with the large retail firms. This staff person would be responsible for your public relations program and ensuring that consumers have a positive experience in dealing with your company. One way to budget for this position would be to add a percentage onto each sale to fund it directly; it is calculated as overhead. Some of the customer-service person's duties would include:

- Follow up with past clients.
- Follow up with present clients having work done.
- Writing press releases and news items for local publications.
- Sending notification of installers' arrival dates.
- Scheduling and sending thank you notes.

The goal of your promotional strategy should be to reach the greatest number of potential customers through the most economical use of your resources (money, personnel and facilities). This means tuning in to those channels of communication (by means of advertising and publicity) most widely used by your target customers. It also means working within the limits of a budget to achieve the desired results.

ADVERTISING

Advertising involves the purchasing of time or space in the various communications media for the purpose of promoting your business. The two categories of advertising are **institutional** and **product**. Institutional advertising promotes your business in general, emphasizing its good name and any contributions that it has made to the well-being of the community. Product advertising promotes the specific products or services you sell, emphasizing the benefits associated with buying them from you. A plumbing-fixture company, for instance, can emphasize the time and money it spends in building new manufacturing facilities (institutional advertising), or it can emphasize the new, improved flushing mechanism of their water closets (product advertising). Your own objectives will determine whether to use one or both of these approaches.

THE MEDIA

The advertising media generally favored are newspapers, magazines, radio, television, direct mail, Yellow Pages and outdoor advertising. Other media includes transit, specialty, movie theaters, flyers, church bulletins, home and garden shows and sponsoring sporting teams.

Each medium has its own unique characteristics and is capable of reaching large numbers of people. Depending on your message, target customers, budget and lead time, some will be more suited to your needs than others.

- Keep your basic **message** simple and direct ("You'll save more money at the ABC Kitchen and Bathroom Company"), and use a more involved, detailed explanation (a list of reasons why the finish on your cabinets is better) for a long advertisement in a magazine or a letter. Does your message lean heavily on words, color, sound or movement to make its point? Create a logo and color for your advertising and use it. Repeat the same message; it takes a while for the public to really "see" your ad. Consider hiring a professional copywriter.

- Is your target customer everyone (the mass market) or just a small segment of the market? The narrower your target, the greater the need to use selective media to reach it. Doctors, for instance, can be reached more effectively by means of an advertisement in a medical journal than on a daytime soap opera.

- Consider your budget. How much money can you spend? Despite the suitability of a particular medium, if you can't afford it, there is no sense in building your promotional strategy around it.

- What is your lead time? Do you want the advertisement to start this week, next week, next year? Lead times vary with the medium, and if you need a quick start, that limits your selection.

Newspapers

Newspapers, which have traditionally been the favorite means of advertising for retailers, account for more than a fourth of all advertising dollars spent in the United States.

Message - Newspapers are one of the best equipped of the media (along with magazines and direct mail) for explaining and describing a product. Not only is the space available, but the only limitation on time is the reader's attention span. The effectiveness of your message can be quickly and easily measured through the use of redeemable coupons in your ads and customer demand for the featured items. If no one brings in a coupon or asks for the product, the ad isn't working.

Target Customer - Since newspapers can be local, they reach the people of your community. Their readers are your potential customers. For greater selectivity, your ad can be placed in the sections most likely to appeal to your target customers (sports, business, world news, entertainment, food, real estate). An ad for a kitchen and bathroom business might run in the home section, entertainment section or food section of the newspaper.

Budget - Newspaper rates are low compared to most other media. Even a business on a very limited budget can generally afford a small ad.

Lead Time - Newspapers have the shortest lead time of the media. Some ads can be placed on as little as two or three days notice. This gives you a great deal of flexibility in deciding when and what to advertise.

Limitations - Newspapers are short-lived; if your ad isn't read today, chances are that it won't ever be read. Reproduction quality is poor; products that require strong visual presentations are better served by other media. Most people don't read every page in a newspaper; unless careful attention is paid to your ad's placement, it could get lost in the shuffle.

Rates - Advertising space is sold in column inches (14 lines to an inch). An ad that is two columns wide by three inches deep occupies six column inches. The rate per column inch is based on a paper's circulation—the larger the circulation, the higher the rates.

Volume Rates - Bigger advertisers are entitled to discounts. This means that the more space you buy, the lower the rate per column inch.

Preferred Position Rates - If you specify a particular page or position on the page, the rate may be higher. But if this gets people to see your ad, it's worth the money. Because of the way we read, ads at the upper right of the page generally have the most drawing power.

Classified Rates - These rates are quoted by lines, rather than column inches. The ideal position is at the front of the classified section. The farther back that your ad appears, the larger the drop-off in readers.

Comparing Costs - Depending on your location, there may be several newspapers to choose from. Based on each paper's rates and circulation, it's an easy matter to compare the costs and determine which is the best buy. This is done by measuring each paper's cost per thousand people reached or CPM. The following CPM equations are provided here to help you determine which newspaper's rates best meet your needs.

$$CPM = \frac{\text{Cost of Ad} \times 1000}{\text{Total Circulation}}$$

$$CPM = \frac{\$500 \times 1000}{650,000} = 77¢ \text{ per } 1,000 \text{ for Newspaper A}$$

$$CPM = \frac{\$460 \times 1000}{575,000} = 80¢ \text{ per } 1,000 \text{ for Newspaper B}$$

As you can see, although an ad in newspaper A is more expensive, its cost per 1,000 readers is actually less. This makes it the better buy.

Magazines

Though used primarily by large advertisers, magazines are now starting to grow in popularity with smaller advertisers as well. This is because of the increase in special-interest magazines. Unlike general-interest magazines, these focus on a single topic enabling advertisers to reach a specific audience.

Message - Like newspapers, magazines are well suited to conveying in-depth information and their effectiveness can be readily measured. Reproduction values are high, so products that need color or strong visuals to make an impact look their best. Furthermore, people tend to read magazines at a more leisurely pace than newspapers and are inclined to save them afterward. This lengthens the life span of your ad.

Target Customer - Magazines enable you to be as selective as you want in pinpointing your target customer. Through careful placement of your ads in the right special interest magazines, you are virtually guaranteed of reaching a receptive audience.

Budget - Magazine ads can be expensive, particularly in national magazines with large circulations, but if you are willing to do some research, there are bargains to be found. For information about rates, check the *Standard Rate and Data Service*, a monthly publication available at many libraries.

Lead Time - Magazines have a much longer lead time than newspapers. Ads normally must be received two or three months prior to publication.

Limitations - The long-lead time reduces your flexibility. Ads must be planned and space purchased well in advance. Magazine ads can get lost, too; position is important.

Rates - Space is usually sold by the page or fraction of a page. Some magazines also have classified or mail-order sections in which space is sold by the line. These sections are generally at the back of the magazines. Rates are determined by circulation. However, a magazine that caters to a particularly affluent or hard-to-reach audience may still be able to charge high rates despite a small circulation. Other determinants of rates are:

- **Color** - An ad that is in color is more expensive than a black and white ad.
- **Quantity Discounts** - These are based on the amount of space purchased in a 12-month period.
- **Frequency Discounts** - These are based on the number of times space is purchased in a 12-month period.
- **Positioning** - If a special position is requested, there generally is an additional charge.

Comparing Costs - As with newspapers, magazines can be compared by the CPM technique to determine which is the most *economical*.

Radio

Radio's main strength is its ability to reach people regardless of where they are or what they are doing. Whether at home, driving to work or on vacation, people have their radios with them. In the United States today, there are almost two radios per person, with 99 percent of all households having at least one radio.

Message - Radio uses words, music and sound effects to communicate its message. It has strong emotional impact, which is derived from its ability to establish a rapport with the audience and move listeners to action. Jingles and slogans are common in radio commercials because listeners remember them later. This helps to reinforce brand identification.

Target Customer - Radio stations, like special interest magazines, gear themselves toward a particular audience. Through the program format you select (top 40 rock, country, classical, middle of the road, easy listening, talk show, news), it's possible to zero in on your target customer.

Budget - The cost of purchasing air time depends on a program's popularity and the frequency of your commercials. To determine costs, check the Standard Rate and Data Service. There may be production costs as well.

Lead Time - Lead times vary. Certain programs may be booked as much as year in advance, while others have immediate openings.

Limitations - Many radio stations are competing for audiences; this may make it necessary to buy time on a number of stations to reach all your target customers. To be effective at all, your commercial needs to be broadcast more than once, and this repetition increases your costs. The life span of your commercial is just seconds; unlike a print advertisement, it gets only one chance to communicate your message. Radio is a medium without visuals; if your product has to be seen to be believed, you are wasting your money.

Rates - Time is sold in units of 60 seconds or less, e.g., 10-, 15-, 30- and 60-second spots. Although 60-second commercials once dominated the airwaves, the trend is now toward shorter ones, with 30-second spots currently the most popular. Rates are based on both a station's **coverage** and its **circulation**. Coverage is the geographical area covered by the station's signal. Circulation refers to the potential number of listeners in the area. Since the number of listeners can vary throughout the day, different rates are charged for different time periods.

Drive Time - Drive time is the most expensive time of day because it covers the intervals from 6:00 a.m. to 10:00 a.m. and from 4:00 p.m. to 7:00 p.m., when people are in their cars driving to and from work.

Run of the Station (ROS) - This is the cheapest time because it allows the station to put your commercial anywhere it pleases.

Weekly Plan - A weekly plan offers a lower rate to advertisers purchasing a package of time. Each package contains a variety of time slots, ranging from drive time to ROS.

Comparing Costs - Stations can be compared by means of the cost-per-thousand technique.

Television

Though television trails newspaper as the most-chosen advertising medium, it is rapidly closing in on the top spot. The reason for television's growing popularity is simple: numbers. Currently 98 percent of all American households have one or more television sets, and the average family watches for more than six hours per day. The newest of the media, television's impact on its audience is still being explored. But the fact that it can shape attitudes and change opinions is already known.

Message - Television is the most intimate of the media, combining sight, sound, color and motion. It takes your presentation right into the viewer's home. Television lets you show off your product, rather than just tell about it. The viewer sees it in a natural setting that encourages acceptance. (If the people in the commercial are satisfied with the product, why shouldn't the viewer be, too?)

Target Customer - More than any of the other media, television is a mass medium. At any one time, millions of viewers are watching. Programs like the Super Bowl, the World Series and the Academy Awards are tuned in by viewers worldwide. The question is: Are these your target customers? In selecting a program on which to advertise, it is as important to check the data describing the viewers (age, sex, income, interests), as it is to check the number of people who are watching.

Budget - Unfortunately, advertising on television is expensive. Regardless of its appeal, the majority of small businesses will find it beyond their budgets. However, local and cable television stations offer considerably reduced rates, and these may be a viable alternative. For further information, check the Standard Rate and Data Service.

Lead Time - Top-rated television shows are likely to be booked a year in advance. Time slots on less-popular shows and new shows are generally available on a few day's notice.

Limitations - Television has less selectivity than the other media; using it to reach a small target audience could be an exercise in overkill. Viewers often leave the room during commercials; getting and holding their attention isn't easy. Television commercials, like radio commercials, become more effective with repetition, and this adds to your costs.

Rates - Time is sold in units of 60 seconds or less, with 30-second spots currently the most favored. Rates vary on the basis of the time period selected and the size of the audience per given program, hence the importance of the Nielsen and Arbitron ratings, which rank programs in the order of their popularity.

Prime Time - This is the most costly time. It covers the hours from 7:00 p.m. to 11:00 p.m., when the greatest number of viewers are watching television.

Discounts - These are available on essentially the same terms as those offered by radio stations.

Comparing Costs - The CPM technique applies.

Direct Mail

Direct mail refers to any printed material of a promotional nature that is mailed directly to the intended customer, such as brochures, letters, price lists, catalogs and coupons. This is currently the third most popular choice with advertisers and is used by the majority of businesses, large and small.

Message - Like newspapers and magazines, direct mail is one of the best formats for conveying in-depth information. It also offers the greatest flexibility, since any message can be sent to anyone at any time. Direct mail is regularly used to:

- Inform customers of sales.
- Introduce new products.
- Announce price changes.
- Solicit mail-order business.
- Solicit phone-order business.
- Maintain customer contact.
- Reach new customers.
- Develop your image.
- Promote in-house promotions.

Target Customers - The success of a direct-mail campaign is primarily determined by the mailing list. Unless your mailing list is going out to the people who are likely to buy your product, you are wasting both time and money. How can you obtain a mailing list that is right for you? You can either purchase it from someone else or build your own list. There are a number of companies in the business of compiling and selling mailing lists. These lists are available in literally thousands of categories (women between the ages of 18 and 45, teenagers, skiers, homeowners, cooking enthusiasts, etc.). Regardless of your target market, there is probably an applicable list. The cost may be as low as $12 per thousand names or as high as $300 per thousand. If you prefer to build your own list, some of the sources you may be able to use are:

- Your own customers.
- Telephone directories.
- Professional, trade and industrial directories.
- Credit bureaus.
- Newspaper announcements (housing permits, weddings, graduations, new business).
- Construction permits on file in municipal and county offices.
- Supplier leads.

Budget - Direct-mail flexibility makes it possible to structure a campaign to meet practically any budget. However, keep in mind that the more extensive the mail, the higher the costs. You should consider:

- The cost of the mailing list.
- The cost of the package (printed materials).
- The cost of postage.
- The cost of labor (addressing, stuffing and sealing envelopes).

Lead Time - You control the lead time.

Limitations - In terms of unit cost, direct mail is expensive; it has the highest cost per thousand of the media. There is only a fine line between direct mail and junk mail; make sure you are sending your mail to the people who really want it.

Rates - Since there is no space or time to be purchased, there are no set rates to be considered.

Yellow Pages

Adding to the appeal of Yellow Pages advertising is a growing number of specialty directories from which to choose: the neighborhood directory, silver pages, business-to-business directory, etc.

Message - A Yellow Pages display ad is an attention-getting device. Since your ad is surrounded by those of your competition, it is important that you focus on the best way to differentiate yourself from the rest with lowest prices, widest selection or friendliest service.

Target Customer - The main advantage of Yellow Pages advertising is its ability to reach your target customer at the time they want to buy. Thus, your audience is pre-sold. Having already decided what to buy, the customers are just looking for the right place to buy it.

Budget - Yellow Pages ads are inexpensive in comparison to the other media.

Lead Time - Your ad must be placed before the closing date for inclusion in the current directory. This will vary during each calendar year for each geographic directory.

Limitations - You can't make changes in your ad; it runs as it is until the next directory printing.

Rates - Any business with a phone is entitled to a one-line listing free of charge. To find out the rates for display ads, contact your local Yellow Pages sales representative.

Outdoor Advertising

Outdoor advertising involves the use of signs, posters and billboards to promote your business. In the simplest sense, it serves as a marker identifying your location. In the broadest sense, it creates an image so that people think of your name when they think of a particular product.

Message - Your message needs to be simple and direct. Concise copy, bold graphics and a recognizable product are essential. Remember, the average passerby spends less than 10 seconds reading your ad.

Target Customer - Although outdoor advertising is visible to anyone who cares to look, a fairly high degree of selectivity can be achieved through the geographic placement of your advertisement.

Budget - The costs of outdoor advertising are among the lowest of the media.

Lead Time - If you are just using signs at your place of business, the only lead time is the production and installation time. In the case of posters and billboards, space is rented on an availability basis and there may be a waiting list for the locations you want.

Limitations - Your advertisement is competing with numerous others; its effectiveness hinges on its ability to command attention. Some people regard outdoor advertising as a form of visual pollution, thus, part of the response to your ads may be negative.

Rates - The rates charged for posters and billboards are based on the size and location of the space being leased. Locations are classified by territories, which are priced according to traffic counts. The higher the count, the higher the cost.

Comparing Costs - The CPM technique can be used to compare territories to determine the most economical purchase.

Other Advertising Media

Some of the other forms of advertising you may wish to consider are:

- *Transit Advertising* - Messages are displayed on the exteriors and interiors of trains, buses and taxicabs.
- *Specialty Advertising* - Your company's name or logo is imprinted on such items as calendars, memo pads, bookmarks, ashtrays, coffee cups, keychains and T-shirts.
- *Flyers* - These can be handed out to passersby or placed on automobile windshields, placed directly at the home, or handed out at home shows, seminars, etc.
- *Theater Screen Advertisements* - Ads are shown during intermissions.

PUBLICITY

In addition to advertising, you can use publicity to promote your business. This involves getting information about your company's activities or products reported in the news media. Such coverage is provided when the information is thought to have news value or to be of interest to the public.

Although publicity and advertising are similar, they differ in three vital areas: costs, control and credibility. Publicity is free; there is no cost to you for the media coverage you receive, nor do you have any control over it. Unlike advertising, publicity can be favorable or unfavorable, as likely to point out your business' flaws as its accomplishments. If a news broadcast chooses to focus on a lawsuit that has been brought against you rather than on your volunteer service to the community, there is nothing you can do about it. This lack of control is what gives publicity its greatest strength and credibility. The fact that it is the news media, rather than a sponsor, delivering your message makes it more believable than advertising.

While it is impossible to control the publicity you get, it is possible to influence it. The way to do this is by maintaining good press relations, providing timely and accurate information in the form of press releases, pointing out the angle that makes your story interesting or news-worthy, being available to answer questions and not making unreasonable demands. By learning to work within the limitations of publicity, you can take full advantage of it.

Press Releases

Far from being anything mysterious, a press release is simply a fact sheet. Explaining who, what, where, when and how, it states the details of the story you want the press to tell. It also makes the reporter's job easier by emphasizing why your story will be of interest to the public. Possible "whys" include:

- Having a unique product or service.
- Staging a special event.
- Helping a charity.
- Winning an award.
- Giving a speech.

This story angle, or hook, as it is called, is the most important information of all in helping to justify your story to the media and to shape the coverage you receive.

To give your press release a professional look, use the format shown below. In so doing, though, don't make the mistake of cramming too much information into one press release. If you find yourself writing a book or trying to tell two stories at once, the situation probably calls for more than one press release or for a media kit.

Although a media kit sounds elaborate and expensive, it needn't be. All it takes is a standard-sized folder with two inside pockets. Then, depending on the information you want to send out, you can fill it with such materials as:

- The press release.
- A business fact sheet/history.
- A list of suppliers and/or customers.
- A brochure.
- Photographs (5" x 7" black and white).

PRESS RELEASE

Business Name
Address
Your Name
Phone Number

Release Date: For immediate release / For release (date)

Start copy here and begin with your angle: Why.

Provide all necessary details:

Who
What
Where
When
How

Write in short, clear sentences and paragraphs. Two pages maximum. Double space, using one-inch margins on all sides. Put your name and phone number on each page.

Type "- End -" after the last line of copy to indicate the end. This is commonly used by marketing and public relations professionals.

- End -

PREPARING AN ADVERTISING BUDGET

In preparing advertising budgets, the majority of businesses base allocations on a percentage of annual past sales, estimated sales or a combination of these. For example, 4 percent of $300,000 in sales equals an advertising budget of $12,000. Some of the reasons for this method's general acceptance are that it gives you more to go on than guesswork, it emphasizes the relationship between advertising and sales, and it is easy to use.

In determining the percent of sales you want to invest in advertising, you should consider your business' needs, the competition and the economic environment. To find out what similar businesses are spending, it is a good idea to check such sources as trade journals and reports published by Dun and Bradstreet, Robert Morris Associates, the Accounting Corporation of America, the Census Bureau and the IRS.

SAMPLE ADVERTISING BUDGET ABC KITCHEN AND BATHROOM COMPANY		
Sales for 19xx:	$300,000	
Ad Budget as Percent of Sales:	4%	
Total Ad Budget:	$ 12,000	
Direct Mail:		$ 5,400
Handouts:		1,200
Yellow Pages (yearly cost):		$1,440
Newspapers:		3,960
Total Ad Budget:		$12,000
Best Selling Times		
Spring		
Summer		
Fall		

Once you have calculated your budget, the next step is to allocate it over the coming year, indicating the amount to be spent each month and the media to receive it. Keep in mind that some months will require greater expenditures than others. Also, don't forget to plan for any sales or special events you wish to promote.

ABC KITCHEN AND BATHROOM COMPANY SAMPLE BREAKDOWN BY MONTH					
Month	Direct Mail	Handouts	Yellow Pages	Newspapers	Total
January			$ 120	$330	$ 450
February			120	330	450
March	$ 650		120	330	1,100
April			120	330	450
May	1,350		120	330	1,800
June		$ 600	120	330	1,050
July	1,350		120	330	1,800
August		600	120	330	1,050
September	700		120	330	1,150
October	1,350		120	330	1,800
November			120	330	450
December			120	330	450
TOTAL	$5,400	$1,200	$1,440	$3,960	$12,000

To help launch your promotional campaign and reach your target market in the most economical way, answer the questions in the following promotional strategy checklist:

PROMOTIONAL STRATEGY CHECKLIST	Yes	No
1. Do you know who your potential customers are?		
2. Have you established a game plan for reaching your target market?		
3. Do you know the difference between institutional and product advertising?		
4. Do you know the benefits and limitations of each of the following media?		
Newspaper		
Magazines		
Radio		
Television		
Direct Mail		
Yellow Pages		
Outdoor Advertising		
5. Can you compare costs between like forms of advertising (CPM)?		
6. Do you know the rates of the different media?		
7. Do you know the difference between advertising and publicity?		
8. Do you know how to maintain good press relations?		
9. Have you prepared an advertising budget?		
10. Have you determined which are the best advertising media for your business?		
11. Do you know what media are being used by the competition?		
12. Do you keep track of competitors' advertising campaigns?		
13. Do you know the best times to advertise during the year?		

For more information on promotions, public relations and advertising, read NKBA®'s Proven Promotions by Jim and Lori Jo Krengel.

SELLING AND SERVICING

Your first priority as a business owner should be to please the customer. Far more important than any single sale that you make is your ability to meet customers' needs and to establish long-term relationships that will keep customers coming back again and again.

Businesses that are more interested in "moving the goods" than in giving customers what they really need and want usually don't last very long. To go the distance, your personal selling and customer-service efforts must be directed at satisfying each customer.

A POSITIVE APPROACH TO SELLING

Personal selling involves more than just giving a sales presentation and writing up the order. Today's top salespeople—the kind you want to be or to have in your business—are problem solvers. Equally good at listening as talking, they are able to correctly identify customers' needs and match them to the products or services they sell. Rather than assuming what customers want or pushing the products they want to sell, the best salespeople find out what customers do want and then show them how they can have it.

The Selling Process

Like any skill, personal selling entails a set of steps, which, when combined, results in a successful outcome, in this case, a satisfied customer. As shown here, there are six steps in the selling process. What you and your salespeople do at each step will directly affect your ability to make individual sales, to get repeat sales and referrals, and to build a positive image.

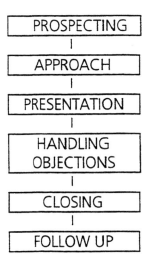

PROSPECTING
|
APPROACH
|
PRESENTATION
|
HANDLING OBJECTIONS
|
CLOSING
|
FOLLOW UP

Prospecting

Many sales experts consider this to be the most important step of all: the search for potential customers, or **prospects**, to whom you can sell your products or services. In developing a list of prospects (through customer referrals, contacts, market research, mailing lists, etc.), your goal is to focus your attention on those who can be considered good prospects. Beyond being able to use your product, a good prospect also has a need for it, can afford it and is authorized to buy it.

Whether prospecting is something you do alone or you have salespeople involved as well, it must be done. Good prospects are the lifeblood of any business. To expand your customer base and raise sales revenues, you need to actively seek out new customers.

For more information on prospecting and sales, read NKBA®'s publication, entitled How to Increase Your Kitchen & Bath Business by 25%...Starting Next Week by Bob Popyk.

Approach

This step calls for you to make initial contact with the prospect. Your main concern at this point is not to make an immediate sale, but rather to open up a dialogue with the prospect and to begin to assess his or her needs. During this step, what you say, how you dress and how you act can either work for you or against you. Everything from your greeting, tone of voice, body language, demeanor and attire should be directed at creating a positive image.

Presentation

Successful sales presentations don't just happen; they are planned. Instead of "winging it" or relying on fast talking and fancy footwork to get through sales presentations, the best salespeople plan their presentations carefully. This does not mean that you should memorize each word—"canned presentations" tend to come off as stilted and one-sided—but rather that you should think about what the customers' needs are, what points you would like to make, and what visual aids or demonstration techniques to use.

In planning your presentation, your goals should be to inform and persuade so that the customer understands what you have to offer and is inclined to buy. Here it helps to do the following:

- Outline the various points you want to make and the order in which to present them.
- Determine how much time you will need (keeping your presentation as concise and to the point as possible).
- Practice your presentation several times until it comes naturally.
- Prepare for different responses so that, as you and the customer interact, you are able to go with the flow.

Two-Way Communication - During the presentation itself, the most important thing to remember is that communication is a two-way street. In addition to telling the customer about your product or your service, you must also tune in to what the customer is telling you. Is the prospect's response positive or negative? Rather than just steamrolling ahead, you must become adept at recognizing both the verbal and nonverbal messages the prospect is sending you. Is the person asking questions? If so, that could either be a sign of interest or a defense mechanism to avoid to having to make a purchase decision. Is the person leaning in to hear more (generally a good sign) or backing away?

The Five Senses - Throughout the presentation, you should also appeal to the prospect's five senses: the ability to hear, see, touch, smell and taste. The more senses you can appeal to, the stronger your presentation will be. Rather than just telling a prospect how comfortable a whirlpool tub might be, ask them to get in it and try it for comfort. In the case of kitchen cabinets, have the prospect open and close drawers to see how fine the glides are and how easily they work. If you sell appliances, do live food demonstrations showing not only how the appliances works, but also the smell, look and taste of the food being cooked. If you sell faucets, ask them to handle the hot and cold handles to experience the easy movement and positive shutoff.

Benefits Versus Features - Another way to strengthen your sales presentations is by emphasizing the benefits rather than features. Whereas features merely describe a product or service, benefits are the advantages the prospect will derive from the purchase. As you can see from these examples, the essential difference is that benefits give the prospect a reason to buy:

FEATURES	BENEFITS
This faucet has ceramic disks.	No washers or replacement maintenance.
The polished brass has a powder coat protective finish.	It won't tarnish and is easy to maintain.
The whirlpool tub is 20" deep.	The body will be totally immersed in the water.
The cabinet boxes are of frameless construction.	Larger openings and more storage space.

Converting features into benefits in this way can significantly increase sales. By shifting your focus from what a product or service is to what it can do for your customers, you enable prospects to more easily envision themselves using it.

Handling Objections

Nice as it would be to conclude each sales presentation with the customer saying, "Yes, I'll take it," that isn't going to happen. You must be prepared for objections. Instead of taking them personally, or letting them upset you, just accept the fact that objections come with the territory. Everyone in sales encounters them at one time or another. Many sales professionals go so far as to insist, "The selling doesn't start until the customer says, 'no.'"

What separates the successful sellers from those who aren't is how they handle the objections. Essentially, when a customer poses an objection, you should take it to be a request for more information. To turn objections into orders, try following these suggestions:

1. Don't get angry or defensive. This will just turn the prospect against you and force an end to the sales dialogue.

2. Deflect the objection in a positive way. For example, if a prospect thinks your price is too high, you can either point out that it is comparable to competitors, if that's the case, or explain why it's higher—because you offer better quality, have better service or provide a warranty.

3. Ask the prospect to restate the objection. Sometimes when you ask the prospect to restate or explain the objection, you get lucky and the prospect deflects it for you. Or the prospect gives you the information to deflect it yourself. For example, "Well, I really wanted a bathtub larger than this." This gives you the opportunity to show the prospect a larger version of the tub, to show different styles or to indicate why the original tub might be the best choice. In any case, you have kept the prospect talking to you, and you have opened an opportunity to better understand the desires of your prospective client.

4. Question the objection. As politely as you can, question the objection that has been raised. Your goal is not to be confrontational, but rather to determine if the stated objection is indeed the real objection. For example, instead of saying that something is too expensive, a prospect will often raise another objection to avoid making a purchase. If the price (or some other factor) is the real reason, then you can address it: "We have financing available." Or, "You can use our installment plan, if you like."

5. Shift the prospect's focus. Ignore the objection, if you can, and shift the prospect's attention to some other aspect of your product or service that you think will be particularly appealing. For example, if a prospect comments that a cabinet line you are showing is too expensive, you might answer, "Yes, but the door style and wood species that you have selected is somewhat higher than the particular cabinet style and wood species in this display."

6. Keep the prospect talking. The most important thing of all is to keep your dialogue with the prospect going. This gives you the opportunity to do more probing—asking questions that enable you to learn more about the prospect's true needs and circumstances. Your prospect will feel that you better understand what he or she wants, and that you have taken a personal interest.

In handling objections, you must also keep in mind that you won't be able to overcome each and every objection. It may be that, for whatever reason (price, style, size, color, fit, purpose, timing or something else), your product or service is not right for the prospect. In that case, not only will it be difficult to make the sale, but you shouldn't make it. Even if you could convince the prospect to buy it, it wouldn't be in his or her best interests, or in yours. Rather than create a dissatisfied customer, you are better off forgoing the sale and trying for the next best thing: a referral.

Closing

Once you have gotten past any objections, you must be able to do one more thing: **close**. This is the moment of truth, when you ask the prospect to buy. This step should be a natural extension of the dialogue you have been having with the prospect. Unfortunately, it is a step that many business owners are reluctant to take because they fear rejection. Instead, they just let their sales presentations trail off into nothing, hoping the customer will ask to buy. They end up saying something like, "Well, that's it. If you need anymore information, just ask." This may be a good fallback position to take later. But it isn't a close, and it's not likely to result in a sale.

You can close in a number of ways. The simplest, most direct method is to ask for the order: "Shall I go ahead and write that up for you now?" This method can get fast results. The main problem with it, though, is that by asking what is known as a yes/no question, you may be setting yourself up for the no.

One way to avoid asking a yes/no question is to assume the order. Rather than asking the prospect to buy, you can simply assume the sale has been made and proceed accordingly: "If you'll just fill in this information, I'll finish writing up the order." This method works fine if the prospect goes along with you. If the prospect doesn't, then be prepared to ask more questions to keep the dialogue going and try for a second close.

Another popular (and effective) close is the **alternative** close. This avoids the problem of a yes/no question by asking the prospect to choose between two or more alternatives: "Would you prefer the cherry or the maple wood?" Or, "Which day would you like to have us deliver the bathtub, Monday or Tuesday?" The beauty of this closing technique is that, as the prospect picks one of the choices, the sale is made.

Two other closes you might use are the **added-inducement** close and the **warning to buy** close. The first one offers a price reduction, free service, gift or some other inducement if the prospect buys now: "If you place your order today, we'll be able to pay the shipping charges." The second close warns the prospect to buy before it's too late: "These are the last faucets of this type that I have in stock. To guarantee delivery, I need to receive your order today." Both closes, while effective, should be used sparingly. The added-inducement close cuts into your profit margins and the warning to buy close, if used too often, can be perceived as a high-pressure tactic.

These and other closing methods that you may decide to use can help you to make more sales. Again, it is important to remember, though, that you don't want to force customers into buying what they don't want. The purpose of a close is to make it easier for prospects to choose what is right for them.

For information on how you can use point-of-purchase financing as a sales tool, read NKBA®'s publication, Leveraging Design: Finance and the Kitchen and Bathroom Specialist by Debi Bach.

Follow-Up

The selling process does not stop when the sale is made. To keep the customer happy and to ensure yourself of repeat sales and referrals, you must do everything possible to see that the customer is satisfied with the purchase. In a sense, this last step is the first, offering you the opportunity to reestablish contact with the customer and to begin the selling process again.

MAINTAINING GOOD CUSTOMER RELATIONS

Considering the time and money that go into finding prospects and convincing them to buy, it makes sense to maintain good customer relations. After all, it is easier to sell to a customer who is already sold on your business than it is to sell to someone who does not know anything about you. This explains why so many businesses claim that, "After the sale, we don't forget the service." To make sure that your customers are getting the service they deserve, it is important for you to do the following:

- Expedite each purchase.
- Provide personal service.
- Answer questions.
- Handle complaints.
- Solve problems.
- Stay in touch.

Expedite the Purchase

Nothing is more frustrating to a customer than deciding to buy something and then having to wait longer than necessary to receive it. As the seller, you want to make sure that there are no delays in getting your product or service to the customer. Once the sale is made, you should do everything possible to expedite the purchase by reassuring the customer that the purchase is the right one, speeding delivery of the goods and overseeing any installation or implementation that may be required.

Provide Personal Service

In an age of "cookie-cutter" service that treats all customers the same or that offers no service at all, providing personal service can be a powerful customer-relations tool for winning customer loyalty. Everyone likes to be thought of as special or enjoys getting something extra. You can meet these needs by addressing each customer by name, paying attention to individual preferences and doing more than is expected.

Contrary to what you might think, providing a personal touch does not have to increase your costs. What it requires more than expenditures of money is thoughtfulness. Examples include:

- The business owner/customer service specialist sending a thank-you note and/or flowers, candy or dinner reservations for a kitchen-cabinet sale and installation.
- Making sure the designer/salesperson visits the job site regularly during installation of a kitchen-cabinet job.
- Doing a complete spec package on plumbing fixtures for a new house construction so that the homeowner, general contractor and plumber all know exactly what has been specified and will be delivered to the job site.

Since these little things often mean a lot to customers, paying attention to them can give you a distinct advantage over businesses that don't.

Answer Questions

Letting customers know that you are available to answer any questions that come up after the purchase is made is another way to serve your customers. Or you might want to set up a telephone/fax hotline that customers can use when they need to get information in a hurry. This not only provides customers with a sense of security, but can keep minor problems from becoming major ones. What's more, by keeping the lines of communication open, you stand a better chance of making more sales in the future.

Handle Complaints

In addition to answering questions, you must also be prepared to handle complaints. Complaints are a fact of business life. Even the most service-oriented businesses can expect to receive them. The issue is not who is right or who is wrong, but rather what needs to be done to satisfy the customer. If there is something wrong with your products or services, you want to determine what you can do to improve them. If a customer is unhappy with a purchase, you must decide how you can remedy the situation.

To handle complaints more efficiently and to let your customers know that you are on their side, it helps to follow these guidelines:

- Listen to what the customer is telling you without interruption.
- Don't become defensive or angry.
- Ask questions to get additional details, if necessary.
- Show the customer that you care.
- Take steps to resolve the problem as quickly as possible.
- Thank the customer for bringing the problem to your attention.

Even if you think that the complaint is unjustified or that the customer is wasting your time, remember that there is something worse than having to deal with a dissatisfied customer who complains. That is having a dissatisfied customer who does not complain and just takes his or her business someplace else.

Solve Problems

The most successful sellers are problem solvers, not just when it comes to making the sale, but in helping customers put the products or services they have bought to the best use. Instead of leaving customers to fend for themselves or saying, "That's your problem," they work with customers to find solutions to their problems. This joint approach to problem solving benefits not only the customer, but you as well. Customers, who might not otherwise have come back, buy again, and recommend you to the people they know.

Stay in Touch

Instead of waiting for customers to contact you, take the initiative yourself. Staying in touch with customers on a regular basis shows that you care and puts you in a better position to anticipate customers' needs and to provide a high level of customer service. Some of the ways that you can stay in touch include:

- Telephoning from time to time to see how customers are doing.
- Sending a card or thank you or small gift to say thank you.
- Sending out mailings with current information on your products, services and prices.
- Making periodic sales calls.

To determine if you are doing everything you can to build a positive relationship with each customer, answer the questions in the following checklist:

CUSTOMER SERVICE CHECKLIST	Yes	No
1. Is your selling strategy oriented toward satisfying each customer?		
2. Do you try to establish long-term relationships rather than just make a sale?		
3. During the selling process, do you find out what the customers' needs are?		
4. Are you a good listener?		
5. How do you interpret the verbal and non-verbal messages customers send?		
6. Do you show customers the benefits of buying your products or services?		
7. Will you forego making a sale if the purchase is not right for the customer?		
8. After a sale is made, do you follow up on it to see that the customer is pleased?		
9. Do you provide personal service?		
10. Are you available to answer any questions that customers may have?		
11. Do you handle complaints quickly and courteously?		
12. Are you a problem solver?		
13. Do you make it a point to stay in touch with customers?		
14. Do you try to give customers something extra for their money?		
15. Do you genuinely care about your customers?		
16. Does your place of business convey a pleasing and professional image?		
17. Have you instructed your employees to treat all customers in a courteous and efficient manner, including installers, subcontractors and delivery people?		
18. Do you believe that the customer is always right?		

If you answered "no" to a question, review this chapter for ideas on how to improve that area of your customer service.

Read NKBA®'s book, entitled _Proven Promotions for Kitchen and Bathroom Businesses_ by Jim Krengel, CKD, CBD and Lori Jo M. Krengel, CKD, CBD.

Now let's teach others what you've learned about the fire.

Chapter 7

TEACHING OTHERS HOW TO BUILD A FIRE
Personnel

Nothing great was ever achieved without enthusiasm. - Ralph Waldo Emerson

Teaching others how to build a fire will help to ensure your own success. Guidelines are included in this chapter for staffing, how to choose who is going to work for you and your kitchen and bathroom business, and also how to monitor progress and evaluate performances. Your staff members are the ones who will often be dealing with customers, selling your products and services, and representing you. Even if you are an expert in all of the areas we've discussed so far in this book, if you don't choose and maintain employees who will embody these principles, they may be dousing your fire as fast as you are building it.

STAFFING

The most valuable asset of any business is its people. Land, buildings, merchandise and equipment may dominate a balance sheet, but they don't make a business successful; people do. The best businesses are the ones that have the best people—capable, creative, energetic people. To attract them requires both ingenuity and initiative on your part. But the payoff in productivity is worth it. Staffing your business with the best people available should be one of your highest priorities.

Placing a sign in your window saying, "Help wanted, apply within," is one way to get results, but not necessarily the results you want. A sign in the window will probably bring in a stream of applicants. But unless they possess the skills to do the job, a great deal of time can be wasted in interviewing and you still would not find anyone you would want to hire. Generally, the sign in the window works only when the position to be filled calls for little or no skills and entails a minimum amount of responsibility.

How then should you go about hiring the people you need? First, its important to realize that hiring is only one element in staffing. This is an ongoing process that involves finding qualified people, hiring them, making the best use of their skills and abilities, and having them stay on the job instead of quitting and taking their talents elsewhere. To control and direct the staffing process, take these steps before you hire anyone:

1. Analyze Each Job

This is the most important step in staffing since it forms the basis for any hiring decisions that you make. Unfortunately, it is often skipped over by employers and managers who, in a rush to get a position filled quickly, would rather hire now and ask questions later. Then, when confronted with poor performance, low morale and high turnover, they wonder why it is so hard to find good workers. Taking a little more time in the beginning is the way to avoid a great many problems later.

During the job analysis step, you should ask yourself:

- What work has to be accomplished?
- Do I need additional help to do it?
- How many people do I need?
- Would part-time help be sufficient?
- What skills am I looking for?
- How much experience is required?
- Is the labor market favorable?
- How much am I able to pay?

You may find that you don't need to hire anyone after all. Perhaps, if you reschedule the work flow or juggle work assignments, your present staff can handle it. Or you may find out that one additional person is not enough. Maybe you need to hire two or more people to keep pace with the workload. A job you thought anyone can do may, in fact, require someone with specific skills. The answer to your questions can be surprising. But that's the point of doing the job analysis. It is better to be surprised before you hire someone, rather than after. The choice is yours. You can be the one saying, "If only I'd known," or you can take the time to find out.

2. Prepare Job Description

A job description is a written record of the duties and responsibilities associated with a particular position. It serves a dual purpose, making it easier for you to match the right person to the right job and informing each employee of what his or her job entails. In preparing a job description, include the following details:

- A general description of the job.
- The duties to be performed.
- The job responsibilities.
- Specific skills needed.
- Education and experience required.

For instance, a receiving clerk in a store might have a job description that looks like the sample shown below. Once you have put everything down on paper, you are ready to start looking for the person who fits the description.

SAMPLE JOB DESCRIPTION	
Job Title	**Receiving Clerk**
Supervisor	Business Owner/Manager
Summary	Responsible for receiving shipments from suppliers. Removes goods from containers and places them on warehouse shelves. Prepares and processes paperwork and maintains receiving files.
Duties and Responsibilities	Removing stock from containers and placing stock on warehouse shelves. Checking invoices to merchandise received. Inspecting merchandise received. Typing miscellaneous forms and labels. Maintaining receiving files. Assisting in physical inventory. Keeping warehouse clean and orderly.
Job Specifications	Education: High school graduate Experience: None required Skills: Must be able to organize material; work with numbers; interact well with people.

NEED ADA LANGUAGE

3. Check Recruitment Sources

The method of recruitment that you decide to utilize depends upon your business. Entry-level positions may be recruited from the local high school, but finding experienced, qualified kitchen and bathroom design/sales people requires a totally different approach. Some of the sources to choose from are:

Public Employment Agencies - Public employment agencies operate throughout each state, finding and placing both blue-collar and white-collar workers. Without charge, they will recruit and screen your applicants, sending you only the ones who meet your specifications.

Private Employment Agencies - Private employment agencies operate much the same as public ones do, except that there is a fee involved. Either you pay it or the person who is hired pays it.

Newspaper and Trade Journal Advertisements - A newspaper or trade journal enables you to reach a large pool of interested job applicants quickly. However, it is important to design your ad in such a way as to attract those who are qualified, while discouraging the unqualified. The way to do this is to make it interesting, give adequate details about the job, indicate the skills needed and specify the education and experience. A general guideline is to stick to a straightforward approach, since cute or exaggerated copy tends to generate a negative reaction.

Local Schools - Contacting placement centers at local high schools and colleges is a good way to find applicants who are long on potential, though usually short on experience. If you are looking for part-time help, this source should particularly be considered.

Trade and Professional Associations - Most trade and professional associations are eager to assist employers in obtaining the services of their members. Whether you need help in finding an accountant, sales manager, management trainee, computer specialist or supervisor, the local association is a good place to check.

Local Colleges and NKBA®-Endorsed Colleges - You may locate potential employees through specific departments, or you may tap into an intern program that will offer you and your employee an excellent relationship. The NKBA®-Endorsed College Program has been established specifically to help kitchen and bathroom business owners find talented design students seeking a career in the kitchen and bathroom industry. Contact NKBA®.

Industry Networking - Make contacts through your industry, including manufacturing and vendor representatives

Word of Mouth - Spreading the word via industry associates, friends and customers can create good leads. Encourage employee referrals and check previous job applications and résumés you may have on file.

4. Utilize Application Forms

Job application forms simplify the hiring decision by helping you screen out unsuitable applicants and focus on qualified ones. The application can also serve as a starting point during an interview, suggesting questions or comments that make it easier to break the ice and establish a rapport with the applicant.

Your application form needn't be long or complicated to be effective. In fact, the simpler you can keep it, the better. The important thing is to cover the information that is relevant to a prospective employee's job performance.

In developing the job-application form you will be using, keep in mind that federal laws prohibit discriminating against anyone on the basis of race, sex, religion, color or national origin. Nor can you automatically rule out an applicant because of age or because of physical handicap. To stay in compliance with the law, your best bet is to restrict your questions to those that focus on the applicant's ability to do the work.

5. Conduct Interviews

Interviewing prospective employees gives you the opportunity to find out more about each applicant's employment background, skills and education. Such additional factors as an applicant's enthusiasm, ability to communicate, poise and personal appearance can also be evaluated.

In conducting interviews, schedule at least an hour so you won't be rushed. Select a private, comfortable location in which to talk. Trying to carry on a conversation over the sounds of machinery or ringing telephones is counterproductive. You want to put the applicant at ease so that you can gather the information you need. The trick is to get the other person talking. Too many interviewers dominate the conversation themselves, and then when it is time to make an evaluation, they have little to go on.

The way to get the most out of interviews is to be ready for them. Review the job application prior to each interview. This will give you some idea of the person you are about to meet. Keep the application with you during the interview as well, so that you can refer to it if needed or make notes on it. Many staffing experts also recommend writing out a few questions in advance. Then, instead of worrying about what to ask next, you can really listen to what's being said. Immediately after the interview is over, jot down your evaluation of the applicant before you forget anything.

There are questions you can ask and those you cannot. These guidelines will help you avoid asking discriminatory questions. To make sure you are in compliance with the law, contact your state's Department of Fair Employment.

Questions You Can Ask:

- Have you ever used another name?
- What is your place of residence?
- If hired, can you show proof of age?
- Are you over 18 years old?
- If hired, can you provide verification of your right to work in the United States?
- What languages can you speak, read or write?
- What is the name and address of a parent or guardian (if applicant is a minor)?
- Do you have any physical condition that would keep you from performing your job?
- Have you ever been convicted of a felony?
- What skills have you acquired through military service?
- What professional organizations do you belong to?

Questions You Cannot Ask:

- What is your maiden name?
- Do you own or rent your home?
- How old are you?
- What is your birth date?

- When did you attend school?
- Are you a U.S. citizen?
- Where were you born? Where were your parents born?
- What is your native tongue?
- With whom do you live?
- Are you married or single? Divorced?
- What does your spouse do?
- How many children do you have? What are their ages?
- Have you made provisions for child care?
- What race are you?
- What color?
- What is your height and weight?
- Do you have any physical disabilities?
- Have you ever applied for Workers' Compensation?
- What religion are you?
- Have you ever been arrested?
- When did you serve in the military?
- What type of discharge do you have?
- What organizations or clubs do you belong to?

6. Verify Information

Even if you are positive that you found the best person for the job, don't hire anyone yet. Before you do, there is one more step: **verify** the information you have been given. Regardless of how favorable the first impression may be, there is no substitute for checking the facts. It is not a matter of doubting your own judgment; it is just good business sense.

In verifying academic information, ask to see an official copy of the applicant's record from each school attended. Dates of attendance, courses taken and grades received should all appear on the record. To check an applicant's work history, contact previous employers. This can be done by phone, by letter or in person. In so doing, though, be prepared to take all comments with a grain of salt; former employers sometimes exaggerate a past employee's attributes or failings. Your job is to try to separate the facts from the fiction.

HIRING DECISION IS MADE

Congratulations! Having gone through the previous steps, with any luck, you are now ready to select the person you want to hire. This is a time to celebrate, but not a time to rest on your laurels. The staffing process continues. To facilitate clear communication, you can use an agreement, signed by both employee and employer, which states the rate of compensation and procedures if employee leaves or is released.

JOB ORIENTATION

Each new employee needs to be made to feel comfortable in your business. Starting a new job is a cause for uncertainty, regardless of how terrific the job is or how well qualified the employee. Getting to know co-workers, keeping track of new duties and responsibilities, and attempting to understand how the organization operates can easily overwhelm a new employee. It takes time to adjust to a new job.

You can facilitate the process by assuring that new employees are introduced to other staff and given a tour to familiarize them with their area and with the business. Don't assume that a new employee has a clear understanding of what you expect; provide an opportunity to communicate exactly what responsibilities are assigned.

A job-orientation program will answer many questions about your business and the new employee's position within it. The employee should be filled in on the company's policies and regulations, as well as duties, responsibilities, compensation and benefits.

PROCEDURES HANDBOOK

Many businesses provide new hires with a procedures handbook which spells out the policies and mission of the company. While not a substitute for personal communication, a procedures handbook can help put your business in the proper perspective and simplify the employee's adjustment. When putting together a handbook, don't feel that it has to be a thick volume, complete with pictures and a fancy cover. A few typewritten pages of clearly presented information can generally do the job. Among the subjects you will want to cover are:

- Mission statement.
- Company's history.
- Explanation of company's products and services.
- Company policies and procedures.
    Work hours.
    Equal opportunity statement.
    Performance reviews.
    Grievance procedure.
    Causes for discipline.
- Employee compensation benefits.
    Employee classifications.
    Salary and wage schedule.
    Sick leave and personal leave, including jury duty, bereavement leave.
    Holidays and vacations.
    Overtime pay.
    Severance pay.
    Leave of absence, military or personal.
    Insurance benefits.
    Pension or profit-sharing plans.
    Tuition assistance.

TRAINING

The welfare of both your business and your employees rests on the quality of training that you are able to provide. To carry out their current jobs and to obtain the skills necessary to advance into more challenging jobs, employees need guidance and training. Without it, skills and motivation begin to stagnate and decline, productivity drops off and the business suffers. A training program helps employees to grow so that they can help your business grow. Some of the kinds generally utilized are:

On-the-job training endeavors to instruct an employee in how to carry out a particular assignment. Equally useful in training new employees and employees who are changing jobs, it consists of four parts:

- *Preparation*   - The *trainer* finds out what the employee already knows about the job.
- *Demonstration* - The *trainer* shows the employee how to do the job.
- *Application*   - The *work* is inspected and suggestions or comments made.
- *Inspection*   - The work is inspected and suggestions or comments made.

Job rotation allows employees to learn new jobs and broaden their skills by working at different assignments on a temporary basis. As a result, workers become more versatile, tedium is reduced and scheduling is simplified because of worker flexibility.

Specialized training can enable an employee to hone old skills or master new ones. Through company-offered courses or outside courses at local colleges or trade schools, employees can learn how to operate a new piece of machinery, type faster, improve sales presentations, read a blueprint or do any number of things beneficial to both the employees and the company.

Management development is geared toward training people to enter management or to advance within the managerial ranks. Through courses such as leadership, decision making, planning and communication, employees can be groomed to accept more responsibility.

In an article appearing in NKBA®'s newsletter, *Perspectives*, entitled "How To Hire and Compensate Kitchen and Bath Sales People," NKBA® suggests "establishing a series of in-house training programs that last three months each. The first three-month interval has the employer paying the sales designer on a salary basis...The idea behind this action is to take the burden of survival off the employee so that the focus is on the training program." The employee receives progressively more challenging tasks and assignments, with regular monitoring and evaluation. "The second three-month period establishes a draw versus a commission payment schedule...The thrust of this stage is to get the employee to sell something and to overachieve on the draw...At this point, the employee should begin to become motivated to get on a straight commission basis as soon as possible." This program needs careful planning and ongoing evaluation, with an eye on profits during the training period, but the results will be worth the effort.

EVALUATE PERFORMANCE

Employees need a yardstick by which to measure their performance and progress and to support a fair compensation system. This can be accomplished by a **performance evaluation**. Conducted at regular intervals, this evaluation should highlight an employee's strengths and pinpoint the areas that need improvement.

One method of evaluation that is popular with employees and employers alike is **management by objectives** (MBO). Its appeal stems from the fact that it contains no surprises or hidden clauses; everything expected of the employee is spelled out in advance as objectives. Furthermore, these objectives are decided upon jointly by the worker and the worker's supervisor. Together, as a team, they set down on paper the targets that the employee will strive to reach.

See sample Employee Performance Evaluation and other employment forms at the end of this chapter.

When the evaluation is completed, it is easy to see which objectives have been met and which ones need additional work. New objectives can then be set and the evaluation process continued.

COMPENSATE EMPLOYEES

To attract and retain high-caliber employees, it is necessary to compensate them at the going wage or better. Trying to get something for nothing just leads to employee dissatisfaction and high turnover. And, if your employees feel that you are taking advantage of them, chances are that they will find a way to take advantage of you. Work slowdowns and theft are just two of the many ways possible.

In addition to comparing favorably with the competition, your policy on wages should be an equitable one that rewards employees on the basis of merit. This instills loyalty and motivates employees to work harder and to expand their skills, so that they can increase their earnings.

Another kind of compensation that employees have come to expect is called **fringe benefits**. These might include a health plan, dental plan, pension plan, life insurance, bonuses and profit sharing. These vary from company to company and may not be applicable or affordable for your business. However, they should certainly be considered.

Other benefits you might consider include sick leave, military leave, a bonus or flexible hours. These will add greatly to the package you offer to prospective employees.

Perform an annual review of your compensation plan, evaluate the results and consider possible changes and/or additions.

PROBLEMS WITH EMPLOYEES

All businesses have the potential for personality conflicts and problems. However, clearly stated policies and procedures will help avoid misunderstandings. When a problem does arise, don't ignore it. Although each situation needs to be handled differently, some general guidelines may help:

- Ensure that employee understands the company's policies and procedures.
- Attempt to determine if the employee has a problem that is interfering with his or her ability to work.
- If there are personality conflicts, try to diffuse the problem. Listen to the parties involved. Try to establish open communication between them.
- If you determine that you need to terminate an employee, when appropriate, inform the employee of your decision. Expect that the reaction may be angry or even hostile; remain calm and listen. At the exit interview, go over your policies so that the employee understands exactly what he or she is entitled to.

MONITOR EMPLOYEE TURNOVER

Once an employee quits, who cares what the employee thinks about your business? You do. It is just as important to pay heed to an employee's reason for leaving as it is to listen to a job applicant's reasons for wanting to work for you. This is your chance to find out something about your business that might help you to make it a better place in which to work. Hiring and training employees is costly and time consuming. Any information associated with reducing turnover is worth listening to.

Before the employee leaves, an **exit interview** should be scheduled. During this interview, the employee should be asked the reasons for leaving (better salary, promotion, dissatisfaction with the job, return to school, spouse's job transfer, etc.). The employee's opinions regarding the company, its policies, and its personnel should also be solicited. Your goal is not to debate the issues or to convince the dissatisfied worker to stay, but to obtain information you can refer to in making future plans.

EXIT INTERVIEW FORM		
Name of Employee		
Date	Date hired	
Address		
Male	Female	
Age		
Marital Status		
Education		
Job Title or Position		
Name of Supervisor		
Would you rehire?		
Previous Training		
Type of Separation	Reasons for Separation	
Indirect Causes for Separation		
Action Taken		

By following these steps, instead of waiting for fate to send you perfect employees or complaining about your current employees, you can control and direct the staffing process.

In order to recruit, hire and retain the best people available for your business, be sure you are knowledgeable in all aspect of staffing. Take a moment to answer the questions in the following staffing checklist:

STAFFING CHECKLIST	Yes	No
1. Have you analyzed each job that you want filled?		
2. Have you prepared job descriptions?		
3. Do you know what sources to use in recruiting employees?		
4. Will you utilize an application form?		
5. Do you know the information that can and cannot be included on an application form?		
6. Do you know what to do to prepare for an interview?		
7. Will you verify the information received from each applicant that you are seriously considering?		
8. Have you decided on the kind of job orientation to give your new employee?		
9. Have you prepared an employee handbook?		
10. Do you know which form(s) of job training to utilize?		
11. Have you determined how often to evaluate your employees?		
12. Do you intend to use an evaluation form when evaluating employees?		
13. Will your employees be adequately compensated for the work they perform?		
14. Are you planning to monitor employee turnover?		
15. Will you use an exit interview report?		
16. Do you intend to listen to the advice of employees who are leaving and take advantage of worthwhile suggestions?		

Do you know the true cost of adding an employee? Read NKBA®'s book, entitled _Managing Your Kitchen and Bathroom Firms' Finances for Profit_ by Don Quigley.

Your carefully chosen employees will help protect your fire, now let's consider how to avoid outside threats to the safety of your fire.

Chapter 7
Forms

The following forms are provided as samples only. You are encouraged to consult with a Human Resource Specialist and other legal advisors as to their appropriate use. NKBA® accepts or provides no warranties for the use of these materials.

- **Hiring Procedures**
- **Open Position Form**
- **Employment Application**
- **Employment Verification**
- **Applicant Voluntary Survey**
- **Receipt and Acknowledgment of Employee Handbook**
- **Lists of Acceptable Employment and Identification Documents**
- **Health Insurance Payroll Deduction Authorization**
- **Employment Status Changes Policy**
- **Employee Status Form**
- **Employee Performance Evaluation**
- **Employee Self-Evaluation**
- **Inside Sales Commission Plan and Agreement**
- **Commission Rate Schedule for Inside Sales Commission Plan**
- **Timekeeping and Payroll**
- **Time Sheet**
- **Leave Request**
- **Vacation and Sick Leave**
- **Work-Related Injuries and Illnesses**
- **Employee Conference Summary**
- **Terminations**
- **Termination Notice**

SAMPLE

YOUR COMPANY NAME
HIRING PROCEDURES

1. The Supervisor or Manager completes the Open Position Form and submits it to the General Manager for approval. The form is forwarded to the President for final approval before submission to Human Resources.

2. Upon receipt, Human Resources contacts the hiring Manager with notification of the approval. The hiring Manager informs Human Resources of recruitment activities or any special needs or issues.

3. Before interviewing for the position, all applicants should complete an employment application.

4. Applicants selected are interviewed by the direct Supervisor and/or Manager. Interview notes should be taken on a separate piece of paper and not on the application or résumé. Interview questions must be directly related to the position.

5. Upon selection of the top applicants, the Supervisor documents employment verifications and reference checks using the Employment Verification Form.

6. If the position includes driving for the Company, the Supervisor contacts Human Resources and requests a DMV check.

7. The Supervisor selects an applicant for the position and reviews the decision with the General Manager and with Human Resources prior to extending an offer to the applicant.

8. The Supervisor offers the position and notifies Human Resources upon acceptance of the offer. The application, résumé, interview notes and Employment Verification Forms must be received by Human Resources at least one day prior to the start date. The Supervisor may make and keep copies of the application and résumé for the employee's store personnel file.

9. Written offers should be extended in cases where there are unique conditions, such as a special commission arrangement. The Human Resources Manager should be contacted to draft and send the written offer.

10. If the job offer includes an agreement for future pay or status changes, the Supervisor submits the appropriate form to Human Resources documenting the changes prior to the effective date.

SAMPLE

HIRING PROCEDURES - PAGE 2

11. All original applications and résumés are to be sent to Human Resources. Written responses will be sent by Human Resources to any applicants not hired unless otherwise instructed by the Supervisor.

12. Human Resources sends the new hire packet to the appropriate Manager so it is received no later than the employee's first day of work. The Manager gives the employee an orientation and returns the completed forms to Human Resources.

13. The New Hire Packet consists of:
    - New Hire Data Form
    - Affirmative Action Program Voluntary Survey
    - Attendance Calendar
    - Federal and State Withholding Forms
    - I-9 Forms
    - Employee Handbook Receipt and Acknowledgment Form
    - Medical Insurance Payroll Deduction Authorization
    - Commission Agreement (if applicable)
    - "Sexual Harassment is Forbidden by Law" Brochure
    - "Facts about Workers' Compensation" Brochure
    - "EDD Disability Insurance Provisions" Brochure

SAMPLE

YOUR COMPANY NAME   *OPEN POSITION FORM*

Job Title: _____   Location: _____
Supervisor: _____   Date Needed: _____
Estimated Starting Pay: $ _____   Budgeted: □ Yes   □ No

REASON FOR HIRE

□ New Position
□ Replacement for: _____   Date Vacated: _____
                    (Name)

TYPE OF EMPLOYMENT *(Check one in each column.)*			
□ Regular, Full Time	□ Exempt	□ Commission	□ Class A Truck Driver
□ Regular, Part Time	□ Non-Exempt	□ Non-Commission	□ Class B Truck Driver
□ Temporary, Full Time			□ Forklift Driver
□ Temporary, Part Time			□ Other □ N/A

WORK EXPERIENCE/SKILLS	PHYSICAL REQUIREMENTS	EDUCATIONAL QUALIFICATIONS
Required:_____	Required:_____	Required:_____
Desired:_____	Desired:_____	Desired:_____

PRIMARY RESPONSIBILITY OF POSITION *(Essential Job Functions)*
_____
_____

ADDITIONAL COMMENTS
_____
_____
_____

APPROVALS

Submitted by: _____   Title: _____   Date: _____
Approved by: _____   Title: General Manager   Date: _____
Approved by: _____   Title: President   Date: _____
Received by: _____   Date: _____
              (Human Resources)

THIS SECTION TO BE COMPLETED BY HUMAN RESOURCES	
SOURCES CONTACTED:	
_____	**Name of Candidate Selected:**
Date Filled: _____	_____
Source: _____	**Position:** _____ **Rate:** _____
Hired by: _____	
Starting Date: _____	

SAMPLE

YOUR COMPANY NAME *EMPLOYMENT APPLICATION* *An Equal Opportunity Employer* **PLEASE PRINT IN INK** Date: _____ Position applying for: _____ Location applying to: _____	**FOR COMPANY USE ONLY** To Start (Date) _____ Emp. # _____ Pay Rate $_____per_____Commission_____ Yes or No Location _____ Position _____ Job # _____ Supervisor: _____ Hired by: _____ Hire Source: _____

Check: □ Full Time □ Part Time □Regular □ Temporary

NAME: First Middle Last	Social Security No.
ADDRESS: Number Street	Telephone No.

CITY	STATE	ZIP CODE

DRIVER'S LICENSE: Number   State

How were you referred to our company?   □ Ad   □ Agency   □ Relative   □ Friend   □ Walk-in   □ Other

Have you been employed by us before:
□ No   □ Yes   Dates: Locations:

Have you ever been convicted of a criminal act? (Conviction will not automatically exclude you from employment.)
□ No   □ Yes   If yes, explain:

Are you legally allowed to work in the United States?
□ No   □ Yes   If hired, federal law requires documentation verifying your identity and legal authorization to work in the U.S.

EDUCATION

NAME	CITY/STATE	# OF YRS COMPLETED	GRADUATED	DEGREE/MAJOR
HIGH SCHOOL				
COLLEGE/UNIVERSITY				
TRADE SCHOOL				
OTHER				

List any other education, training, special skills or certificates that you possess related to the job for which you are applying.

List any machines or equipment that you are qualified and experienced at operating.

List all computer software programs and systems with which you are experienced.

Salary Desired

May we contact your present employer?
□ Yes   □ No   If yes, please indicate telephone number _____

SAMPLE

EMPLOYMENT APPLICATION - PAGE 2

WORK HISTORY
Start with your most recent employment, include self-employment, military and voluntary experience.
This section must be completed even if submitting a résumé.

Employer			Telephone
Address			
Employed From (Mo/Yr) — To (Mo/Yr)	Income Starting $ — Ending $		Title
Job Duties:			Supervisor
Reason For Leaving			
Employer			Telephone
Address			
Employed From (Mo/Yr) — To (Mo/Yr)	Income Starting $ — Ending $		Title
Job Duties:			Supervisor
Reason For Leaving			
Employer			Telephone
Address			
Employed From (Mo/Yr) — To (Mo/Yr)	Income Starting $ — Ending $		Title
Job Duties:			Supervisor
Reason For Leaving			
Employer			Telephone
Address			
Employed From (Mo/Yr) — To (Mo/Yr)	Income Starting $ — Ending $		Title
Job Duties:			Supervisor
Reason For Leaving			

IMPORTANT - READ BEFORE SIGNING

I certify that the information in this application is true and complete. Any false statements, concealments or omissions are grounds for refusal to hire or immediate dismissal, if hired.

I authorize (Your Company Name) to investigate and verify the information contained in this application which may include contacting my schools and former employers, and for (Your Company Name) to keep and preserve such records. I understand that, if hired, my employment is *at will* and may be terminated without cause and without notification by either the Company or me. THIS APPLICATION DOES NOT CONSTITUTE A CONTRACT FOR EMPLOYMENT, EXPRESS OR IMPLIED.

If employed, I agree to adhere to the Company's rules and regulations.

_____ _____
   Signature   Date

SAMPLE

YOUR COMPANY NAME
EMPLOYMENT VERIFICATION (SENT TO PREVIOUS EMPLOYERS)

Position: _____ *Location:* _____

Applicant's Name: _____ *SS#:* _____

Person Contacted: _____ *Title:* _____

Company: _____ *Telephone:* _____

---

1.   Confirm dates of employment: From _____ To _____

2.   Confirm earnings: From _____ To _____

3.   What were his/her job duties?

4.   How would you rate the quality and quantity of his/her work?

5.   How did he/she get along with others?

6.   What are his/her strong points?

7.   What are his/her weak points or areas which needed development?

8.   How would you rate his/her attendance and reliability?

9.   How attentive was he/she to safety?

10. How successful was he/she as a supervisor, if applicable?

11. What were his/her reasons for leaving?

12. Would you rehire him/her?

13. Additional comments:

Conducted by: _____ *Date:* _____

SAMPLE

APPLICANT VOLUNTARY SURVEY

Name: _____ Date: _____

Location: _____ Job Applied For: _____

Please read carefully:

Solely to help us comply with government record keeping, reporting, and other legal requirements, please complete this form. We appreciate your cooperation. This form will be kept completely separate from any application and will not be used to make any personnel decisions. Applicants are considered for all positions and employees are treated without regard to race, color, religion, sex, national origin, age, marital status, physical or mental disability, veteran status or sexual orientation. All information requested below will be protected as confidential. If you want assistance in completing this form, please ask the interviewer or Human Resources.

SEX	RACE
☐ Male	☐ White
☐ Female	☐ Black
	☐ Hispanic
	☐ Asian/Pacific Islander
	☐ American Indian/Alaskan Native

Check if any of the following apply:

☐ Vietnam-Era Veteran
☐ Special Disabled Veteran
☐ Handicapped Individual

Definitions:

WHITE: (Not of Hispanic origin) - All persons having origins in any of the original peoples of Europe, North Africa or the Middle East.
BLACK: (Not of Hispanic origin) - All persons having origins in any of the Black racial groups of Africa.
HISPANIC: All persons of Mexican, Puerto Rican, Cuban, Central or South American or other Spanish culture or origin, regardless of race.
ASIAN OR PACIFIC ISLANDER: All persons having origins in any of the original peoples of the Far East, Southeast Asia, the Indian Sub-continent or the Pacific Islands. This area includes, i.e., China, Japan, Korea, the Philippine Islands and Samoa.
AMERICAN INDIAN OR ALASKAN NATIVE: All persons having origins in any of the original peoples of North America.
VIETNAM-ERA VETERAN: A person who served on active duty for a period of more than 180 days and was discharged or released therefrom with other than a dishonorable discharge or was discharged or released from active duty because of a service-connected disability. Any part of eligible active duty must have occurred between August 5, 1964, and May 7, 1975.
SPECIAL-DISABLED VETERAN: A veteran entitled to disability compensation under laws administered by the Veteran's Administration for disability rated at 30 percent or more, or a person who was discharged or released from active duty because of a service-connected disability.
HANDICAPPED: Any person who has a physical or mental impairment which substantially limits one or more of such person's major life activities, has a record of such impairment or is regarded as having such an impairment. Please explain your limitations and specify accommodations required. (PLEASE USE THE BACK OF THIS FORM IF NECESSARY.)

SAMPLE

YOUR COMPANY NAME
RECEIPT AND ACKNOWLEDGMENT OF EMPLOYEE HANDBOOK

I, _____, acknowledge receipt of the Employee Handbook. I agree to familiarize myself with the information in this handbook and to observe the procedures set forth herein. I understand that the contents of this handbook do not form a contract between (Company Name) and me, but are only intended as a general statement of Company policies. I also understand that the Company may change, rescind or add to any procedures, benefits or practices described in the handbook from time to time in its sole discretion, with or without prior notice to any employee. I further understand that I have the right to terminate my employment at any time and for any reason, and likewise the Company has the right to terminate my employment at any time and for any reason. I acknowledge that no agreement contrary to the foregoing has been made with me by any person. Finally, I understand and agree that no person, other than the President of the Company or the Human Resources Manager, has the authority to enter into any agreement for a specified term of employment or to modify the contents of this handbook, either orally or in writing, and that any such agreement or modification must be in writing to be effective.

THIS IS NOT A CONTRACT.

_____

Employee's Signature

_____

Employee's Name (please print)

_____

Date Signed

LISTS OF ACCEPTABLE EMPLOYMENT AND IDENTIFICATION DOCUMENTS

List A

Documents That Establish Both Identity and Employment Eligibility

1. U.S. passport (unexpired or expired).

2. Certificate of U.S. citizenship (INS Form N-560 or N-561).

3. Certificate of Naturalization (INS Form N-550 or N-570).

4. Unexpired foreign passport, with I-551 stamp or attached INS Form I-94 indicating unexpired employment authorization.

5. Alien Registration Receipt Card with photograph (INS Form I-151 or I-551).

6. Unexpired Temporary Resident Card (INS Form I-688).

7. Unexpired Employment Authorization Card (INS Form I-688A).

8. Unexpired Reentry Permit (INS Form I-327).

9. Unexpired Refugee Travel Document (INS Form I-571).

10. Unexpired Employment Authorization Document issued by the INS which contains a photograph (INS Form I-688B).

OR

List B

Documents That Establish Identity

1. Driver's license or ID card issued by a state or outlying possession of the United States provided it contains a photograph or information such as name, date of birth, sex, height, eye color and address.

2. ID card issued by federal, state or local government agencies or entities provided it contains a photograph or information such as name, date of birth, sex, height, eye color and address.

3. School ID card with a photograph.

4. Voter's registration card.

5. U.S. Military card or draft record.

6. Military dependent's ID card.

7. U.S. Coast Guard Merchant Mariner Card.

8. Native American tribal document.

9. Driver's license issued by a Canadian government authority.

For persons under age 18 who are unable to present a document listed above:

10. School record or report card.

11. Clinic, doctor, or hospital record.

12. Day-care or nursery school record.

AND

List C

Documents That Establish Employment Eligibility

1. U.S. Social Security Card issued by the Social Security Administration (other than a card stating it is not valid for employment.

2. Certification of Birth Abroad issued by the Department of State (Form FS-545 or Form DS-1350).

3. Original or certified copy of a birth certificate issued by a state, country, municipal authority or outlying possession of the United States bearing an official seal.

4. Native American tribal document.

5. U.S. Citizen ID Card (INS Form I-197).

6. ID Card for use of Resident Citizen in the United States (INS Form I-179).

7. Unexpired employment authorization document issued by the INS (other than those listed under List A).

SAMPLE

YOUR COMPANY NAME
HEALTH INSURANCE PAYROLL DEDUCTION AUTHORIZATION

I. INSTRUCTIONS
Complete Sections II, III and IV.
Complete the applicable enrollment forms in Section II.
Return ALL forms to HUMAN RESOURCES within five days.

II. ELECTION OF COVERAGE

     1. _____ NO   I waive health insurance. I understand that if I initially waive health coverage, I may be subject to late enrollment limitations. For more information, please call the Human Resources Department.

     2. _____ YES   I elect health insurance coverage. Health insurance is effective the first of the month following 90 days of employment.

                        HEALTH PLAN NAME
                        Complete Enrollment Application, including signature and date.

                        DENTAL PLAN NAME
                        Complete Enrollment Application, including signature and date.

III. COVERED INDIVIDUALS

I elect coverage for:

_____ Employee Only   _____ Employee + One   _____ Employee + Family

IV. AUTHORIZATION (sign and date)

I hereby request coverage for the group health insurance for which I am or may become eligible. I certify that the individuals I have enrolled are eligible dependents. I authorize my employer to make the necessary payroll deductions required for this insurance.

This payroll deduction authorization supersedes and cancels any health insurance deduction authorization I currently have on file.

Name: _____   Signature: _____

Date: _____   Location: _____

                                 Company Use Only: Effective _____

SAMPLE

YOUR COMPANY NAME
EMPLOYMENT
STATUS CHANGES POLICY

1. An Employee Status Form is completed by the Manager to reflect any change to an employee's status, location, position or pay.

2. A change to status or pay should always have an effective date of the first or the 16th of the month.

3. The Manager submits the completed form to the General Manager for approval. The General Manager then submits the form to the Human Resources Manager for a compliance review. The President gives final approval.

4. Once approved, Human Resources returns two copies to the Manager. The Manager keeps one copy for his/her file and gives one to the employee.

5. Changes must be submitted, approved and forwarded to Human Resources prior to the end of the pay period in which the change is effective.

SAMPLE

YOUR COMPANY NAME
EMPLOYEE STATUS FORM

EMPLOYEE NO. _____   EMPLOYEE NAME: _____

CURRENT POSITION/WAGE

JOB TITLE: _____   BRANCH/DEPT: _____

PAY RATE: _____   PER: _____   SINCE: _____

NEW POSITION/WAGE/STATUS

Changes checked below are to be effective: _____

_____Status Change: From _____ To _____
(Exempt/Nonexempt, Commission/Non-commission, Part time/Full Time)
_____Transfer: From _____ To _____

_____Job No: _____   Job Title: _____

_____Wage Rate: _____   Per _____

APPROVALS (Route in the following order):

DATE

Manager: _____   _____

General Manager: _____   _____

Human Resources Manager: _____   _____

President: _____   _____

SUPPORTING INFORMATION

Duties to be added or deleted:

Comments on performance:

Other:

NOTE: Once approved, two copies of this form will be returned to the requesting Manager for appropriate distribution.

TO BE COMPLETED BY HUMAN RESOURCES

Copies sent: _____   HRIS Updated: _____

SAMPLE

YOUR COMPANY NAME	EMPLOYEE PERFORMANCE EVALUATION

Name _____ Title _____

Location/Department _____ Due Date _____ Period Covered _____

Appraisal Type: __ Introductory __ Promotion/Transfer __ Annual __ Other _____

EVALUATION CODES

E	=	Excellent	Performance consistently above standards with minimal supervision
C	=	Competent	Performance fully meets Company's standards
U	=	Unsatisfactory	Performance falls below minimum standards
NA	=	Not Applicable	

SUPERVISOR RATING OF EMPLOYEE

Rate the following	Evaluation Code	Comments (Attach additional page, if necessary.)
1. PROFICIENCY IN FIELD/SPECIALTY Degree of competence. Professional manner.		
2. ADMINISTRATIVE EFFECTIVENESS Skill in planning, organizing and implementing work assignments or project.		
3. LEADERSHIP Skill in getting work done through formal or informal direction of others.		
4. JUDGMENT/DECISION MAKING Degree of analysis, objectivity and foresight used to make decisions.		
5. RELATIONSHIPS Ability to work effectively with subordinates, peers and superiors.		
6. INITIATIVE AND RESOURCEFULLNESS Amount of drive and creativity. Ability to start and accomplish work. Degree of supervision needed.		
7. SUPERVISORY SKILL Demonstrated ability to select, train, motivate and develop subordinates. Degree of sustained contribution from work group.		
8. COMMUNICATION Expression of verbal or written ideas. Method and manner of speaking. Ability to observe and listen.		
9. PROFESSIONAL DEVELOPMENT Commitment to professional growth through development of skills and knowledge.		
10. ADAPTABILITY Efficiency under stress. Receptiveness to change/new ideas. Poise and/or courtesy in tough situations.		
11. ATTITUDE AND COOPERATION Degree to which employee is supportive of Company's directives, decisions and policies. Accepts and profits from constructive criticism.		
OVERALL RATING: When determining this rating, take into consideration the rating for the major accomplishments.		

SAMPLE

EMPLOYEE PERFORMANCE EVALUATION - PAGE 2	
STRENGTHS	**AREAS FOR IMPROVEMENT**

EVALUATION SUMMARY
Briefly summarize employee's performance:

FOR INTRODUCTORY PERIOD EMPLOYEES	FOR REGULAR EMPLOYEES
__ Satisfactory completion of introductory period.	__ Satisfactory completion of employment year.
__ Delay introductory period. Reevaluation date _____.	__ Delay continued regular status and reevaluate on _____.
__ Less than satisfactory completion of evaluation. Recommend termination effective _____.	__ Continued unsatisfactory performance. Recommend termination effective _____.

SIGNATURES

(The employee's signature means that the performance evaluation was reviewed with him/her. It does not necessarily indicate that employee agrees with evaluation.)

EMPLOYEE	**DATE**
DIRECT SUPERVISOR	**DATE**
GENERAL MANAGER/DATE	**PRESIDENT/DATE**

EMPLOYEE COMMENTS: (Write below any comments you wish to make regarding your evaluation.)

SAMPLE

EMPLOYEE SELF-EVALUATION

EVALUATION CODES

E	= Excellent	Performance consistently above standards with minimal supervision
C	= Competent	Performance fully meets Company's standards
U	= Unsatisfactory	Performance falls below minimum standards
NA	= Not Applicable	

RATE THE FOLLOWING	EVAL CODE	COMMENTS (Attached additional page, if necessary.)
1. *Proficiency in Field/Specialty* Degree of competence. Professional manner.		
2. *Administrative Effectiveness* Skill in planning, organizing and implementing work assignments or project.		
3. *Leadership* Skill in getting work done through formal or informal direction of others.		
4. *Judgment/Decision Making* Degree of analysis, objectivity and foresight used to make decisions.		
5. *Relationships* Ability to work effectively with subordinates, peers and superiors.		
6. *Initiative and Resourcefulness* Amount of drive and creativity. Ability to start and accomplish work. Degree of supervision needed.		
7. *Supervisory Skill* Demonstrated ability to select, train, motivate and develop subordinates. Degree of sustained contribution from work group.		
8. *Communication* Expression of verbal or written ideas. Method and manner of speaking. Ability to observe and listen.		
9. *Professional Development* Commitment to professional growth through development of skills and knowledge.		
10. *Adaptability* Efficiency under stress. Receptiveness to change/new ideas. Poise and/or courtesy in tough situations.		
11. *Attitude and Cooperation* Degree to which employee is supportive of Company's objectives, decisions and policies. Accepts and profits from constructive criticism.		
OVERALL RATING		

SAMPLE

EMPLOYEE SELF-EVALUATION - PAGE 2

MAJOR ACCOMPLISHMENTS DURING EVALUATION PERIOD			
EMPLOYEE: Briefly identify goals/projects or other accomplishments.	**Eval Code**	**EVALUATOR: Briefly summarize employee's performance.**	**Eval Code**

GOALS AND OBJECTIVES FOR NEXT EMPLOYMENT YEAR
List your goals and objectives. Your Manager may modify these during the review of your performance.

_____   _____
Employee's Signature   Date

Return this completed form to your Supervisor by the agreed-upon date.

SAMPLE

YOUR COMPANY NAME
INSIDE SALES COMMISSION PLAN AND AGREEMENT

Employee/Location #

Effective Date

The Inside Sales Commission Plan applies to employees classified as plumbing or kitchen cabinet salespersons for the Company. Outside salespersons are not eligible for this Plan.

The Plan is as follows:

1. The purpose of the Plan is to increase sales and maximize gross margins. To fulfill the Plan's purpose, participants agree to make regular calls to solicit new orders, follow up on orders and problems, assist with the collection of past due accounts, handle complaints, build sales through selling companion items, assist customers in any way possible to maximize sales and support the sales efforts of other employees.

2. Participants are compensated through both base pay and commission earnings. Participants earn commissions on invoices they generate and submit which are billed. Invoices must be approved by the Manager before they will be credited for payment of commissions. In order for commissions to be earned, the participant must attain a monthly minimum of $_____ in billed sales, or a minimum ___ percent gross profit. If this is achieved, commissions are paid on all billed sales for the month according to the Commission Rate Schedule currently in effect.

    Commission will not be paid to a participant for sales in which the monthly minimum in billed sales or the minimum gross profit is not achieved.

3. For invoices written by a participant for an account assigned to an outside salesperson, the participant will receive credit for ___ percent of the gross commission earned. However, the Manager may unilaterally authorize another commission percentage be paid (more or less than ___ percent) as deemed appropriate for a specific invoice. In addition, the Manager may authorize a commission split between inside salespeople.

4. In addition to commission earnings, participants are eligible for vendor Sales Performance Improvement Fund (SPIF) monies offered by the Company as an incentive. If the Company pays the SPIF, all mandatory federal and state taxes will be deducted and withheld. For SPIFs paid directly to participants by vendors, the participant is responsible for all federal and state taxes.

5. Commission payment will be processed with the second pay period of the month following the month in which the invoice was billed.

SAMPLE

INSIDE SALES COMMISSION PLAN AND AGREEMENT - PAGE 2

6.   In the event a participant's employment with the Company terminates, commissions will be paid on invoices generated and billed prior to the termination date. Commission payment will be processed according to the Company's usual practice and schedule.

7.   To continue participating in this Plan, participants must achieve minimum expectations of billed sales dollars, gross profit dollars and gross margin percent.

Inside Sales Commission Plan Agreement

I understand that as an inside salesperson, I am a participant in the Inside Sales Commission Plan as of the Effective Date.

My signature below acknowledges that I have read and understand the Plan as stated above and agree to its terms and conditions.

I also understand that any and all terms and conditions of this Agreement and the Plan are subject to change without notice, prospectively as well as retroactively. The Company may terminate the program or my eligibility for the program at any time without notice. I understand that nothing in this Agreement nor anything in the Plan constitutes a contract of employment, or continuation of the program described in this Agreement or the Plan, and that my employment with the Company is at-will. I also understand this supersedes all prior agreements, promises or understanding, whether verbal or in writing, and that no purported modification to this Agreement will be binding on the Company unless it is in writing and signed by the President of the Company.

_____   _____
Employee's Signature/Date   Manager's Signature/Date

Copy Distribution:

Personnel File (original)
Employee
Branch Manager
General Manager
President
Accounting

SAMPLE

YOUR COMPANY NAME
COMMISSION RATE SCHEDULE FOR INSIDE SALES COMMISSION PLAN

_____   _____

Employee/Location #   Effective Date

_____

Date of Previous Schedule

	Gross Profit Percent	**Commission Rate (% paid)**
Plumbing products, kitchen and bathroom cabinets, door and cabinet hardware	42.00 and over	13
	40.00 - 41.99	12
	38.00 - 39.99	11
	36.00 - 37.99	10
	34.00 - 35.99	9
	32.00 - 33.99	8
	30.00 - 31.99	6
	25.00 - 29.99	4
	Less than 25.00	0
Appliances and Countertops	20.00 and over	12
	17.00 - 19.99	10
	14.00 - 16.99	8
	10.00 - 13.99	5
	Less than 10.00	0

I understand that this Commission Rate Schedule is subject to change without notice.

_____   _____

Employee's Signature/Date   Manager's Signature/Date

Copy Distribution:

Personnel File (original)
Employee
Branch Manager
General Manager
President
Accounting

SAMPLE

YOUR COMPANY NAME
TIMEKEEPING AND PAYROLL

1. Nonexempt employees are required to complete a time sheet to record their time worked. Employees are responsible for recording their work hours accurately.

2. Time sheet entries for time worked are made at the beginning and end of a shift and for the length of a meal break. Work shifts must be for a minimum of two hours.

   Time worked is recorded in 15 minute increments in military time. Time that is less than 7.5 minutes into the quarter hour is to be rounded down. Time that is 7.5 minutes or more into a quarter hour is to be rounded up to the next quarter hour. (Example: 1:07 p.m. is recorded as 13:00. 1:08 p.m. is recorded as 13:15.)

3. Time sheet entries for time not worked are made by using the following abbreviations:

Abbreviation	**Non-worked Time**
D	Docked, not paid and not worked
H	Holiday
S	Sick leave
V	Vacation
S/V	Pay sick first, then vacation
F	Funeral leave
SDI	State Disability Insurance
WC	Workers' Compensation
C	Training Class

   For partial day absences, the amount of time not worked must also be recorded on the time sheet.

4. A meal break of at least 30 minutes must be taken and recorded on the time sheet after a work period of no more than five hours in length. Six consecutive hours may be worked without a meal break if the six hours completes the end of the workday and the employee does not return to work.

5. Rest periods are not recorded on the time sheet.

6. Employees are required to sign their time sheets at the end of each pay period after reviewing all entries. Time sheets are then reviewed and signed by the Manager before forwarding them to Accounting.

SAMPLE

TIMEKEEPING AND PAYROLL - PAGE 2

7. Employees report vacation, sick and other leave days by submitting the Leave Request Form to their Supervisor.

    For non-exempt employees, leave days are recorded on the time sheets using the codes listed above in Item 3.

    For exempt employees, the Manager records absences each pay period using the Vacation and Sick Leave Absence Record. This form must be submitted each pay period for each department even when no absences are recorded.

8. Time sheets (nonexempt employees) and Vacation and Sick Leave Absence Records (exempt employees) must be forwarded to Accounting by 08:00 of the day following the last day of a pay period (the first or 16th of the month).

9. Overtime hours are paid at one and one-half times the regular rate of pay and include:
    *   All hours worked in excess of 8 hours in a single day.
    *   All hours worked in excess of 40 hours in a single week.
    *   The first 8 hours worked of the 7th consecutive workday.

10. Double-time hours are paid at two times the regular rate of pay and include:
    *   All hours worked in excess of 12 hours in a single day.
    *   All hours worked in excess of 8 hours on the 7th consecutive work day in any one work week.

11. Exempt employees are not eligible for overtime or double-time pay.

12. Paid vacation, sick and holiday hours are not included when calculating the weekly hours worked for computing weekly overtime.

13. Commissions or incentives earned by nonexempt employees are included in the employee's regular rate of pay for the purpose of computing overtime due. Additional overtime pay due is calculated and paid after commissions have been determined. Bonus pay is not included in these calculations as it is discretionary income.

14. Employees may not receive compensatory time off in lieu of overtime pay. *SAME WORK WEEK*

15. Employees may request the Company to automatically deposit their paychecks to their bank account by submitting a completed Authorization Agreement for Automatic Deposits Form to Human Resources.

SAMPLE

YOUR COMPANY NAME
TIME SHEET

RECORDING INSTRUCTIONS: Round off all items to the nearest quarter hour. Use Military Time. Example: 1:00 to 1:07 record as 13:00; 1:08 to 1:15 record as 13:15.

DAY	DATE	TIME IN	MEAL BREAK	TIME OUT	TIME OUT	TIME IN	EXPLANATION OF HRS NOT WORKED: (Use Codes below and indicate number of hours absent.)	ACCOUNTING USE ONLY	
								REGULAR	OVERTIME
	01/16								
	02/17								
	03/18								
	04/19								
	05/20								
	06/21								
	07/22								
	08/23								
	09/24								
	10/25								
	11/26								
	12/27								
	13/28								
	14/29								
	15/30								
	XX/31								

_____
Employee's Signature/Date

_____
Supervisor's Signature/Date

CODES

SICK	= S
VACATION	= V
HOLIDAY	= H
DOCK	= D
SICK/VACATION	= S/V
JURYDUTY	= JD
WORKERS' COMP	= WC
STATE DISABILITY	= SDI

MILITARY TIME CONVERSION CHART

HRS:
7:00 am	=	07:00
8:00 am	=	08:00
9:00 am	=	09:00
10:00 am	=	10:00
11:00 am	=	11:00
12:00 noon	=	12:00
1:00 pm	=	13:00
2:00 pm	=	14:00
3:00 pm	=	15:00
4:00 pm	=	16:00
5:00 pm	=	17:00
6:00 pm	=	18:00
7:00 pm	=	19:00

MINS:
15 = .25
30 = .50
45 = .75

Routing Instructions:
1. The immediate Supervisor and employee must sign the time sheet prior to submitting to Accounting.
2. Completed time sheets are due in Accounting on the 1st and 16th day of each month.

SAMPLE

YOUR COMPANY NAME
LEAVE REQUEST

Employee	Date
Position	Full Time ☐ Part Time ☐
Dept/Location	

TYPE OF LEAVE REQUESTED

Vacation ☐	Sick Leave ☐	Military☐
Maternity ☐	Other _____	

1ˢᵗ day off work _____ **Date return to work** _____

 # work days off _____

Reason for request _____

_____
Employee's Signature

ELIGIBILITY

   # Vacation hours accrued _____

   # Hours sick leave available _____

APPROVALS

_____   _____
Personnel or Payroll   Date

_____   _____
Supervisor   Date

_____   _____
Owner/Manager Representative   Date

SAMPLE

YOUR COMPANY NAME
VACATION AND SICK LEAVE

ELIGIBILITY

Regular, full-time employees. Part-time, temporary, on-call and commission-only employees are ineligible.

SICK LEAVE

- Sick leave begins accruing on the first of the month following or coinciding with the completion of six months of regular, full-time employment.
- Sick leave is accrued at a rate of four hours per month.
- If you are in an unpaid status for more than 80 hours, sick leave does not accumulate for that month.
- The maximum amount of sick leave which can accrue is 48 hours.

VACATION

Length of Time Employed	Days Earned Per Year	Maximum Hours Accrued/Month	Ceiling in Hours
Employment date through 1 year	5	3.34	60.00
2 yrs through 8 yrs	10	6.67	120.00
9 yrs through 14 yrs	15	10.00	180.00
15 yrs or more	20	13.34	240.00

- Vacation accrual begins with the first day of full-time, regular employment.
- Vacation accrual is prorated for any month during which you are paid less than 120 hours.
- Vacation accrues monthly at the rate indicated in the above table, effective January 1, ____.
- Vacation will accrue until the ceiling is reached and then will cease accruing until the hours accrued drops below the ceiling. The ceiling will become effective January 1, ____.
- Only earned vacation can be taken. If you have no vacation hours, the time-off is unpaid.
- You may not receive pay in lieu of vacation except at the time of termination.

SAMPLE

YOUR COMPANY NAME
WORK-RELATED INJURIES AND ILLNESSES

1. If an employee requires treatment, he/she should be sent to the doctor or clinic specified below. Employees have the right to be treated by their personal physician provided they have given written notice to the Company of the doctor's name and address prior to the injury. The written notice should be forwarded to Human Resources.

   Clinics:

   (Name, address, phone number)   (Name, address, phone number)

2. Upon being notified of a work-related injury, the Supervisor or Manager completes and signs the Employer's Report of Occupational Injury or Illness (Form 5020). The employee may not complete or sign the form for his/her own injury. The form is sent to Human Resources within one day of the date of the injury or knowledge of the injury.

   Additional information regarding the claim may be written in the box above the form's signature line, i.e., "restricted work activity." This area should also be used to note the date the employee was given the Employee's Claim for Worker's Compensation Benefits.

   If there are any concerns regarding the validity of the claim, a separate note or letter can be attached.

3. Human Resources reviews the claim form for completion and forwards it to the insurance company for processing.

4. The Supervisor should also complete the Supervisor's Accident Investigation Loss Source Identification Form after investigating the details of the injury and accident. The purpose of this form is to provide information which the Manager can use to take action to prevent a recurrence of the same type of accident. This form should be submitted with the Employer's First Report. However, if the investigation is not completed within one day, submit the form separately.

5. Upon being informed of the injury, the Supervisor or Manager gives the employee the pamphlet, "Facts for Injured Workers" and the "Employee's Claim for Worker's Compensation Benefits."

SAMPLE

WORK-RELATED INJURIES AND ILLNESSES - PAGE 2

6. The Employee's Claim Form must be provided to the employee within one working day of actual or constructive knowledge of the injury. After receiving the form, the employee completes the first section and returns it to the Manager at his/her leisure. There is no requirement that the employee complete the form or return it within any specified time frame.

    Upon receiving the form from the employee, the Manager completes the second section of the form and returns a copy of the completed form to the employee within one working day of receipt of the completed form from the employee. The original form is sent to Human Resources immediately for submittal to the insurance company.

7. Any doctor's note or pertinent documentation should be forwarded to Human Resources upon receipt.

8. A death or serious injury must be reported immediately by phone to Human Resources.

9. If the employee is out for an extended length of time, the Manager should arrange for weekly communication with the employee.

10. The Company will attempt to return the injured worker to modified work whenever possible.

SAMPLE

YOUR COMPANY NAME
EMPLOYEE CONFERENCE SUMMARY

To: _____ Date: _____

From: _____

Subject: _____

Issues Discussed:

Specific Examples:

Employee's Response:

Requirements Set and/or Actions Taken:

Time Lines and Specific Goals Set:

Plan for Follow-up:

Signatures:

_____   _____
Employee   Supervisor/Date

_____   _____
Date   Owner/Manager, as necessary/Date

SAMPLE

YOUR COMPANY NAME
TERMINATIONS

Voluntary Terminations

1.   Upon being informed of an employee's resignation, ask the employee to put the reason for leaving and last day of work in writing. If there are any new or unresolved issues or comments, investigate them at this time.

2.   The supervisor is responsible for immediately notifying the Manager of any terminations. The manager then notifies Human Resources of the resignation as soon as possible including any outstanding or unresolved issues.

3.   If appropriate, Human Resources will review the resignation with the Manager including any relevant issues, i.e., commission pay, Company property.

Involuntary Terminations

1.   Prior to an involuntary (dismissal or lay-off) termination, the Manager must first contact the General Manager to discuss the situation. The Manager is to then contact the Human Resources Manager (or designee) and review all information regarding the proposed termination. This should include previous performance appraisals, Employee Conference Summary forms, documentation of meetings, warnings, relevant policies and any other related documentation.

2.   The Human Resources Manager reviews the situation and the Manager's request to terminate the employee with the president. No action may be taken prior to the President's approval.

3.   If necessary, the employee may be suspended without pay to give the Company an opportunity to investigate the circumstances giving rise to the termination. The investigation may include an interview of the employee. A Supervisor or Manager may suspend an employee without prior approval if the situation requires immediate action, i.e., employees fighting.

4.   If the decision is made to terminate the employee after a review of the relevant information, the Manager interviews the employee and notifies the employee of the reason for termination.

SAMPLE

TERMINATIONS - PAGE 2

Last Day of Work

1. In the case of either a voluntary or involuntary termination, Human Resources must be notified by noon of the day before the last day of work.

2. Human Resources provides the Manager with all necessary documents and information for the employee on the last day.

3. On the last day of work, the manager meets with the employee to:
   - Complete the termination notice
   - Issue the final paycheck
   - Receive returned Company property
   - Ensure all vouchers owed have been settled

   COBRA forms for the conversion of medical insurance are mailed directly to the employee's home.

   If the employee resigns without giving notice, the final check and necessary forms may be mailed to the employee's home within 72 hours of the resignation.

4. After the meeting, the Manager forwards the Termination Notice along with any other documents to Human Resources.

5. Any commission owed will be calculated during the normal course of business and mailed to the employee's home at the usual time.

SAMPLE

YOUR COMPANY NAME
TERMINATION NOTICE

TO BE COMPLETED BY THE EMPLOYEE

Employee: _____   Position: _____

Address: _____   Phone: _____

Dept/Location: _____   Last day of work: _____

Reason for Termination: _____

I have received my final pay and vacation check in the amount of $ _____.

I have returned all items, equipment or documents with the exception of _____

to be returned by _____.

I will receive any commissions due me at the time normally computed.

I have been informed of my right to continue any group health insurance I now have at my own expense. This employer has no other obligations to me, as I acknowledged at hire, that I accept that this employment is at the will of the employees and the employer and may be terminated at any time without cause.

_____   _____
Employee's Signature   Date

TO BE COMPLETED BY THE MANAGER

Employee's Name: _____   Position: _____

Last day of work: _____   Type of Termination: Voluntary ☐   Discharge ☐   Other ☐

Reason: _____

Company Property	Date Returned		Date Issued
Car	_____		
Keys	_____		
Credit Cards	_____		Final Check: _____
Uniform	_____		Insurance Forms: _____
Company Manuals	_____		
Employee Receivables	_____		

Completed by: _____   Date: _____
Return completed forms to Human Resources Department along with any employee-related materials.

TO BE COMPLETED BY HUMAN RESOURCES

Date Received: _____   LDW: _____   Effective Date of Term: _____

Chapter 8

WATCH FOR THOSE BURNING EMBERS
Protecting Your Business

There can't be a crisis next week. My schedule is already full. - Henry Kissinger

We have been very fortunate in our business. Other than a few small truck accidents and Worker's Compensation claims, we have not had to call on the various business insurances we carry. It's kind of a "Catch-22." Why pay all that money if we haven't had to use it? That's pretty easy. It would only take one incident to put us out of business. I have friends who have experienced fires, hurricanes, embezzlement, product liability, floods, etc. If they hadn't safeguarded their businesses, they might have lost them, and more.

SAFEGUARDING YOUR BUSINESS

The very act of forming your own business entails risk. The rewards of prosperity and self-fulfillment must be balanced against the risks of financial loss and personal dissatisfaction. There are no sure things in business. Still, such factors as planning, experience, adequate financing, managerial expertise, creativity and a willingness to work hard can swing the odds in your favor. For these to be effective, though, you need an ongoing program of risk management.

Suppose any of the following should happen:

- Your building is damaged by fire.
- A customer is hurt in your store.
- An employee steals merchandise.
- A car drives through your store window.
- Your accountant embezzles a large sum of money.
- An employee is injured on the job.
- Your store is burglarized.
- Your business is suffering because of shoplifting.
- A partner dies.

What would you do? A likely answer is, "Call my insurance agent." But relying on insurance is only one of the ways to deal with these hazards.

RISK MANAGEMENT

An effective program of risk management enables you to cope with risks by eliminating them, reducing them, accepting them or transferring them. These methods can be used singly or in combination, depending on the risk as well as your own circumstances.

Eliminating the Risk

Certain risks can be entirely eliminated. Among these are the risks of employee injury because of substandard materials or unsafe equipment, the risk of customer injury because of a hazardous store layout and the risk of fire because of faulty wiring. There is no excuse for allowing risks that are solely the result of negligence or indifference. One who persists in doing so could wind up not only financially liable, but criminally liable as well. And, it is not enough merely to carry insurance. Gross negligence, the flagrant violation of health and safety standards, is sufficient grounds for an insurance carrier to void your policy.

Reducing the Risks

It would be impossible for you to eliminate every business risk, even if you were aware of every one. Your best bet, then, is to reduce the risks. Close evaluation of your workplace, your workers and your customers will enable you to take precautionary actions so as to reduce most of your business risks.

The risk of falling off a ladder cannot be eliminated, but the use of safety ladders, with guard rails on either side, can reduce the risk. Keeping all merchandise boxes, cleaning supplies, tools and electrical cords clear of customer walkways reduces the risk of having customers trip and injure themselves. The risks of breakage and theft can be reduced by displaying merchandise in locked cases. Electronic tags on merchandise, alert salespeople, closed-circuit cameras, burglar alarms and security guards can also help you to combat theft.

Accepting the Risk

Self insurance, a method whereby you create your own contingency fund to pay for whatever business losses might arise, is another way of coping with risk. This enables a business to protect itself while at the same time avoiding payment of insurance premiums. Unfortunately, the protection this method provides is usually inadequate. Given current high replacement costs for buildings, equipment, furniture and fixtures, as well as the staggering amounts of some judgment claims in liability cases, a small business that relies solely on self insurance could easily be wiped out.

A policy of accepting the risk might be applied however, when the risk cannot be eliminated and buying outside insurance is not profitable. For instance, if your losses from shoplifting are less than the insurance premiums to protect yourself against it, accepting the losses makes more sense. Furthermore, even when you do carry insurance against a particular type of risk, part of the risk usually must be accepted because of the policy's deductible provision.

Transferring the Risk

The purchase of coverage from an insurance company enables businesses to transfer their risks. In exchange for a fee, the insurance company accepts the risks that the business wishes to be protected against. In effect, when you buy insurance, you arrange to absorb small periodic losses (premiums) rather than a large uncertain loss. If your property is to be adequately protected and large damage claims that result from public liability or employee injury suits are to be avoided, insurance is a necessity.

If you shop for insurance every year and submit an environmental claim, you may have difficulty collecting because insurance companies will not take responsibility if the date of the environmental spill or incident cannot be determined.

TYPES OF INSURANCE COVERAGE

Fire Insurance

In a standard fire insurance policy, your building, the property contained within it and property temporarily removed from it because of fire are protected against damage inflicted by fire or lightning. This coverage does not extend to accounting records, bills, deeds, money, securities or manuscripts. Nor are you protected against such hazards as windstorms, hail, earthquake, smoke, explosions, vandalism, automatic sprinkler leakage and malicious mischief. To guard excluded valuables and protect yourself against loss in these hazards, you must obtain additional coverage. Neither fire resulting from war nor actions taken under the orders of a civil authority are covered by insurance.

Depending upon the terms of your policy, compensation may be made in any of three ways:

- The insurance carrier may pay you the current cash value of the damaged property.
- The property may be repaired or replaced.

- The property may be taken over by the insurer, who then reimburses you at its appraised value.

Most fire insurance policies are written for a three-year period, and both you and the insurer have the right to cancel. You may cancel your policy at any time. The insurer, however, must give you five days notice before canceling. In either event, you will be reimbursed for any premiums that have been paid in advance. But if you are the one to cancel, a penalty as set forth in your policy may be assessed against your refund.

To keep your fire insurance policy valid, it is your responsibility to use all reasonable means to protect the insured property, both before and after a fire. If you knowingly increase the fire hazard, by renting part of your building to a fireworks manufacturer, for example, this could void your policy. Hiding pertinent information from the insurer, or leaving your building unoccupied for more than 60 days, is also cause for voiding your policy.

Should it become necessary for you to file an insurance claim, you will be required to provide the insurance company with a complete inventory list, detailing the types, quantities and values of the damaged property. Unless an extension is granted, you generally have 60 days in which to do this.

Liability Insurance

As the operator of your own business, you are responsible for the safety of your employees and customers. If a customer slips on a wet floor, you may be liable for damages. You are also responsible for the products or services you sell. For instance, the owner of a garage could be held liable for using a car wax that strips the paint off of a customer's car, or if a mechanic forgets to set the hand brake on a car and it rolls into the street and causes an accident. In the first case, the garage owner might have to cover the cost of a new paint job. In the second, there is no telling how much the cost might be. Was the car damaged? Were other cars damaged? Was anyone injured in the accident? These are just the physical damages for which the garage owner may be liable. What about the mental anguish of the parties involved in the accident? By the time all the costs have been added in, the entire assets of the garage could be wiped out.

Most liability policies cover losses stemming from bodily injury, property-damage claims, medical services required at the time of the accident, investigation and court costs.

The actual amount that your policy will pay depends on both the limit per accident and the limit per person provided for in it. For example, if your policy has a per accident limit of $1,000,000 and a per person limit of $300,000, and if one person receives a $500,000 judgment against you, the insurance company will pay only $300,000. This means you are responsible for paying the remaining $200,000 even though it is within your per accident limit. The guide word here is caution. Make sure you understand and agree with any limitations in your policy. If the limit is $300,000 per person, is that adequate coverage?

If an accident does occur, even if it seems minor, contact your insurance agent immediately. This enables the insurance company to begin its investigation while the relevant information is readily available. Failure to notify the company can void your policy.

The most common types of liability insurance are:

- **General Liability Insurance** - The most far-reaching type of liability insurance available, it provides basic coverage against all liabilities not specifically excluded from the policy.

- **Product Liability Insurance** - This insurance protects you against financial loss in the event that someone is injured by a product you manufacture, distribute or sell.

- **Professional Liability Insurance -** For doctors, lawyers, consultants and others who provide advice or information or perform a service, this insurance protects you against damage claims brought by dissatisfied clients.

Motor Vehicle Insurance

If you plan to use one or more cars or trucks in your business, motor vehicle insurance is a must. Coverage can be provided to protect you against:

- Bodily Injury Claims.
- Property Damage Claims.
- Medical Payments.
- Uninsured Motorist Damages.
- Damage to Your Vehicle.
- Towing Costs.

The amount of coverage you need and the cost of a motor-vehicle insurance policy depend on:

- The number of cars or trucks being insured.
- Their value.
- The kinds of driving to be done (making deliveries, hauling equipment, driving clients).
- Your location.

When five or more motor vehicles are used in your business, you can generally insure them under a low-cost fleet policy. As far as deductibles go, the higher they are, the lower your premiums.

You may find that motor vehicle insurance is a good buy even if you don't plan to use any motor vehicles in your business. This is because you could be held liable for employees or subcontractors who operate their own vehicles, or those of customers, while on company business.

Workers' Compensation Insurance

Common law requires that employers:

- Provide employees with a safe place to work.
- Hire competent coworkers.
- Provide safe tools.
- Warn employees of existing danger.

An employer who fails to do so is liable for damages, including claims for on-the-job injury and occupational diseases. Sometimes payment can be required for the remainder of a disabled worker's life.

Under Workers' Compensation Insurance, the insurance pays all sums you are legally required to pay a claimant. One way to save money on this insurance is to make sure your employees are properly classified. Since rates vary with the degree of hazard associated with each occupational category, improperly classifying an employee in a high-risk occupation raises your rates. Another way to save money is to use safety measures that will lower your accident rate and thereby reduce premiums.

Business Interruption Insurance

Many business owners fail to purchase business interruption insurance because they don't think they need it. If a building burns downs, they think a standard fire insurance policy will suffice. But, what about the loss of business income during the months it takes to rebuild? What about the expenses that continue to mount up even though your doors are closed—taxes, interest on loans, salaries, rent, utilities? Yet not until it is too late do many business owners realize that fire insurance alone is not enough.

Only business interruption insurance covers your fixed expenses and expected profits during the time your business is closed down. Examine these policies very carefully. Make sure that the policy is written to provide coverage in the event that your business is not totally shut down, but is seriously disrupted. Some policies pay only in the event of a total shutdown. You should also remember that an indirect peril could force you to suspend operations as well. What if an important supplier or customer's plant burned down, temporarily interrupting your business? What if your power, water or phone service were disrupted? Protection against these hazards can be written into your policy, but you have to ask for it.

Glass Insurance

Although it may seem insignificant, glass insurance is something most businesses should have. The cost of replacing broken plate glass windows, panels, doors, signs and display cases is so high that you cannot afford to be without it. Furthermore, delays in making the replacement can result in vandalism or theft, which in turn results in additional property loss.

A glass-insurance policy covers the cost not only of replacing the glass itself, but of redoing any letter or ornamentation on the glass, installing the glass (including temporary glass or boards, if needed) and repairing any frame damage. The only exclusions in the standard all-risk, glass-insurance policy are for glass damage from fire or war, and, in the case of fire, your fire-insurance policy provides coverage.

Fidelity Bonds

Most new business owners are unaware that, on the average, thefts by employees far surpass business losses from burglary, robbery and shoplifting. The accountant who embezzles thousands of dollars and then goes to Acapulco and the sales clerk who dips into the cash drawer come readily to mind. Less obvious examples include:

- Putting fictitious employees on the payroll and pocketing their paychecks.
- Ringing up lower prices on merchandise sold to friends or accomplices.
- Stealing merchandise, equipment or supplies.
- Misappropriating company property for personal use.
- Lying on expense vouchers.
- Falsifying time cards.

Unless you or members of your immediate family handle all phases of your business operation, you should obtain fidelity bond protection. This is available in three formats:.

- **Individual Bonds** cover theft by specifically named individuals.
- **Schedule Bonds** list every name or position to be covered.
- **Blanket Bonds**, the most encompassing of the three, cover all employees without reference to individual names or positions.

Before an employee is bonded, the insurance company issuing the bond conducts a character investigation to determine whether anything is known of past acts of dishonesty. Then, if the employee is deemed bondable, coverage is provided. If a prospective employee refuses to be bonded, this could be a tipoff that the applicant has something to hide.

Crime Insurance

Crime insurance covers you against business losses resulting from the criminal activities of people who are not associated with your business. The three categories of crime insurance are:

- **Burglary Insurance** which protects your safes and inventory against thefts in which there is evidence of forcible entry. This means that if a thief enters through an unlocked door or window without disturbing the premises, your burglary policy does not cover any losses. Nor does the standard burglary policy protect accounting records, manuscripts or certain valuables such as accessories that are kept in display windows. To cover these, additional insurance is necessary. Besides protecting you against losses from stolen property, burglary insurance provides coverage for damage sustained during the burglary.

- **Robbery Insurance**, which differs from burglary in that it involves a face-to-face confrontation. The robber actually uses force, or the threat of violence, to take property from the person guarding it. A robbery insurance policy covers the money, property or securities taken, as well as property damage that occurs during the robbery. Another feature of this policy is that it is not limited to robberies that take place inside your building. Thus, if you are robbed while making a delivery, you are covered.

- **Comprehensive Insurance** which is popular because, in addition to protecting you against burglary and robbery, it also protects against a variety of other hazards, including counterfeit money and forged checks. For instance, deception does not constitute robbery. If a con artist tricks you or an employee into parting with property, no force or threat of violence is involved. Therefore, it is not robbery, and unless you have a comprehensive policy, you are not covered. Coverage is also provided against the thief who gains entry to your business without any apparent use of force.

Personal Insurance

Just as there is a need to insure your property against loss, there is an equal need to insure both yourself and your employees. **Group health and life insurance, retirement plans and key personnel insurance** all help to do this. The need for these may seem a long way off, but more and more small businesses are offering an employee benefits package that includes health and life insurance as a way of retaining valued personnel. If you decide to incorporate a retirement plan, too, there is another advantage—contributions made to the plan for yourself and employees are deductible from your federal income tax.

Key personnel insurance, long a staple in the insurance portfolio of major corporations, can be just as necessary for the small-business owner. Could your business survive the death or disability of a partner or key employee? If not, key personnel insurance can at least ease the loss. The proceeds from the insurance are exempt from income tax and payable directly to the business. The policy itself has a cash value and may be used as loan collateral.

RECOGNIZING WARNING SIGNALS

The old adage that "an ounce of prevention is worth a pound of cure" readily pertains to risk management. But before you can take precautionary measures to head off impending danger, you have to recognize the danger. The way to do this is to be alert to the warning signals around you.

The following examples indicate a fire, accident or theft waiting to happen, if it hasn't already:

Fire

- Overloaded circuits.
- Fuse blowouts.
- Frayed electrical cords.
- Overheating of equipment.
- Fire extinguishers inoperative or inaccessible.
- Trash piled up.
- Smoking permitted in high-risk areas.
- Improper procedures in use, storage or disposal of inflammable materials.
- Power plant, heating, ventilation and air-conditioning equipment not checked at regular intervals.

Accidents

- Workers inadequately trained for their jobs.
- Lack of safety rules or failure to enforce them.
- Use of substandard materials or equipment.
- Poor quality control.
- Hazardous layout.
- Admitting customers to the work area.
- Letting customers use equipment themselves.
- Lack of knowledge about products you sell.

Employee Theft

- Inadequate employee reference checks.
- An employee who refuses to take an annual vacation.
- An employee who never leaves the work area during lunch.
- An employee who always arrives at work early and stays late.
- One employee handling all bookkeeping procedures.
- Expenses that are higher than predicted.
- Inventory shortages.
- Finding merchandise or equipment in trash bins.
- Checks and cash left sitting on desk tops.
- Unfamiliar names on the payroll.
- An increase in sales returns.
- Slow collections.

On the surface, none of these examples is proof of embezzlement, but their occurrence does indicate the need for additional investigation or tightened management controls.

Crime

Protect yourself and your business:

- Don't accept checks without asking to see proper identification.
- Don't accept checks that have been endorsed twice.
- Don't accept blank checks that do not have computer-coded characteristics.
- Don't leave large amounts of cash in cash registers or cash boxes.
- Pay attention to customers when:
  - They are wearing loose-fitting clothing.
  - They are carrying large purses or shopping bags.
  - They seem nervous or anxious.
  - They wander into restricted areas.
  - They are left unsupervised for long periods of time.
  - Products are displayed with easily removable sale and price tags.
  - All items being purchased are not recounted before customer leaves store.
  - Display areas are large or messy where it would be hard to spot products that might be missing.
  - Lighting is poor.
  - There are unsuitable locks on doors and windows.
  - There is loose handling of keys.

To make sure that you have adequately insured your business, use the following insurance checklist to review the coverage you need:

INSURANCE CHECKLIST		
Type of Insurance	Purchase	Do Not Purchase
Property Insurance		
Fire?		
Windstorm?		
Earthquake?		
Water Damage?		
Hail?		
Smoke?		
Explosion?		
Vandalism?		
Glass? Breakage?		
Liability Insurance		
General?		
Product?		
Professional?		
Motor Vehicle Insurance		
Fire and Theft?		
Comprehensive?		
Collision?		
Fleet?		
Workers' Compensation		
Business Interruption		
Fidelity?		
Robbery?		
Burglary?		
Comprehensive?		
Personal		
Health?		
Life?		
Key Personnel?		

Contact NKBA® for Business Management Advisories.

How do you find outside help, advice and support for your business?

Chapter 9

FAN THE FLAME
Outside Help

I was brought up to believe that the only thing worth doing was to add to the sum of accurate information in the world. - Margaret Mead

Even when you are armed with facts and knowledge, such as the information found in this book, you may require some outside assistance in various areas of your kitchen and bathroom business. The following professionals, agencies and resources can help you tend your fire and assist in assuring your success.

GETTING HELP

The major cause of most business failures is management that lacks the knowledge, skills, experience or simply the time needed to run a business efficiently. Since new or small businesses can rarely afford to hire the specialists which enable big businesses to carry out their objectives, they are at a distinct disadvantage. However, the way to compensate for this, and still keep payroll expenses to a minimum, is to utilize outside services.

Many outside services are willing and eager to help your business succeed. Whether you need help in obtaining financing, keeping your books in order, coming up with new concepts for products and ways to promote your business, training and motivating personnel, or solving a variety of business problems, there are services available. Some of these services cost money, but surprisingly, many of them are provided free of charge.

If possible, have professionals meet with you at your place of work, so they will have an opportunity to observe your business and have first-hand knowledge enabling them to do a better job.

SOURCES OF OUTSIDE HELP

Listed below in alphabetical order are some of the individuals and institutions that can assist you in operating your business. Each source can provide you with specific and useful information that otherwise might not be readily accessible to your business.

ACCOUNTANTS

An accountant can be instrumental in helping you to keep your business operating on a sound financial basis. Even if you are already familiar with record-keeping procedures, or employ a bookkeeper to maintain your records, the services of an outside accountant may still be required. In addition to designing an accounting system that is suitable for your specific needs, an accountant can also assist in the following areas:

- Determining cash requirements.
- Budgeting.
- Forecasting.
- Controlling costs.
- Preparing financial statements.
- Interpreting financial data.
- Obtaining loans.
- Preparing tax returns.

How To Locate

You can find public accountants listed in the Yellow Pages of the telephone directory, but for best results it is advisable to try to locate one through a personal recommendation. Ask your banker or attorney or another business associate to suggest an accountant. Since their work causes them to communicate with accountants regularly, all three should be able to provide the names of accountants who could meet your requirements. Another approach is to contact one of the national or state accounting associations. One of the larger associations is:

American Institute of Certified Public Accountants
1211 Avenue of the Americas
New York, NY 10036

ADVERTISING

Advertising Agencies

An advertising agency can help you to plan, produce and place your business' advertising. Advertising agencies perform the following activities:

- Develop promotional strategies.
- Create advertising pieces (writing copy, designing graphics and layout, producing the finished product).
- Choose the appropriate media.
- Make sure that ads are run according to schedule.

Whether you need to use an advertising agency depends upon the amount of advertising you intend to do.

How To Locate

To find out which advertising agencies offer which services and how to contact them, check the Standard Directory of Advertising Agencies, available at many public libraries. Another source of agency information is to talk to media sales representatives and to get their opinions about the various advertising agencies. The advertising agencies in your area should also be listed in the Yellow Pages.

The Internet

Countess stories in the popular press recently have focused on computers, the Internet and "the information superhighway." With so many stories and so much information, it is easy to get confused. Before one can really take advantage of all of the new technology, one must understand it, learn what it can do, why it is needed and how much it costs.

What Is The Internet?

The Internet is basically a network of computers linked together not unlike the network that links our telephones together. The network of computers provides a collection of services, including:

- Electronic mail (e-mail)
- World Wide Web
- File Transfers

Some Of The Terms Used.

Internet site - A computer that is connected to the Internet.

World Wide Web - An immense network of linked documents on the Internet that point to other documents on related topics.

Hyperlink - Connections between one piece of information and another.

Page - A hyperlinked document on the web.

Home Page - The first document or the entry to a site.

Service Provider - A company that provides access or connections to the Internet.

Browser Software - Software used to view or navigate hyperlinked pages on the Internet.

Where Did It Come From?

The Internet was born about 20 years ago as a United States Defense Department network called ARPAnet. ARPAnet's primary purpose was to provide a network of defense computers capable of sustaining a nuclear attack, yet still continue to maintain communications.

About 10 years ago, the National Science Foundation (NSF) built its own network based on ARPAnet technology to support collaborative research efforts by teams located in different parts of the country.

The Internet, as we read and hear about it in the popular press, evolved out of this early work and has become widely accessible to the general public only within the last few years.

Who Governs The Internet?

There is no single company running the Internet. There is no president or CEO. For that matter, there is no single authority figure. Instead, there is a voluntary membership organization called the Internet Society whose purpose is:

- To promote global exchange through Internet technology.
- To appoint a council of volunteers called the Internet Architecture Board (IAB).
- To approve standards and allocate resources through the IAB.

Who Maintains The Internet?

As with our telephone network, portions of the physical network are owned by various organizations. Collectively, the various owners voluntarily cooperate to keep the networks operating as a single entity.

What Can I Use The Internet For?

The most frequent service used on the Internet is electronic mail. This is the electronic equivalent of the United States Post Office. Messages can be mailed to anyone with an e-mail address.

The second most popular feature is the World Wide Web. This is the service most often referred to as "the web" in the popular press. The web consists of electronic equivalents to paper pages in a book, linked together by hyperlinks or pointers to one or many other pages.

While this may be hard to visualize without a demonstration, consider the table of contents for a book. With a paper book, we need to find a topic of interest, thumb to the appropriate page, and start to read. With a hyperlinked version of the book, we would point a cursor to the topic, click on our mouse and the page would be displayed on the screen.

If the topic contained a term such as "work triangle," the words "work triangle" could be hyperlinked to a glossary of terms. Clicking on "work triangle" would display the glossary contents for work triangle. The glossary might contain hyperlink references to NKBA® guidelines for work triangles. The possibilities are endless.

Since the web is global in nature, a single page of material could contain hyperlinks to anywhere in the world. A local distributor for ceramic tile could have a web page stating pricing information from a local web site and link to photographs of the tile maintained by the manufacturer in Italy on their corporate web site.

What Do I Need To Access The Internet?

A significant factor in the explosive growth of the Internet is that most office and home computers are capable of accessing the Internet with little or no additional equipment. As a minimum, the following is required:

- Microsoft Windows- or Apple Macintosh-compatible PC
- Modem, 9600 bits per second or higher
- Internet browser software
- Internet service provider

What Does It Cost?

Costs to access the Internet vary depending upon the service provider. A realistic range is $15 to $30 per month. An on-line service will provide up to 20 hours per month for this price range. In addition to major service providers, there are local providers in most areas, including rural areas, that are competitive. With a dedicated Internet service provider, this price range could provide unlimited access.

Where Do I Start?

The best approach is to find someone who already has experience using the Internet. Ask for a demonstration. A few minutes spent with a friend who knows what to do will be time well spent. If she or he is happy with the service provider, consider using the same service until you are comfortable enough to make your own choices.

If you must be a pioneer, try one of the on-line services with Internet access. Software to access on-line services can be found attached to popular computer magazines at almost any bookstore, supermarket or newsstand. While the on-line services may be a bit more expensive and not as fast as dedicated Internet providers, their support services tend to accommodate the new user. Most important—enjoy the learning experience.

Helpful Web Site Information Resources

Associations/Trades

NKBA®   www.nkba.org
NARI   www.nari.org
NAHB   www.nahb.com
ASID   www.asid.org
Kitchen and Bath Business Magazine   www.kitchen.net
Remodeling Magazine   www.remodeling.hw.net

Government/Industry

General Site   www.whitehouse.gov
Economic Statistics   www.whitehouse.gov/fsbr/esbr.html
                                                 www.lib.lsu.edu/bus/economic.html
Household Economic Statistics   www.census.gov/ftp/pub/hhes/www
U.S. Department of Commerce   www.doc.gov
U.S. Census Bureau   www.census.gov
Business Management and Finance   www.smartbiz.com
Dun & Bradstreet Business Management and Finance www.dnb.com

ALLIED PROFESSIONALS

Another approach to providing excellent service and products to our clients is the allied professional relationship. Identify professionals in industries that complement your business, i.e., a retail kitchen and bathroom dealer might want to establish a mutual relationship with a flooring retailer or a paint and wallpaper retailer. The allied professional is clearly an asset to our business. For any allied professional program to become successful, it must incorporate four basic ingredients: it must be mutually beneficial for two professionals or trades who have common interests; it must generate a profit to remain viable; it must seem like a 'natural' alliance to those involved; and it must be organized and structured in order to be recognized as a professional partnership. "

An example of the trades you might want to contact in order to establish a relationship are:

- Cabinet Installers
- Plumbing Contractors
- Remodeling Contractors
- Electricians
- Lighting Designers
- Flooring Retailers

- Home Builders
- Houseware Retailers
- Decorative Plumbing and Hardware Retailers
- Architects
- Interior Designers
- Retail Bed and Bath Stores

ATTORNEYS

An attorney can be useful to your business from the very start, helping you to determine which legal form of business is right for you, drawing up agreements, filing government paperwork, negotiating the lease or purchase of your building. Later on, your attorney can continue to help you by:

- Representing you in court, if the need should ever arise.
- Providing legal advice.
- Interpreting legal documents.
- Assisting in tax planning.
- Helping you to comply with employment laws.
- Working out arrangements with creditors.
- Organizing and/or reorganizing the business, if needed.

How To Locate

Your accountant or banker should be able to recommend an attorney. If not, your state bar association can provide you with names of attorneys in your area. Other sources of information include business acquaintances, friends and the Yellow Pages.

BANKERS

Your banker can be a valuable ally to your business, if you take the time to establish good rapport—preferably before you ask for a loan. The advice or information your banker can provide includes:

- How to open a checking account.
- How to obtain a line of credit.
- How to apply for a loan.
- How to prepare financial reports.
- How to bill customers.
- How to set up your payroll.

Furthermore, since bankers are constantly interacting with various segments of the community, your banker is likely to hear news that affects your business before you do.

CHAMBER OF COMMERCE

The chamber of commerce is traditionally the information agency of a community. Each chamber's goal is to represent and promote its area's economy, to encourage business and industrial investment and to provide employment. As a new business owner, you should get in touch with your local chamber to find out what it has to offer (moral support, research data, general information about the community). You might also decide to become a member. Chambers of commerce offer these benefits:

- Promote local businesses.
- Protect business interests.
- Act as the political voice of the business community.
- Unite businesses.
- Offer educational seminars.
- Offer networking opportunities.
- Provide community demographic information.

COLLEGES AND UNIVERSITIES

The colleges and universities in your area are a vast resource of information, skills and training. They offer access to:

- The school's library for books, periodicals, government reports, reference works, maps, charts, audio-visual aids.
- Professional consultants in a variety of business-related areas.
- Labor in the form of students who are receiving training in your field.
- Additional education in the form of classes in management theory, business operations, advertising, etc.
- Seminars especially for small-business owners (often tied to the Small Business Administration).

GOVERNMENT AGENCIES

Agencies of government at the local, state, provincial and federal levels can provide you with an abundance of useful information at little or no cost.

Department Of Commerce

One government agency that specializes in businesses' concerns, the Department of Commerce, oversees the research and distribution of information of direct interest to the economic community. This data is collected and made available to the public in the form of publications and reports, including:

- Survey of Current Business, a monthly periodical that provides updates on changes in the nation's economy and the levels of business production and distribution.
- Census Bureau reports, covering such areas as population statistics (age, income, level of education, family status and other demographic data) and manufacturing, business and agriculture trends.

In addition to these reports, Commerce Department specialists can advise you on such specific areas as domestic and foreign market opportunities, contacting foreign representatives and deciphering tariff and trade regulations.

How To Locate

Department of Commerce publications are available at many public libraries or at the various department offices located throughout the United States. To find out the office that is closest to you, check your local phone directory under "United States Government" or write to the Department of Commerce in Washington, DC.

Economic Development Offices

Many communities maintain their own economic development offices. These differ from chambers of commerce in that they are maintained by local governments rather than local businesses. They can provide you with current statistical information regarding the economy, building activity, housing units, sales trends, population demographics, zoning, transportation, utilities, labor force, wages and salaries, community services, banks and savings and loan associations, traffic flows and important telephone numbers.

Federal Trade Commission

The Federal Trade Commission regulates trade practices to protect the public against unfair methods of competition. It is empowered to collect information pertaining to business conduct and activities, and distribute this to both the government and the public. The information that is available includes guidelines on what constitutes deceptive pricing, deceptive guaranties, bait advertising and other legal practices. For more information, write to the Federal Trade Commission, Washington, DC 20580.

Government Printing Office

The Government Printing Office oversees the publication and distribution of government documents, pamphlets, reports and books on a variety of subjects, many of which are directly related to business. These are for sale, usually at nominal prices, at local government printing office bookstores, which are generally located in federal buildings. If one isn't near you, or it doesn't stock a publication you want, write directly to the U.S. Government Printing Office, Superintendent of Documents, Washington, DC 20402. You will be sent a catalog of the publications available and any publications you request.

Internal Revenue Service

The Internal Revenue Service (IRS) can answer any questions you have concerning your federal income taxes. Tax specialists in local IRS offices can handle specific questions, or you can refer to any of the numerous IRS guides and publications. One particularly valuable guide is the *Tax Guide for Small Businesses*, which is updated annually. It contains approximately 200 pages of information covering such subjects as books and records, accounting periods, determining gross profit, deductible expenses, depreciation, tax credits and ways to report income. This is available free of charge at your local IRS office.

Small Business Administration

The Small Business Administration (SBA) is designed to aid small businesses in these ways:

- Helping to obtain financing.
- Providing management and technical assistance.
- Conducting business seminars and workshops.
- Assisting and procuring government contracts.

This is achieved through the operation of more than 100 district offices, the distribution of publications and the activities of the Service Corps of Retired Executives (SCORE) and the Active Corps of Executives (ACE), volunteer groups or professionals who assist the SBA in advising small businesses.

Financing by the SBA takes the form of direct and indirect loans to businesses. Loan proceeds can be used for working capital, for purchase of inventory, equipment and supplies, or for building construction or expansion. The SBA also makes loans to help small businesses comply with federal air and water pollution regulations and meet occupational health and safety standards. In addition, economic-opportunity loans are available to help persons who are socially or economically disadvantaged.

The SBA offers management and technical assistance in many forms. There are numerous titles to choose from in its list of business publications. SBA Form 115A lists publications that are for sale for a nominal fee. Contact your local SBA office for a list of these publications.

In-depth counseling is also provided by SBA management assistance staff, augmented by SCORE and ACE volunteers. Among the subject areas in which you can receive guidance are opening a business, marketing, advertising, profit goals, borrowing, accounting, bookkeeping, personnel, inventory controls, customer analysis, forecasting and insurance. Meetings with these business counselors can be arranged through your local SBA field office. There is no charge for their services.

To help small entrepreneurs protect their investments, the SBA offers a variety of seminars and workshops. Some topics covered in workshops or seminars include:

- Sales promotion and advertising.
- Basic business operations.
- Business planning.
- Women in business.
- Foreign trade.
- Retail store security.

The SBA's procurement assistance officers can guide you in the process of selling to the government and obtaining government contracts. They can help you to win subcontracting assignments, too. The SBA works closely with large government contractors to make sure that they use qualified small businesses as subcontractors on their projects.

Small Business Development Centers

Entrepreneurs seeking one-on-one business consulting services, technical assistance and training can find this and more at Small Business Development Centers (SBDCs) throughout the United States. Generally operated by colleges and universities, SBDCs draw on a combination of government, education and private sector resources to provide business owners with such services as:

- Individualized counseling.
- Assistance in planning.
- Workshops and seminars.
- On-site employee training.
- Information about government programs.
- Referrals and networking opportunities.
- Access to economic and business data, books, reports, pamphlets, software, video and cassette programs.

The goal of the SBDC is to stimulate the economy by helping small- and medium-sized businesses to function more effectively. Toward this end, SBDC counselors and outside experts in such areas as accounting, law, computers, marketing and finance work closely with entrepreneurs to achieve their goals. Serving the needs of both prospective and current entrepreneurs, SBDCs assist small businesses at all stages of their development.

To find out if there is an SBDC near you, check your Yellow Pages or contact your local college's business department for information.

INDEPENDENT CONTRACTORS

When selecting independent contractors and subcontractors:

- Ensure that they possess the necessary skills and talents to complete your project in a professional manner.
- Verify that they possess the necessary certification or licenses where required.
- Ask if they obtain necessary permits.
- Determine if they provide training, supervision and support for their personnel.
- Determine what insurance coverage do they carry. Are they bonded?
- Ask what their policies are regarding safety and security on the job site.
- Ask about policy regarding cleanliness of the job site, and concern for customer's residence or business.
- Can they provide you with referrals?

Be sure to review the IRS 20-point test for classifying employees.

GUIDELINES FOR SELECTING SUBCONTRACTORS

PROFESSIONAL

Do they possess the necessary skills and talents to complete this project in a professional and appealing manner to the customer's satisfaction?

Yes ☐   No ☐

Do they possess the necessary certification or licenses where required?

Yes ☐   No ☐

Do they provide training and support for their personnel?

Yes ☐   No ☐

What type of training and how often?

ADMINISTRATIVE PRACTICES

What types of insurance do they have in place?

Comprehensive general liability insurance   ☐

Workers' Compensation   ☐

Other _____   ☐

Are certificates of insurance available for the above policies and do they show the name of the broker, the insured and the beginning and ending dates of coverage?

Comprehensive general liability insurance   Yes ☐   No ☐

Worker's Compensation   Yes ☐   No ☐

Other _____   Yes ☐   No ☐

GUIDELINES FOR SELECTING SUBCONTRACTORS   Page 2

If bonds are required can they provide them?   Yes   ☐   No   ☐

    Bid Bond   Yes   ☐   No   ☐

    Performance Bond   Yes   ☐   No   ☐

    Payment Bond   Yes   ☐   No   ☐

    Lien Bond   Yes   ☐   No   ☐

BUSINESS PRACTICES

Do they obtain the necessary permits for their jobs?   Yes   ☐   No   ☐

Will their supervisory personnel be employed on the project?

                                          Yes   ☐   No   ☐

Do they use change orders, so that you will be informed of all changes or field modifications before they are made?

                                          Yes   ☐   No   ☐

What are their policies with respect to job safety, security and job cleanliness?

Job Safety

Job Site Security

Job Cleanliness

GUIDELINES FOR SELECTING SUBCONTRACTORS   Page 3

CLIENT EVALUATIONS

Are they able and willing to provide you with referrals from other contractors and customers?

Yes ☐   No ☐

Be sure and follow up on these referrals, as they may provide you with some valuable insights as to the quality of workmanship and the business relationship you are about to enter into.

Ask at least the following questions:

Was the customer generally satisfied with the quality of the workmanship? If their response is "no," what was the cause of their dissatisfaction?

Yes ☐   No ☐

Did they begin the project on time and was it completed without delay? (If the response is "no," look for an indication that they may have overextended themselves either with their scheduling or their financing.)

Yes ☐   No ☐

Would their client describe their business demeanor as one of being customer oriented, or did they find some specific problem in dealing with them? Was the problem addressed to them and did they handle it to the client's satisfaction?

Yes ☐   No ☐

Would they deal with them again or recommend them to others. If not, why not?

Yes ☐   No ☐

INDEPENDENT CONTRACTOR VS. EMPLOYEE
IRS 20 QUESTIONS

The U.S. Internal Revenue Service (IRS), in its Training Manuals 8463 and 3142-01, lists 20 factors used to determine whether an individual is an independent contractor or an employee. If you, as an employer, have any doubts, you would be wise to check with a certified public accountant.

1.   Is the individual providing services required to comply with instruction on when, where and how the work is done?
2.   Is the individual provided with training to enable him or her to perform the job in a particular manner?
3.   Are the services performed by the individual a part of the contractor's business operations?
4.   Must services be rendered personally?
5.   Does the contractor hire, supervise or pay assistants to help the individual performing under the contract?
6.   Is the relationship between the parties a continuing one?
7.   Who sets the hours of work?
8.   Is the individual required to devote full time to the party for whom the services are performed.
9.   Does the individual perform work on another's business premises?
10.   Who directs the sequence in which the work must be done?
11.   Are regular oral or written reports required?
12.   What is the method of payment—hourly, weekly, commission or by the job?
13.   Are business or traveling expenses reimbursed?
14.   Who furnishes the tools and materials necessary for the provision of services?
15.   Does the individual have significant investment in the tools or facilities used to perform his or her services?
16.   Can the individual providing services realize profit or loss?
17.   Can the individual providing services work for a number of firms at the same time?
18.   Does the individual make his or her services available to the general public?
19.   Can the individual be dismissed for reasons other than non-performance of contract specifications?
20.   Can the individual providing services terminate his or her relationship at any time without incurring a liability for failure to complete a job.

INSURANCE AGENTS

An insurance agent can analyze your business' specific needs and help you to obtain adequate coverage. Aspects of risk management that you should discuss with your agent include how to protect your assets, workers and earnings, and how to stay in compliance with the law. Since the welfare of your business is dependent on the safeguards you provide, finding a good insurance agent should be given a high priority.

How To Locate

The best ways to find an insurance agent are through personal recommendations (your accountant, attorney or banker may be able to suggest someone) and comparison shopping. Talking to different agents not only lets you evaluate the levels of coverage and compare the costs of different insurance plans, but gives you an idea of which agent is the most knowledgeable about your type of business. You can find the names of insurance agents and companies in the Yellow Pages.

LIBRARIES

Much of the information you need in order to operate your business can be obtained free of charge from libraries. The answers to many of your everyday business questions can be found not only in the books, but in the assortment of magazines, newspapers, reference works, government publications, maps, charts and audio visual aids that are available. Management and marketing approaches, technical explanations, statistical data, industry information, trends and economic forecasts are just some of the subject areas in which you can find information.

Other resources you will find at the library include:

- American Demograhics Magazine
- Lifestyle Market Analyst™ (SRDS)
- Sourcebook of Zip Code Demographics (CACI Marketing Systems)
- American Tally: Statistics for over 3,165 US Cities and Towns
- AMA Complete Guide to Small Business Marketing (Cook)
- Data Sources for Business and Market Analysis (Ganly)
- SRDS: Direct Marketing List Source
- Entrepreneur and Small Business Marketing Problem Solver (Cohen)

How To Locate

In addition to public libraries, there are also libraries sponsored by colleges and universities, private industry, trade and professional associations, labor unions and research centers. The most useful of these generally have separate business reference sections. To find the libraries in your area, check your local telephone directory.

MANAGEMENT AND MARKETING CONSULTANTS

Management and marketing consultants can detect weaknesses in your methods of operation or your marketing strategy and recommend corrective measures. They can also be of help before problems arise, providing advice on new product development, marketing research, business expansion, administration, employee motivation, human resource issues, cost control, security, etc.

Many businesses make a practice of calling in a management or marketing consultant whenever a major decision in these areas needs to be made. This enables the business owner to benefit not only from the consultant's knowledge and experience, but from something equally valuable: the consultant's objectivity. Unlike employees, consultants have nothing to gain or lose from the outcome of a decision. Furthermore, the variety of their contacts in the business community usually gives them a broader perspective.

The kitchen and bathroom industry is made up primarily of small business owners. This generally means that many may need consulting help, but they can neither afford it or would allow their egos to admit that they needed the assistance.

How To Locate

The best way to locate a management or marketing consultant is through recommendations, preferably from the consultant's satisfied clients. Otherwise, you can check the listings in one of the several directories of consultants available at public libraries or in the Yellow Pages. Another source would be trade associations or business newspapers such as *The Wall Street Journal*.

TEMPORARY HELP SERVICES

There are temporary-help service firms throughout the United States, providing experienced and well-qualified temporary help at a moment's notice. You may contract for a typist, receptionist, bookkeeper, salesperson, engineer, machinist, or other office professionals and industrial workers. Temporary-help service firms take care of all screening, interviewing and testing of applicants, as well as the checking of references. Using temporary help may save you money, and you won't have to be involved with personnel issues.

How To Locate

Temporary help service firms can be located through personal recommendations, local chambers of commerce or the Yellow Pages.

TRADE ASSOCIATIONS

Trade associations are organizations whose members are in the same business or industry (kitchen and bathroom, remodeling, interior design, etc.). The concerns and services of trade associations are directed at helping members improve their operating efficiency and cope with business problems. This help is in the form of:

- **Accounting Services** - providing accounting forms and manuals, ratio data, cost studies and consultations.

- **Advertising and Marketing Services** - providing advertising materials and forecasts of future demand levels and trends.

- **Publicity and Public Relations Activities** - providing members and the mass media with information about industry activities.

- **Educational Programs** - providing a variety of training courses and aids to assist business owners and employees in developing their skills.

- **Research Activities -** providing members and government with statistics about the industry, such as method of operation, product standards and certifying and grading.

- **Employee Relations Programs** - providing members with information about industry wages, work schedules and fringe benefits, as well as assisting in the negotiation of labor contracts.

- **Government Relations Programs** - providing members with a collective voice to use in communicating with the government and informing members of government of actions pertaining to their businesses.

In addition, trade associations are active in public service, consumerism, environmental safety and legislative issues. Of course, not all associations provide all of these services.

How To Locate

To obtain information on trade associations or find out which ones represent our industry, check the National Trade and Professional Associations of the United States and Canada, Columbia Books, Inc., Washington, DC, available at most public libraries.

Specific information about the National Kitchen & Bath Association is provided here.

National Kitchen & Bath Association
687 Willow Grove Street
Hackettstown, NJ 07840

908 852-0033
908 852-1695 Fax

E-mail - educate@nkba.org
Web site - www.nkba.org

THE NATIONAL KITCHEN & BATH ASSOCIATION

Fact Sheet

Description: The National Kitchen & Bath Association (NKBA®) is an international organization which serves and represents the firms and individuals involved in all aspects of the residential kitchen and bathroom industry. The Association was incorporated in 1963 as the American Institute of Kitchen Dealers, and, in 1982, changed its name to NKBA® to represent the entire industry.

**Mission
Statement:** The mission of the National Kitchen & Bath Association is to enhance member success and excellence, promote professionalism and ethical business practices, and to provide leadership and direction for the kitchen and bathroom industry.

Membership: NKBA® is comprised of the following member groups in the United States and Canada:

- Dealers
- Certified Kitchen Designers/Certified Bathroom Designers
- Multi-Branch Retailers
- Associates
- Distributors
- Manufacturers
- Manufacturer's Representatives
- Decorative Plumbing/Hardware
- Cabinet Shops
- Fabricators

Following is a list of member services available from NKBA® by membership category:

NATIONAL KITCHEN & BATH ASSOCIATION
MEMBER BENEFITS
Dealer, Multi-Branch Retailer, Decorative, Plumbing and Hardware

- Consumer marketing and advertising which promote the value of working with NKBA® members and provide member referrals to consumers.

- Fax-on-demand consumer leads that include hot prospects generated by NKBA® advertising and public relations.

- An official consumer magazine, sold on newsstands across the United States and Canada, that helps raise consumer awareness of NKBA® members and offers advertising discounts for manufacturers.

- Local chapter membership, without the expense of additional dues, providing networking, education and leadership opportunities.

- Timely, informative education programs designed to increase design and business knowledge and help you remain successful.

- Comprehensive business management tools, including forms, checklists and marketing materials, to help your business run smoothly.

- Design competitions that reward excellence and provide substantial trade and consumer exposure.

- Current design and business trend reports.

- Newsletters which bring you association news, business management information and news of pending legislative issues.

- Comprehensive industry conferences featuring timely seminar topics and events.

- K/BIS®, the kitchen and bathroom industry's largest trade show.

NATIONAL KITCHEN & BATH ASSOCIATION
MEMBER BENEFITS
Associate Member

- Public relations efforts that promote the value of working with NKBA® members.

- Fax-on-demand, Internet-based consumer leads that include hot prospects generated by NKBA® advertising and public relations.

- An official consumer magazine, sold on newsstands across the United States and Canada, that helps raise consumer awareness of NKBA® members.

- Local chapter membership, without the expense of additional dues, providing networking, education and leadership opportunities.

- Timely, informative education programs designed to increase design and business knowledge and help you remain successful.

- Comprehensive business management tools, including forms, checklists and marketing materials, to help your business run smoothly.

- Design competitions that reward excellence and provide substantial trade and consumer exposure.

- Newsletters which bring you association news, business management information and news of pending legislative issues.

- Comprehensive industry conferences featuring timely seminar topics and events.

- K/BIS® the kitchen and bathroom industry's largest trade show.

- Design and product trends research that lends insight into the consumer market.

NATIONAL KITCHEN & BATH ASSOCIATION
MEMBER BENEFITS
Distributor, Fabricator, Manufacturer
And Manufacturer Representatives

- Consumer marketing and advertising programs that raise consumer awareness and provide a database of remodeling consumers for research and marketing programs.

- Fax-on-demand consumer leads that include hot prospects generated by NKBA® advertising and public relations.

- An official consumer magazine, sold on newsstands across the United States and Canada, that helps raise consumer awareness of NKBA® members and offers advertising discounts for manufacturers.

- Local chapter membership, without the expense of additional dues, providing networking, education and leadership opportunities.

- Design competitions that reward excellence and provide substantial trade and consumer exposure.

- Newsletters which bring you association news, business management information and news of pending legislative issues.

- Comprehensive industry conferences featuring timely seminar topics and events.

- K/BIS®, the kitchen and bathroom industry's largest trade show.

- Design and product trends research that lends insight into the consumer market.

- Business research results that will provide management, sales and operations with information about the dealer market and the kitchen and bathroom industry.

NATIONAL KITCHEN & BATH ASSOCIATION
MEMBER BENEFITS
Subscriber

- Public relations efforts that promote the value of working with NKBA® members.

- Fax-on-demand consumer leads that include hot prospects generated by NKBA® advertising and public relations.

- An official consumer magazine, sold on newsstands across the United States and Canada, that helps raise consumer awareness of NKBA® members.

- Local chapter membership, without the expense of additional dues, providing networking, education and leadership opportunities.

- Timely, informative education programs designed to increase design and business knowledge and help you remain successful.

- Comprehensive business management tools, including forms, checklists and marketing materials, to help your business run smoothly.

- Newsletters which bring you association news, business management information and news of pending legislative issues.

- Comprehensive industry conferences featuring timely seminar topics and events.

- K/BIS®, the kitchen and bathroom industry's largest trade show.

- Design and product trends research that lends insight into the consumer market.

PUBLICATIONS

Internal Revenue Tax Publications

The following publications can provide you with additional information about business taxation. These publications should be available at your local IRS office; if not, you can obtain them by writing to the Internal Revenue Service, Washington, DC 20224.

TITLE	No.
Your Rights as a Taxpayer	1
Employer's Tax Guide (Circular E)	15
Your Federal Income Tax	17
Tax Guide for Small Business	334
Fuel Tax Credits and Refunds	378
Travel, Entertainment and Gift Expenses	463
Tax Withholding and Estimated Tax	505
Excise Tax	510
Moving Expenses	521
Tax Information on Selling Your Home	523
Residential Rental Property	527
Miscellaneous Deductions	529
Residential Rental Property	527
Tax Information for Homeowners	530
Self Employment Tax	533
Depreciation	534
Business Expenses	535
Net Operating Losses	536
Accounting Periods and Methods	538
Tax Information on Partnerships	541
Tax Information on Corporations	542
Sales and Other Dispositions of Assets	544
Non-Business Disasters, Casualties and Thefts	547
Investment Income and Expenses	550
Basis of Assets	551
Record Keeping for Individuals	552
Federal Tax Information on Community Property	555
Examinations of Returns, Appeal Rights and Claims for Refunds	556
Retirement Plans for the Self-Employed	560
Taxpayers Starting a Business	583
The Collection Process (Income Tax Accounts)	586A
Business Use of Your Home	587
Tax Information on S Corporations	589
Individual Retirement Arrangements (IRAs)	590
The Collection Process (Employment Tax Accounts)	594
Guide to Free Tax Services	910
Tax Information for Direct Selling	911
Business Use of a Car	917
Employment Taxes for Household Employers	926
Business Reporting	937
How to Begin Depreciating Your Property	946
Filing Requirements for Employee Benefit Plans	1048
Per Diem Rates	1542

Small Business Administration Publications

The following publications can provide you with additional information about small business operations. To purchase these nominally priced publications, write to the Small Business Administration, Washington, DC 20417, to obtain an order form.

TITLE	No.
Products/Ideas/Inventions	
Ideas into Dollars	P11
Avoiding Patent, Trademark and Copyright Problems	P12
Trademarks and Business Goodwill	P13
Financial Management	
ABCs of Borrowing	Fm 1
Basic Budgets for Profit Planning	Fm 3
Understanding Cash Flow ·	Fm 4
A Venture Capital Primer for Small Business	Fm 5
Accounting Services for Small Service Firms	Fm 6
Analyze Your Records to Reduce Costs	Fm 7
Budgeting in a Small Service Firm	Fm 8
Sound Cash Management and Borrowing	Fm 9
Record Keeping in a Small Business	Fm 10
Simple Break-Even Analysis for Small Stores	Fm 11
A Pricing Checklist for Small Retailers	Fm 12
Pricing your Products and Services Profitably	Fm 13
Management and Planning	
Effective Business Communications	MP 1
Locating or Relocating your Business	MP 2
Problems in Managing a Family-owned Business	MP 3
Business Plan for Small Manufacturers	MP 4
Business Plan for Small Construction Firms	MP 5
Planning and Goal Setting for Small Business	MP 6
Should You Lease or Buy Equipment	MP 8
Business Plan for Retailers	MP 9
Choosing a Retail Location	MP 10
Business Plan for Small Service Firms	MP 11
Checklist for Going into Business	MP 12
How to Get Started with a Small Business Computer	MP 14
The Business Plan for Home-Based Business	MP 15
How to Buy or Sell a Business	MP 16
Buying for Retail Stores	MP 18
Small Business Decision Making	MP 19
Business Continuation Planning	MP 20
Developing a Strategic Business Plan	MP 21
Inventory Management	MP 22
Techniques for Problem Solving	MP 23
Techniques for Productivity Improvement	MP 24
Selecting the Legal Structure for Your Business	MP 25
Small Business Risk Management Guide	MP 28
Marketing	
Creative Selling: The Competitive Edge	MT 1

TITLE	No.
Marketing for Small Business: An Overview	MT 2
Marketing Checklist for Small Retailers	MT 4
Researching Your Market	MT 8
Advertising	MT 11
Crime Prevention	
Curtailing Crime - Inside and Out	CP 2
A Small Business Guide to Computer Security	CP 3
Personnel Management	
Checklist for Developing a Training Program	PM 1
Employees: How to Find and Pay Them	PM 2
Managing Employee Benefits	PM 3

How can you keep the sparks flying?

Chapter 10

ALL FIRED UP!
Management and Motivation

Don't agonize. Organize. - Florynce R. Kennedy

The key to entrepreneurial success is getting others to commit to your vision and to work at making it a reality. Few successful businesses are the result of one person's solo efforts. It is not enough for an entrepreneur to be good at producing a product or performing a service. If your business is to grow and prosper, you must be a leader.

In addition to finding the most qualified people to work in your business, you need to come up with effective ways to manage and motivate them. Technical skills alone won't do it. Your technical skills can get your business started, but it's your human relations skills that will keep it going.

How you are perceived by your employees will make a difference in your ability to manage. Set high standards for yourself. Demonstrate a strong work ethic. Be fair. Keep your word. Encourage others. Don't be pompous. Everyone knows you're good at what you do or you wouldn't be the manager. You don't have to tell them. As Robert Fulghum says, "All I needed to know, I learned in kindergarten."

DEVELOPING YOUR OWN MANAGEMENT STYLE

No one management style is best for everyone. It is a matter of finding a style that you feel comfortable with and that works well in your situation. In the broadest sense, there are as

many ways to manage as there are managers. When focusing on the most commonly used management styles, though, three become clear: **autocratic**, **democratic**, and **free-rein**.

Autocratic Management

Business owners who use an autocratic management style keep most of the authority to themselves, making decisions without consulting others. More inclined to give orders than to ask for advice, they generally adopt a take-charge approach to management. When the situation calls for a fast, decisive action, they are ready to move.

The autocratic management style works best in fast-paced, volatile industries where there isn't time to confer with others and in situations where employees are lacking in experience or motivation. The drawback to this style is that it can generate resentment and frustration among workers who feel that their input is being ignored. Furthermore, by making all the decisions alone, entrepreneurs can end up limiting their business' growth potential by failing to develop the employee-management talent needed to run a larger operation.

Democratic Management

As the name implies, a democratic management style gives employees a much greater say in decision making. Rather than making unilateral decisions and expecting employees to carry them out, the entrepreneur encourages employees to get involved in the process. Business owners who take a participative approach to managing delegate authority whenever possible, but retain the final right to approval.

The democratic management style works best with employees who have strong job skills and require only minimum supervision. Among its advantages are the feelings of belonging, pride and commitment that it can instill in workers and its ability to tap employees' ideas and ingenuity for the good of the business. The main disadvantages of this management style are the time it takes to get employees' input and the weakening or "watering down" of decisions that can occur in reaching a consensus.

Free-Rein Management

A free-rein management style, also called *laissez-faire* style, from the French expression, "leave it alone," gives employees the most authority of all. Business owners who use this style hire the best workers they can find and let them make the majority of the decisions concerning their job functions and responsibilities. Utilizing a hands-off approach to managing, the entrepreneur sets goals and objectives for the business, but leaves the employees relatively free to perform their duties as they see fit.

The free-rein management style works best with professionals, such as engineers, scientists, writers and others who are expected to function independently. It is often used with outside salespeople who operate in the field and must determine the best ways to manage their time and serve customers' needs. The main weakness of this style is that, by letting employees set their own agendas, workers can end up pursuing their own interests rather than the ones most beneficial to the business.

To find the right management style for you, you should look at three factors:

- **Look at Yourself** - Being a good manager is not just knowing what makes people tick, but what makes *you* tick. The more you know about yourself, your management abilities and temperament, the better you will be able to capitalize on your strengths and compensate for your weaknesses. How willing are you to share authority with others? Have you ever managed people before? How many? For how long? In what capacity? What's your approach to problem solving? Are you more comfortable working alone or as part of a team?

- **Look at Your Employees** - Just as managers are different, so are the people they manage.   Part of choosing a management style involves matching it to the work force. Are your employees more likely to:

  a. Show initiative, work independently without supervision, accept responsibility, be creative problem solvers, take pride in doing their jobs well?

  b. Or, avoid work when they can, goof off, wait for someone to tell them what to do, cut corners when no one is looking?

  In the first instance, less supervision is needed; a management style that gives employees more say in decision making should work well. In the second instance, though, a more authoritarian management style is called for that provides closer supervision and tighter controls.

  Consider implementing a supervisor's procedures manual which would include specific instruction for each process, e.g., hiring, termination, sick leave, raises, vacation, etc. That way you and your supervisors will be working with the same information.

- **Look at the Work Environment** - The nature of the work being done also plays a big part in determining which management style is most effective. Are your employees performing creative, varied tasks that change from day to day or from one project to the next? Or are they performing repetitive tasks that basically remain the same? Workers that perform varied tasks generally respond best to a management style that offers a high degree of freedom to carry out their respective tasks in the manner they think best. Workers that perform repetitive tasks usually need a management style that is more direction-oriented, clearly stating what needs to be accomplished and when. This is not to say that their input is not equally valuable or should not be sought out. It should be, but in a more structured way, possibly through **quality circles**—meetings where workers discuss ways to increase productivity and job satisfaction.

Once you have taken these factors into consideration, you should be able to arrive at the management style that provides the best fit for your specific business. If you don't hit on it immediately, though, don't get upset or discouraged. Developing a management style takes time, and, once you have found a method that works for you, you have to keep fine tuning it. As people and circumstances change, so does the need for one management style or another.

To be effective, you need to be in control of your operation. If paperwork is overwhelming, assess how you and your staff are working. Are people handling paper too often? Can you streamline the process? Is everyone using the same method for taking phone messages? Are papers and reports being filed?

As the manager, you need your own daily, weekly and monthly checklists to monitor and assess the health of your business. Check your financial status, including sales, cash flow, accounts receivable, direct expenses, net profit, ratio of gross profit to net sales. Determine your inventory levels on a regular basis.

Are you using computers to track finances and inventory, produce correspondence, keep mailing lists?

Review your organization chart. Is work flowing smoothly? What possibilities exist to improve your operation?

Look at your physical plant. Are repairs or improvements needed? What can you afford? Do you have a short- and long-range plan for projects? Is your facility safe?

Are you satisfied with the product and/or service you are offering? Are changes warranted?

Look over every aspect of your business on a set schedule and you will be in control of your operation.

KNOWING WHEN TO DELEGATE

Unlike corporate managers who are used to getting things done through people, entrepreneurs often want to do everything themselves. Whichever management style you choose, you must become proficient at delegating authority. Whether you delegate the minimum amount possible (autocratic management) or the maximum amount (free-rein management), there will be times when you have to let someone else make the decision. It is not a question of whether to delegate, but when. One person simply cannot do it all.

To make the delegation process go smoothly and get positive results, try following these suggestions:

1. *Go low* - One of the first rules of management is to delegate authority to the lowest *competent* level in an organization. How low can you go? To the person who has the knowledge, skills and willingness needed to carry out the job. A clerk may be competent enough to order office supplies, but you wouldn't expect that person to choose a new site for your business. Pushing decisions down to the lowest competent level possibly frees you and high-level workers to focus your attention on more important matters.

2. *Give enough authority* - The most common mistake in delegating is not giving workers enough authority to carry out their duties and responsibilities. Expecting salespeople to satisfy customers, but not giving them the authority to make exchanges or refunds, is an example.

3. *State what's expected* - Let employees know the scope of the work involved and what you want them to accomplish, such as buying merchandise, negotiating a contract, training a new employee.

4. *Be supportive* - Make it clear to employees they can come to you for help if they need it. Just knowing that you are available to offer advice or information should help to relieve some of the job anxiety the employee may have.

5. *Keep communication channels open* - The easier it is for employees to communicate with each other and with you, the easier it will be for them to carry out their assignments. Making the information the workers need to have readily accessible not only speeds things up, but helps to keep mistakes from happening.

6. *Establish controls* - Although the act of delegating involves giving up control, it also calls for you to establish controls. Controls, in this sense, are guidelines or limits within which the work must be performed. For example, telling a supervisor to increase the productivity in his or her department does not go far enough. How much should it be increased? Within what time frame?

7. *Create opportunities to succeed* - Rather than setting employees up for failure, set them up for success. By picking the right person for a job and providing the resources (people, time, money, information) needed to succeed, you can develop strong, confident managers capable of making your business thrive.

FINDING WAYS TO MOTIVATE

One of the biggest challenges a business owner can face is finding ways to motivate employees. It should be simple if all employees wanted the same thing from a job and were driven by the same needs. But they aren't. People are different, and what motivates one person may not motivate another. An employee may be struggling with personal or health problems, or might be experiencing some discontent at work. If you are alert to your employees, you will notice changes. You may be able to rectify or improve the situation or at least reduce the stress level. Your concern and effort to find a solution will in itself be a motivator.

Identifying Needs

Just as important as the ability to identify your customers' needs is the ability to identify your employees' needs. What is important to them? What needs do they expect to be fulfilled by working for you? The need for money? Achievement? Recognition? Power? Creativity? Interaction with others? Security? Personal satisfaction?

One of the mistakes business owners make is thinking that money is the only motivator. Their common refrain is, "I pay a fair wage. I expect a fair day's work." Then when they don't get it, they wonder why employees are so lazy or don't care about doing a good job anymore.

The thing to realize is that money is just one of many motivators. In some situations, it may not even be a motivator. For example, a construction worker who has just put in two months of 60-hour work weeks may be less than thrilled by the prospect of earning additional overtime pay. Instead of being a motivator, the overtime is actually a de-motivator. What the worker really wants is some time off to spend with family and friends.

You can use a number of incentives to increase workers' productivity, such as:

- Interesting work
- Opportunities for advancement
- Competitive salaries
- Bonuses
- Ownership in the business
- Job training
- Recognition
- Responsibility

- New challenges
- Fair treatment
- Good fringe benefits
- Positive work environment
- Flexible hours
- Job security
- Praise
- Respect

The trick, of course, is knowing which incentives to use. Through careful observation and by taking the time to know your employees, you should be able to determine which incentives will work best with which people. For instance, an employee who is in debt or barely making ends meet is obviously going to be more motivated by financial incentives than by opportunity to make friends on the job. The very opposite could be true, though, for someone who is new in the area or who worked in a business where the employees did not get along. A person with low self esteem is likely to respond to praise. A high achiever, who is already doing well, might do even better if given additional responsibilities or a stake in the business.

To be effective, the incentives you offer must meet both the needs of the individual employees and of your business. There aren't very many small businesses that can match the salaries and benefit packages offered by major corporations. But they can often have other incentives employees want even more: the chance to be part of a growing business, greater responsibility, enthusiastic co-workers, opportunities for creativity and recognition, or a piece of the pie (through partnerships, stock options, etc.). Rather than just being another cog in the wheel following long-set policies and procedures, they can have a real impact on your business, if you'll let them.

To make sure that the incentives you use have the desired effect of motivating workers, rather than de-motivating them, keep in mind that:

- The incentive must be something that the employee wants. In other words, it must meet some unfulfilled need.

- The incentive must be seen as something positive. If you give an employee additional responsibilities, will that be viewed as a reward for a good job performance or as a ploy to get more work done?

- The incentive must be known. Employees must be aware of the incentive before it can motivate them. Praising an employee's work to a business associate, but not to the employee, for example, will not provide an incentive.

- The incentive must be fair. Showing favoritism and rewarding some workers for their accomplishments, but not others, demoralizes employees and divides the work force.

- The incentive must be attainable. Setting a sales quota needed to qualify for a bonus beyond employees' reach will have a reverse effect, causing them to cut back, rather than increase, their sales efforts.

- The incentive must change as workers' needs change. Once a need is fulfilled, it no longer is a motivator. An employee whose primary motivation was money is likely to want other things, such as recognition, personal satisfaction, once the need for financial security has been met.

Sharing Your Vision

The best way to motivate your employees is by sharing your vision for the business with them and showing how your success relates to their success. You need to make employees feel that they have a vested interest in the business, that it is theirs, too, and that the work they do is important.

To share your vision, you must be able to put it into words and communicate it to others. Every employee should know what your business stands for, what it hopes to accomplish, and the rewards to be earned by contributing to its success. Only when employees see that the business' future is interlocked with their own will they be willing to fully commit to your vision and do the things necessary to enable you to achieve it.

Richard Baynton, a well-known and very successful distributor in the kitchen and bathroom industry, has developed a 14-point guide for managing a business today. Every business owner and manager would do well to employ them. They are listed for you here:

1. Develop a vision of what you want your company to be and where you want it to go.
2. Create and publicize your company mission statement.
3. Produce a business plan annually for 1 to 3 years.
4. Focus on the bottom line—not the top line; growth is the reward for profitable planning.
5. Forge partnerships with employees, customers and suppliers.
6. Communicate plans and ideas to all partners.
7. Hire and keep outstanding people.
8. Increase productivity and quality with relentless training.

9.   Empower employee partners; they will help achieve lofty goals.
10. Exercise leadership; people respect and often emulate great leaders.
11. Evaluate all activities; get and use feedback.
12. Seek, develop and manage niches carefully.
13. Sell quality and value; they are permanent. Price is temporary.
14. Produce more than you promise.

To evaluate your leadership skills and determine if you are effectively managing and motivating your employees, answer the questions in the following leadership checklist:

LEADERSHIP CHECKLIST		
	Yes	No
1. What are strengths and weaknesses of the three most common management styles?		
Autocratic?		
Democratic?		
Free-Rein?		
2. In evaluating each style, have you considered the major factors affecting your business?		
Your own abilities/preferences?		
Your employees?		
The work environment?		
3. Have you chosen the management style that is best for you?		
4. Do you know what responsibilities and authority you are willing to delegate?		
5. Are you familiar with how the delegation process works?		
6. Have you identified the various needs of your employees?		
7. Have you determined the types of incentives that you want to use?		
8. Do you know which incentives will be the most effective at motivating which workers?		
9. How can you keep incentives from having a reverse effect and becoming de-motivators?		
10. Can you put your vision for your business into words?		
11. Are you ready to share your vision with others?		
12. Will helping you achieve your goals enable employees to achieve their own goals?		

For more information on management styles, motivation and operating your business using total quality management principles, read NKBA®'s book Bringing Total Quality Management To Your Kitchen and Bathroom Business by David Newton.

And, remember the quote by Robert Johnson:

Success is not spontaneous combustion.
You have to set yourself on fire.

AFTERWORD

Throughout this book, we have been learning how to start, build and grow a fire. Most of us have forgotten how much knowledge and energy it takes to build a roaring bonfire. But, honestly, once that fire really got going, wasn't it great?

Starting, building and growing our business sure has been a thrill. After my family, friends, and good health, managing my business has been the highlight of my life.

I started working on this book more than two years ago, and have put many hours into it. I've had the pleasure of sharing with you—fellow kitchen and bathroom industry peers—ways to run a successful business. My hope is that you will use this information, incorporate it into your management style and make your business just a little better. As more and more of us improve, get smarter, manage better and service better, we will upgrade an already wonderful industry. We're "moms and pops" trying our best, but, in many cases, it hasn't been good enough. We need more successful businesses burning brightly.

Possibly the hardest part of running my own business has been learning to balance family, friends, industry, community, church and business. The next hardest thing was motivation. I'm basically a very "up" person, filled with enthusiasm and self-confidence. I love people, I love getting up in the morning and I love life. But there were several times during the past 15 years that I was plumb worn out. My fire was almost out. But, I was able to reach deep down in myself, turn the fire over and come back more determined and energetic. I hope that the information in this book will inspire, motivate and excite you, and that you can use it as fuel for your own fire.

Take some of this new kindling and help your employees light their fires. You know how it feels when that spark catches! Your responsibility is to take part of your flame and pass it to your co-workers and encourage them to do the same.

You can be successful, very successful and make a great deal of money because you have a broader vision and have laid a good foundation.

Hank Darlington

You never get a second chance to make a first impression. - Anonymous

Bibliography

BOOKS

HOW TO BE A BETTER MANAGER, Hank Darlington, Kitchen and Bath Business, New York, NY, 1997.

MODEL BUSINESS PLANS FOR PRODUCT BUSINESSES, William A. Cohen. John Wiley & Sons, Inc., New York, NY, 1995.

THE ENTREPRENEUR MAGAZINE - SMALL BUSINESS ADVISOR, John Wiley & Sons, Inc., New York, NY, 1995.

THE ENTREPRENEUR'S GUIDE TO BUILDING A BETTER BUSINESS PLAN: A STEP-BY-STEP APPROACH, Harold J. McLaughlin. John Wiley & Sons, Inc., New York, NY.

THE HUMAN RESOURCE PROBLEM-SOLVERS HANDBOOK, Joseph P. Levesque. McGraw/Hill, Inc., New York, NY, 1992.

THE PORTABLE MBA IN ENTREPRENEURSHIP, William D. Bygrave. John Wiley & Sons, Inc., New York, NY, 1997

THE SMALL BUSINESS HANDBOOK, Irving Burstiner, Simon & Schuster, Inc., New York, NY, 1989, 1994.

THE VEST POCKET ENTREPRENEUR, David E. Rye. Prentice Hall, NJ, 1995.

PUBLICATIONS

SMALL BUSINESS ASSOCIATION
- List of Publications (See Chapter 9 under *Publications*.)

INTERNAL REVENUE SERVICE
- *Independent Contractor vs. Employee 20 Questions* (See Chapter 9 under *Independent Contractors*.)
- List of Publications (See Chapter 9 under *Publications*.)

NKBA® PUBLICATIONS

BRINGING TOTAL QUALITY MANAGEMENT TO YOUR KITCHEN AND BATHROOM BUSINESS, David Newton. NKBA®, Hackettstown, NJ, 1996.

INCREASE YOUR KITCHEN & BATH BUSINESS BY 25%...Starting Next Week!, Bob Popyk. NKBA®, Hackettstown, NJ, 1996.

LEVERAGING DESIGN: Finance And The Kitchen And Bathroom Specialist, Debi Bach. NKBA®, Hackettstown, NJ, 1996.

NKBA® PERFORMANCE ANALYSIS REVIEW (PAR) STUDY, NKBA®, Hackettstown, NJ, 1996.

PROVEN PROMOTIONS, Jim and Lori Jo M. Krengel. NKBA®, Hackettstown, NJ, 1997.

MANAGING YOUR KITCHEN AND BATHROOM FIRM'S FINANCES FOR PROFIT, Don Quigley. NKBA®, Hackettstown, NJ, 1997.

THE GREAT CASH HUNT, Stephen P. Vlachos and Leslie L. Vlachos. NKBA®, Hackettstown, NJ, 1997.

Glossary

accounting period: Period of time covered by a financial statement, usually a year, although interim reports are sometimes prepared.

accounts payable: Money you owe your suppliers and other creditors for purchases you have made and charged to your account.

accounts receivable: Revenues from sales which you have agreed to accept on a delayed payment schedule.

allied professional: A professional in an industry that complements your business, i.e., a retail kitchen and bathroom dealer might want to establish a mutual relationship with a flooring retailer or a paint and wallpaper retailer

assets: Any type of property possessed by the business which may be of some future financial benefit. This could be tangible property (buildings, land, equipment) and non-tangible property (patents, copyrights, formulas, designs) valued on your balance sheet.

balance sheet: A financial report designed to accurately represent the ownership and debt of the business.

bond: 1. A financial commitment that certain work will be completed if the contractor defaults. It protects third parties only; contractor remains responsible to bonding company. 2. A written promise to repay money furnished the business, with interest at some future date, usually more than one year hence.

bookkeeper: One who records the accounts or transactions of a business.

books of original entry: Journals which are chronological records of your business transactions. Each entry contains the date on which the transaction occurred, the specific accounts to be debited and credited and the amount of debit and credit.

books of secondary entry: Ledgers where information of the same kind is separated from the other journal data and entered into its respective account.

browser: Software used to view or navigate linked pages on the Internet.

build out: Capital investment made to a business property to ready it for occupancy. Otherwise known as leasehold improvement which will appear on an annual balance sheet.

business plan: Detailed strategy designed to communicate to you, your investors, employees and others, your mission and plans to execute these strategies.

capital: The long-term financing of a business. Its components are debt, equity (capital stock and retained earnings) and deferred taxes.

capital stock: A balance sheet account showing the amount that the shareholder contributed in exchange for stock. This, plus retained earnings, equals owners' equity in a corporation.

cash flow: Measurement of cash generated by a business.

certified public accountant (CPA): An individual recognized for educational and professional achievement and licensed the state in which he or she practices.

chart of accounts: A structure of the various accounts your business uses to account for all its financial transactions.

checklist: An affordable, convenient organizational tool which can be used to make better use of time and resources.

collateral: Security for a loan. A physical asset that has some unencumbered equity remaining.

commission: Compensation for salespeople paid as a percentage of gross sales.

controls: A built-in system of checks and balances, such as checklists and standard operating procedures, that you can employ in your business to avoid problems.

copyright: A copyright protects the right of an individual to keep others from copying his or her creations. Although most commonly associated with literary works, copyright protection extends to your kitchen and bathroom designs, graphic designs, paintings, sculpture, musical compositions, sound recordings and audio/visual works. All you need to do is to provide public notice of the copyright of the work itself and file an application form. The fee is currently $20, and, once granted, the copyright is for up to 50 years after the holder's death.

cost of goods sold: Represents the total amount spent by the business to purchase the product sold during the accounting period.

cost of sales: Same as cost of goods sold, except it also applies to the cost of services sold.

cost per thousand (CPM): Amount spent in advertising to reach each 1,000 "viewers" of your advertisement.

creditor: Person who lends money or extends credit to a business.

current assets: Those assets which can typically be converted to cash within the next 12 months. They may be cash, securities, accounts receivables, inventory or checking account.

current liabilities: Obligations that become due within a short period of time, usually one year.

current ratio: This ratio compares current assets to current liabilities, and is used to assess your business' ability to meet its financial obligations within the coming year. This best known and most widely used of the ratios is computed by dividing current assets and current liabilities

dividend: The portion of profit distributed to shareholders.

double-entry accounting: An accounting method where for every transaction that is recorded, two entries are required. This is because any change in one account automatically results in a change in another account. For instance, if a customer purchases merchandise from you and pays cash for it, the balance in your cash account increases and at the same time your merchandise inventory decreases. Both changes must be recorded. The means for doing this is by way of debit and credit entries.

earnings: Net income.

economic order quantity: The number of units you must order to achieve the lowest total cost.

e-mail: Electronic mail.

employee: An individual compensated to work where, when and how he or she is directed to by a supervisor, owner or manager according to the IRS guidelines.

employer identification number: The federal government requires you to have an employer identification number, if you employ one or more persons in your business. This enables the government to verify that you are paying all appropriate employer taxes and withholding the proper amounts from employee paychecks. There is no fee for it, just fill out the IRS Form #FS-4 and submit it to the IRS.

estimate: Frequently confused with a quote, an estimate is a price for your customer, generally based upon available information with respect to how much you intend to complete on a project and how long you calculate it will take.

expense: Costs incurred as a result of operating a business. These can be divided into two categories: *selling expenses* (expenses such as sales, commissions and advertising, that are directly related to the business' sales activities), and *general and administrative expenses* (expenses incurred through activities other than selling, such as clerical salaries, rent and insurance).

fictitious business name statement: If you are planning to operate your business under a name other than your own, such as ABC Kitchens, then you will probably need to file a Fictitious Name Statement with the county clerk's office. The purpose of this statement is to inform the public of your identity and the identities of any others who are co-owners in the business.

financial reports: Reports prepared for and used by management and others to evaluate the company's financial performance. Most commonly these refer to the balance sheet, the statement of income and expenses and the statement of cash flow.

fiscal year: An accounting period of 12 months.

fixed assets: Property, plant and equipment that usually have a service life over a year, with the exception of land. Usually can be depreciated.

gross margin: Represents the difference between the net sales and the cost of goods sold. Though it is also frequently referred to as *gross profit*, it is not a true profit since overhead has not been deducted yet.

gross profit: See *gross margin*.

home page: The first document or the entry to a web site.

hyperlink: Connections between one piece of information and another.

income and expense statement: A financial report designed to determine whether or not the business' income exceeded its expenses or vice versa during a given period of time.

independent contractor: A self-employed person offering services to other companies. To be classified as an independent contractor, an individual must be truly independent from the companies for which the person does work.

intangible asset: Consists of items that are usually non-physical assets. Included in this category are trademarks, patents, copyrights and goodwill.

interest: The amount paid for the use of money. A loan requires payment of both interest and principal.

Internet: The Internet is a network of computers linked together, not unlike the network that links our telephones together. It provides a collection of services, including electronic mail, world wide web and file transfers.

inventory: Materials, parts and products sold by the business and maintained on hand, such as cabinets, countertops, hardware and laminates.

inventory turnover: A ratio that shows how many times inventory was totally replaced during the year, calculated by dividing the average inventory into cost of sales.

journal: A record in which transactions are recorded in chronological order.

layout: The physical setup of furniture and fixtures, equipment, merchandise and supplies within your building.

lease: An agreement under which the owner of property permits someone else to use it. Often thought of as long-term rental. The owner is the lessor; The user is the lessee.

ledger: A group of accounts. Entries are posted to the ledger from the journal.

leverage ratio: Used to measure firm's indebtedness.

liability: A creditor's claim against the assets of a business, i.e., accounts payable, accrued expenses.

liquidity ratio: Measures your business' ability to pay its bills and convert assets into cash.

line of credit: Prior arrangement for funds as needed, with a cap, through your bank or commercial lender.

marketing: An educational opportunity to get your customer to interact with you so as to correctly identify your market's trends and then to develop a strategy to meet those demands.

markup: The calculation of the correct amount of charges required to produce a selling price that will cover the seller's cots, overhead and provide and the seller with a margin of profit.

mentor: Tutor, coach, trusted counselor or guide.

net income: Also known as the bottom line, this figure is a measure of your ability to create wealth. It is arrived at only after you have subtracted all costs, expenses and taxes associated with the operation of your business. This is the net profit amount reflected on your income and expense statement.

net loss: Figure left when total expenses exceed the gross margin.

net profit on sales: *Profit Margin or Net Profit on Sales* compares net profit to net sales. Used to assess the ability of your business to turn a profit on the sales it makes, it is computed by dividing net profit by net sales.

net sales: Represents the total sales during the accounting period, less sales tax and deductions for sales discounts, returns or allowances.

owner's equity: The difference between the assets of a business and its liabilities equals its capital or owner's equity. Also known as partner's equity or stockholder's equity, this is direct (investments) or indirect (retained earnings) accounting of the owner's claims against the assets of the business, and appears on your balance sheet.

ownership ratio: This measures the levels of ownership in the business, comparing the claims of owners to those of creditors.

partnership: An unincorporated business with two or more owners.

patent: In granting a patent to a business, the federal government gives it the right to exclude all others from making, using or selling the invention in the United States. Patents for new and useful products or purposes are valid for 17 years. A design patent, covering only the style or appearance of a product, may be valid for a period ranging from 3½ to 14 years. If you develop a product, process or design that you believe has commercial possibilities, obtaining a patent may be advisable, given the protection it affords.

press release: A press release is simply a fact sheet. Explaining who, what, where, when and how, it states the details of the story you want the press to tell.

profit: Residual value or surplus from a sale or investment transaction that remains after satisfying any claims for goods and/or services rendered, relative to that transaction, and after deducting the seller's expenses.

profit margin: Profit Margin or Net Profit on Sales compares net profit to net sales. Used to assess the ability of your business to turn a profit on the sales it makes, it is computed by dividing net profit by net sales:

profitability ratio: Shows where the profits are being generated and where the investor's money is being used to create wealth.

quick ratio: This ratio compares cash and accounts receivable to current liabilities, and is used to assess the ability of your business to meet its current financial obligations in the event that sales decline and merchandise inventory cannot readily be converted to cash. Also called the *acid test* because it measures only ready assets, it is computed by dividing cash and accounts receivable by current liabilities:

quote: Also known as a proposal or bid, this is a written document which lays out the scope of the work, the specifications and related documentation such as drawings.

ratios: Relationships between financial calculations which allow for meaningful interpretations of management's abilities, including profit ratios, leverage ratios and turnover ratios.

retained earnings: A portion of the net income used to satisfy some of the outstanding debt of the corporation, or to be invested in other capital expenditures, in either case increasing the value of the stockholder's existing investment.

return on investment (ROI): Compares net profit to total assets. Used to assess the ability of your business to turn a profit on the assets it holds, it is computed by dividing net profit by total assets:

s corporation: If you are interested in forming a corporation, but hesitant because of the double taxation, you can make your business an s corporation. The Internal Revenue Service (IRS) permits this type of corporation to be taxed as a partnership rather than as a corporation. However, to qualify for "s" status, your business must meet the specific requirements set forth by the IRS. These include limits on the number and type of shareholders in the business, the stock that is issued and the corporation's sources of revenues.

Sales Performance Improvement Fund (SPIF): Incentive paid to help increase the sales of a particular product or service.

seller's permit: This permit exempts you from paying sales tax on the merchandise you purchase for resale through your business, and authorizes you to collect sales tax from your customers. Usually there is no fee to obtain a seller's permit, but, depending on your estimated growth sales for the year, you may be required to post a bond. This is to ensure that you collect and remit to the state all sales tax due.

service provider: A company that provides access or connections to the Internet.

single-entry accounting: This is an accounting process which provides a simple way to keep track of your accounts receivable, accounts payable, depreciable assets and inventory. Based on your income statement, rather than your balance sheet, a single-entry system does not require you to balance the books or record more than one entry for each transaction.

sole proprietorship: A business owned by just one person.

standard markup: The amount, often expressed as a percentage, of the original cost that you are adding to the cost to determine the *sell price*.

stockholder: The owners of a corporation.

subcontractor: A person or business that agrees to render services and/or provide materials necessary for the performance of a project under contract to another contractor, retailer/dealer/designer, or installer.

sublease: A lease by a tenant or lessee of part or all of leased premises to another person for a shorter term than his or her own and under which he or she retains some right or interest under the original lease.

target market: Those people most likely to use your product or service.

trademark: Any word, name, symbol, device or combination of these used to identify the products or services of a business and to distinguish them from those of other enterprises.

universal product code: Bar codes, or universal product codes (UPCs) as they are officially called, are the vertical lines on packages and price tags that get scanned at electronic cash registers when a purchase is made.

working capital ratio: This ratio compares current assets and current liabilities, and is used to assess the ability of your business to meet unforeseen expenses or weather a financial setback. It is computed by subtracting current liabilities from current assets:

world wide web: An immense network of linked documents on the Internet that point to other documents on related topics.

worth to debt: This compares net worth to total debt. It is used to assess the ability of your business to protect creditors against losses. To compute it, divide net worth by total debts:

zoning: Regulations and restrictions used to protect the rights of people and property, a business that is noisy, smelly or unsightly can expect to run into trouble.. Typically regulated things include the type of businesses that are acceptable, the size and placement of signs, exterior merchandise displays, inventory storage, parking and hours of operation.

Index